T5-DGH-637

PEASANT AND FRENCH

Cultural Contact in Rural France During the Nineteenth Century

James R. Lehning

Peasant and French examines the relationship between French peasants and the development of the French national identity during the nineteenth century. Drawing on methods from cultural studies and social history, as well as a broad range of literary and archival sources, Lehning argues that modern France has in part defined itself as different from the peasantry. Rather than seeing rural French history as a process in which peasants lose their identities and become French, he views it as an ongoing process of cultural contact in which both peasants and the French nation negotiate their identities in relation to each other. The book suggests a new kind of rural history that places the countryside in its national context rather than in isolation.

Peasant and French

Peasant and French

Cultural contact in rural France during the nineteenth century

JAMES R. LEHNING

University of Utah

 CAMBRIDGE
UNIVERSITY PRESS

Published by the Press Syndicate of the University of Cambridge
The Pitt Building, Trumpington Street, Cambridge CB2 1RP
40 West 20th Street, New York, NY 10011-4211, USA
10 Stamford Road, Oakleigh, Melbourne 3166, Australia

First published 1995

Printed in the United States of America

Library of Congress Cataloging-in-Publication Data

Lehning, James R., 1947–
Peasant and French : cultural contact in rural France during the
nineteenth century / James R. Lehning.
p.   cm.
Includes bibliographical references.
ISBN 0-521-46210-X. – ISBN 0-521-46770-5 (pbk.)
1. National characteristics, French.   2. Nationalism – France –
History – 19th century.   3. Peasantry – France – Political activity.
4. France – Cultural policy – History – 19th century.   I. Title.
DC34.L5   1995   94-22859
944.06–dc20   CIP

A catalog record for this book is available from the British Library.

ISBN   0-521-46210-X hardback
ISBN   0-521-46770-5 paperback

This one is for Chuck

Contents

~~~~~~

Tables

Figures

ix

Acknowledgments

Writing this book has been a lengthy process, and in the course of it I have incurred many debts. I have imposed the project on many of the people I have conversed with over the years, and to those people I am grateful for their wisdom and forbearance. Others assisted more specifically. The participants in the social history seminar at the University of Utah in 1986–89 helped me begin the theoretical process of transforming this from a monograph on population history; a year with nonhistorians at the Humanities Center at the University of Utah in 1993–94 furthered that learning process. Yves Lequin, Jean-Pierre Gutton, and Phil Hoffman helped with their knowledge of Lyonnais history and archives, and the staffs of the Archives nationales de France in Paris, the Archives départementales de la Loire in Saint-Etienne, and the Archives de la Diana in Montbrison have over the years provided more assistance than anyone has a right to expect. Anand Yang, Gay Gullickson, Joan Wallach Scott, and an anonymous referee for the press read the entire manuscript. Harvey Graff, Ray Gunn, Susan Cotts Watkins, Nancy Fitch, Daniel Scott Smith, Srinivas Aravamudan, Solomon Namala, Mark Fiege, and David Gordon read various chapters. All provided useful comments and criticism, which, in the long-standing authorial tradition, I have sometimes taken to heart and other times ignored. Also in that tradition, I remain responsible for the finished product. Linda Burns, Noel Case, and the rest of the interlibrary loan staff of the Marriott Library helped overcome the deficiencies of that library. Steve Thomas and Connie L. S. Bartos of the DIGIT Laboratory of the University of Utah helped prepare the maps.

I must also express my appreciation to JAI Press for permission to use portions of my articles "The Timing and Prevalence of Women's Marriage in the French Department of the Loire, 1851–1891," *Journal of Family History* 13 (1988), 307–323; "Socioeconomic Change, Peasant Household Structure and Demographic Behavior in a French Department," *Journal*

of *Family History* 17 (1992), 161–181; and "Nuptiality and Rural Industry: Families and Labor in the French Countryside," *Journal of Family
History* 8 (1983), 333–345.
    I have benefited from financial support as well. The very beginnings of
this project came at the end of a year in France supported by a Social
Science Research Council training fellowship in 1974–75. It progressed
during a year as a fellow at the Population Studies Center of the University of Pennsylvania supported by Grant No. 1 F32 HDO 54 17-01 from
the National Institute of Child Health and Development. Further support came in the form of grants from the American Council of Learned
Societies in 1981, and from the University of Utah Research Committee
in 1983 and 1988.

Books that take fifteen years to write require not only scholarly and
financial support but personal encouragement as well, and I have received
this especially from Anand Yang, Ray Gunn, Joan Wallach Scott, Gay
Gullickson, and my parents and brother. My daughter Amanda and my
son Charles have spent their entire lives hearing about this book, and have
over the years provided their own kind of assistance in its writing. I have
always thought of it as "Chuck's book." Now it is finally done, complete
with the dedication to him, and I hope it is worth the wait.

Salt Lake City
March 28, 1994

1

Introductory positions

I

This history is about rural France during the nineteenth century. But we might begin with a story of a Frenchman in a different place at a different time. In Brazil in 1935, the young anthropologist Claude Lévi-Strauss met his first non-European civilization, the Tibagy Indians. Lévi-Strauss was a product of French civilization and its educational institutions, someone who had, almost on a whim, headed off to study primitive civilizations. His description of the Tibagy brings out his appreciation of the value of the indigenous civilization as well as his disappointment in the contamination by Europeans of his objects of study. But he saw their culture through the paradigm of Europe and France: while conscious of himself as an observer of the Tibagy, he viewed that civilization through its relationship to his own. Reading his account half a century later, we can notice how difficult it was for Lévi-Strauss to fit the Tibagy into the categories he brought with him to Brazil – "primitive" and "civilized." They were, he wrote, "former savages" on whom civilization had been abruptly forced.[1]

Like ethnographers everywhere, Lévi-Strauss described himself as he searched for words to describe a foreign culture.[2] These ambiguities of description and the construction of identities also run through past constructions of country dwellers in his own country. Educated, urban Frenchmen have typically placed country dwellers in the category of "peasants," an ambivalent identity different from themselves, curious,

1 Claude Lévi-Strauss, *Tristes tropiques*, trans. by John Russell (New York: Criterion, 1961), 134–135.
2 James Clifford, *The Predicament of Culture* (Cambridge, Mass.: Harvard University Press, 1988); Clifford Geertz, *Works and Lives: The Anthropologist as Author* (Stanford, Calif.: Stanford University Press, 1988).

1

and at times dangerous.[3] Country dwellers have almost always been time-less repositories of virtues, but this view has coexisted with a more malev-olent one: "peasants" were superstitious savages, potentially given to irrational violence, a dead weight on French development, under the control of priests, politically conservative, and resistant to change. After the middle of nineteenth century those who lived in the countryside began to seem like an acceptable alternative to the militant urban working class, and the bourgeois politicians of the Third Republic came to rely on rural votes to hold off the Socialist challenge. For the Vichy regime during World War II, "peasants" even became the repository of every-thing that was good about France, and since World War II, they have been a symbol of opposition to a centralized, unitary national identity. In all of these variations, they have been an important part of the French nation's perception of itself as, in different ways, participants in French culture have found in the countryside both sources of personal and national regeneration and a civilization profoundly at odds with their own selves and with the nation.

These images of the country dweller were founded on the view that "peasant" was different from "French," whether the latter was con-structed as the aristocrat of the ancien régime, an educated bourgeois of the nineteenth century, or the worker of the twentieth; and one can find these representations in literature, administrative records, and politicians' speeches. But they are present in histories as well. As "peasants," in their sixteenth- to eighteenth-century incarnations, became the subjects of his-tories, they were portrayed as relatively isolated from others, living in a "peasant civilization."[4] This image has also marked analyses of the rural culture of more recent centuries.[5] But most historians of rural France agree that in the last several centuries "civilization" came to French peas-ants. National and urban culture found its way into the countryside, whether through the extension of markets, improved transportation, state building and the spread of political participation, secularization, or the intrusion of primary education. Differences of opinion exist over when this happened, but few doubt that at some point those living in the French countryside were touched by events, institutions, and culture

3 Pierre Barral, "Note historique sur l'emploi du terme 'paysan,'" *Etudes Rurales* 21 (1966), 72–80; Susan Carol Rogers, "Good To Think: The 'Peasant' in Contemporary France," *Anthropoligical Quarterly* 60 (1987), 56–63; and this volume, Ch. 2.
4 See, among others, Emmanuel Le Roy Ladurie, *Les Paysans de Languedoc* (Paris: S.E.V.P.E.N., 1966); Pierre Goubert, *Beauvais et les beauvaisis de 1600 à 1730* (Paris: S.E.V.P.E.N., 1960); and Pierre de Saint-Jacob, *Les Paysans de la Bourgogne du Nord au dernier siècle de l'ancien régime* (Paris: Belles Lettres, 1960).
5 See Judith Devlin, *The Superstitious Mind: French Peasants and the Supernatural in the Nineteenth Century* (New Haven, Conn.: Yale University Press, 1987).

from outside of their villages.[6] Rural French history, then, is a progress of integration of country dwellers into the French nation: local loyalties, customs, and languages were broken down and replaced by a national culture. The story of this contamination of the countryside can be told several ways, but it is almost always done in cataclysmic terms. For some, especially those with a primarily national point of view, it was a relatively benign process, a comedy with a happy ending. For others, however, it has the tragic aura of cultural destruction.[7]

A guiding assumption of this book is that these ways of describing country dwellers make up a French discourse about the countryside that placed those who lived there in specific positions with regard to the rest of France. The category of "peasant" has made and continues to make country dwellers a distinct part of the French nation. Contemporaries knew that "peasants" were different, and their history revolves around the process by which they lost their Burgundian, Breton, Norman, Provençal, or other (peasant) identities and were made French. While the story can be told from different perspectives, all versions rest on categories that imply essential differences between two civilizations, while effacing differences within each category. Peasants were not French because they were peasants; French were not peasants because they were French.

This French discourse about the countryside has been an instrument by which one culture creates its own version, in its own terms, of another.[8] It is a process similar to the ones in which Western European scholars

---

6 See for example David Pinkney, *Decisive Years in France, 1840–1847* (Princeton, N.J.: Princeton University Press, 1986); Eugen Weber, *Peasants into Frenchmen* (Stanford, Calif.: Stanford University Press, 1975); P. M. Jones, *Politics and Rural Society: The Southern Massif Central c. 1750–1880* (Cambridge, Mass.: Cambridge University Press, 1985); Maurice Agulhon, *La République au village* (Paris: Plon, 1970); Edward Berenson, *Populist Religion and Left-Wing Politics in France, 1830–1852* (Princeton, N.J.: Princeton University Press, 1984). For critiques of this view, see Charles Tilly, "Did the Cake of Custom Break?" in John M. Merriman, ed., *Consciousness and Class Experience in Nineteenth-Century Europe* (New York: Holmes & Meier, 1979), 17–44; and Peter McPhee, *The Politics of Rural Life* (Oxford University Press [Clarendon Press], 1992).

7 See Weber, *Peasants into Frenchmen*, for a general argument, and many community studies for specific examples, such as: Laurence Wylie, *Village in the Vaucluse* (Cambridge, Mass.: Harvard University Press, 1974); Pierre-Jakez Hélias, *Le Cheval d'orgueil* (Paris: Fayard, 1967); and Rogers, "Good to Think," 58–59.

8 Peasants joined other groups in this. See, for example, Susanna Barrows, *Distorting Mirrors: Visions of the Crowd in Late 19th-Century France* (New Haven, Conn.: Yale University Press, 1981); Joan Wallach Scott, *Gender and the Politics of History* (New York: Columbia University Press, 1989), esp. ch. 5; William B. Cohen, *The French Encounter with Africans: White Response to Blacks, 1530–1880* (Bloomington: Indiana University Press, 1980); and Tony Judt, *Past Imperfect: French Intellectuals, 1944–1956* (Berkeley and Los Angeles: University of California Press, 1992), 187–204.

created an "Orient" of their own imagination,[9] the Renaissance viewed the indigenous peoples of the Western Hemisphere as without a culture of their own,[10] and British views of bonded laborers or *kamias* in colonial India placed those individuals within a (British) discourse about individual rights.[11] Marie-Noelle Bourguet has begun the work of analyzing French history from this perspective by showing how the administrative reports of early nineteenth-century French prefects also created a particular version of the peasant.[12] In each case, various texts crystallize and develop discourses that identify the subjects of the discourse. Scholarly studies, literary works, and administrative reports describe Oriental peoples, indigenous Americans, South Asian laborers, and French peasants in a way that creates their identity. These discourses also served to organize power relations and make them appear natural: the Middle East came under the control of the European colonial powers; Prospero, by his culture, controlled Caliban; Spanish soldiers held sway over those who greeted them on the beaches of Mexico; *kamias* came under the "protection" of the British colonial administration; and Napoleonic prefects administered French peasants. But while in each case the apparent aim of the discourse was to separate the subject from the dominant group, both parties were inextricably linked to each other, since each was necessary to define the other.

The power of these discourses lies in their ability to attribute ahistorical and essential qualities to the discourses themselves and to the others that they describe.[13] If we are to retell the story of the men and women who lived in the French countryside as they came into contact with French civilization, we must first question the categories of "peasant" and "French" that serve this discourse. Rather than erecting barriers between the two categories, denying their interrelationship, and making rural history a process of moving counters from one to the other, we need to see

---

9 Edward Said, *Orientalism* (New York: Random House, 1978), esp. ch. 1; and idem, "Orientalism Reconsidered" in Francis Barker et al., eds., *Literature, Politics and Theory* (London: Methuen, 1986), 210–229.

10 Stephen J. Greenblatt, "Learning to Curse: Aspects of Linguistic Colonialism in the Sixteenth Century," in idem, *Learning to Curse: Essays in Early Modern Culture* (New York: Routledge, 1990), 16–39.

11 Gyan Prakash, *Bonded Histories: Genealogies of Labor Servitude in Colonial India* (Cambridge University Press, 1990).

12 Marie-Noelle Bourguet, "Race et folklore: l'image officielle de la France en 1800," *Annales E.S.C.* 31 (1977), 802–823; and idem, *Déchiffrer la France: la Statistique départementale à l'époque napoléonienne* (Paris: Archives contemporaines, 1988).

13 See Michel Foucault, *L'Ordre du discours*, published in English as *The Discourse on Language* in *The Archaeology of Knowledge*, trans. by Rupert Swyer (New York: Pantheon, 1972); and Richard Terdiman, *Discourse/Counter-Discourse: The Theory and Practice of Symbolic Resistance in Nineteenth-Century France* (Ithaca, N.Y.: Cornell University Press, 1985).

how these categories interacted with each other over time. That is, we must recognize these categories as constructed and historical, not essential and timeless. Our intention should not be to find when and how peasants became French, but to discover the ways in which they served to define what being French meant, and the ways in which French culture defined what being a peasant meant.[14]

Rather than being about peasants as defined by the French discourse about the countryside, therefore, this book is about the relations between French and rural cultures, the ways in which French discourse about the countryside has controlled that relationship, and the part played by those who lived in the countryside. It is, then, a history of cultural contact, a history that focuses on the changing constructions over time of the category I will refer to as "peasant," the point of tension between French and rural versions of what is going on in the countryside. The ethnohistorian Greg Dening has described a history of cultural contact as one seeking to understand the processes by which cultural artifacts are "transferred and transformed from one cultural system to another." The advantage of this definition of the task is to emphasize that cultural artifacts do not have inherent meanings, but rather acquire their meanings as parts of cultural systems. For Dening, "cross-cultural perception is about understanding words, perceiving gestures with the meaning with which they were offered."[15] My assumption, while similar, is that the roles, rituals, symbols, and material artifacts that Dening speaks of are both offered and received with multiple meanings, differing from person to person and time to time, and that there is a history in these shifting meanings.

But how are we to discover and write this history? Histories of the countryside have themselves contributed to the creation of the category "peasant" by presenting universalized, transparent accounts of what happened in the past, whose part in the discourse is not articulated. But the very existence of sources for a history of the French countryside is not the result of random accidents of creation, destruction, and preservation of documents. On the contrary, the most prevalent sources were created by agents of the powerful French state or by other representatives of French culture, at particular times, for particular reasons, and these sources are therefore as much about French visions of the countryside as they are about that place itself. The state generated and archived the most "systematic" sources in its various censuses and *enquêtes*. The bourgeoisie created and saved versions of the countryside and its residents that made

14 Caroline Ford, *Creating the Nation in Provincial France* (Princeton, N.J.: Princeton University Press, 1993); Peter Sahlins, *Boundaries: The Making of France and Spain in the Pyrenees* (Berkeley and Los Angeles: The University of California Press, 1989).

15 Greg Dening, *Islands and Beaches: Discourse on a Silent Land: Marquesas, 1774–1880* (Honolulu: University of Hawaii Press, 1980), 44.

"peasant" and "folklore" synonymous. Painters whose works were and still are displayed in museums portrayed country dwellers who resembled bourgeois.[16] That we have sources for a history of the countryside, then, owes little to those who lived there, and a great deal to those who held positions of authority over the countryside. The sources we have are, in fact, not so much about the countryside as they are about the category in French culture called "peasant." Obviously narratives can be pieced together from such primary sources, but these necessarily are part histories shaped not only by what can be read in the sources but also by conventional notions of what a history of "peasants" looks like, the models of the historical discipline that utilize archives and categories such as "French" and "peasant" as if they were transparent.[17]

With these concerns in mind, what follows may be described as a series of "little narratives" that move toward totalization but are framed within an attempt to recognize their conceptual and factual limits. These little narratives are held together by the metaphor of a cultural landscape, a field marked by specific locations in which the contacts between rural culture and French culture took place. Chapter 2 outlines the various and contradictory ways in which representatives of French culture have placed country dwellers in the developing French nation since the Revolution of 1789. My emphasis in this chapter is on the countryside and its inhabitants as they appeared in novels, histories, and visual media, but these forms only stand for a much wider range of cultural representations. These images do not form a seamless pattern, for it proved difficult

16 On inquiries into the countryside, see Bourquet, "Race et folklore," and idem, *Déchiffrer la France*. On folklore, see Charles Rearick, *Beyond the Enlightenment: Historians and Folklore in Nineteenth-Century France* (Bloomington: Indiana University Press, 1974); and Michael R. Marrus, "Folklore as an Ethnographic Source: A 'Mise au Point,'" in Jacques Beauroy, Marc Bertrand, and Edward T. Gargan, eds., *The Wolf and the Lamb: Popular Culture in France* (Saratoga, Calif.: Anma Libri 1977), 109–125. On artistic versions of peasants, see Richard Brettell and Caroline Brettell, *Painters and Peasants in the Nineteenth Century* (New York: Rizzoli, 1983). For similar comments about the sources of labor history, see William M. Reddy, *The Rise of Market Culture* (Cambridge University Press, 1984), 15–16.

17 For works influenced by these concerns, see David Warren Sabean, *Power in the Blood: Popular Culture and Village Discourse in Early Modern Germany* (Cambridge University Press, 1984); Joan Wallach Scott, *Gender and the Politics of History*; Dorinne K. Kondo, *Crafting Selves: Power, Gender, and Discourses of Identity in a Japanese Workplace* (University of Chicago Press, 1990); Tzvetan Todorov, *The Conquest of America: The Question of the Other*, trans. by Richard Howard (New York: Harper & Row, 1984); Richard Price, *First-Time: The Historical Vision of an Afro-American People* (Baltimore: The Johns Hopkins University Press, 1983); and idem, *Alabi's World* (Baltimore: The John Hopkins University Press, 1990). For a materialist critique of these influences on historical writing, see Bryan D. Palmer, *Descent into Discourse: The Reification of Language and the Writing of Social History* (Philadelphia: Temple University Press, 1990).

to reconcile the claims made for the French nation and its culture, on the one hand, with those made for the countryside on the other. Chapter 3 moves to a specific locale, the department of the Loire in southeastern France, and gives a baseline account of the landscape of rural civilization there in the late eighteenth and early nineteenth centuries. By describing the physical organization of the countryside, the economic, social, and demographic structures of the population, and the village community, this chapter develops the contours of the metaphors in which rural identities in that period were externalized, both by the French discourse about the countryside and by the actions of the country dwellers themselves. Succeeding chapters take up specific aspects of the movement and alteration of different sites on this terrain, as the French discourse reshaped the landscape, and as the men and women of the Loire countryside transformed their identities. Chapter 4 presents the experience of economic, social, and demographic change in the second half of the nineteenth century. A fundamental geographic division in the department begins to appear in these activities, as the center and East adopted new agricultural techniques, patterns of family formation, and sociability, while older patterns persisted in the western mountains. There were reasons that made sense within the context of rural families for the adoption of these different types of behaviors. As important, however, is that the evolving French discourse about the countryside enclosed these different regions in its descriptions of economic development, reproduction, and family behavior. Elaborated in scientific, administrative, and moral terms, these included some elements of the changes but were unable to describe others. These descriptions illuminate a subtle shift in the positioning of "peasants" in French culture. One part of the department, the western and southwestern mountains, was defined as traditional and stagnant, while those regions adopting new techniques and behaviors came under the rubric of "progressive." Chapter 5 addresses the ways in which gendered differences were imprinted in particular cultural spaces and roles, and the relative inflexibility of these differences as time passed. For women, our attention is drawn to the farm and family, the principal sites in which they played the roles of housewife, mother, daughter, spinster, and widow. But also apparent is the ability of men to move more freely across the physical and cultural landscape, as they acted not only in the family and on the farm, but also in the village community and beyond. This gendering is perhaps the most visible location in which rural and French cultures found common ground. The final chapters explore three preeminent sites of cultural contact between "peasant" and "French," the school, the Church, and the new system of electoral politics. In each of these areas, there is a shifting of the landscape as older places, such as the parish church, move to the background, while new ones, such as the primary school, gain prominence. In these areas as well, we can see the way in which the French concept of "peasant" limited and positioned country dwellers with regard to the French nation and its culture.

In telling these stories I run the risk of drowning in traditional historiographical concerns, such as grain prices. But the reader must keep in mind that we are involved in reading rural history against the grain in two ways. In focusing on the interaction between French creation of the countryside and the actions of the people who lived there, I seek to avoid simply recapitulating "peasant history." But we must look for the identities of people in sources that, as a product of French rather than rural culture, construct a category, "peasant," that seemed natural to the creators of those sources.

II

We will view the contact between "peasant" and "French" cultures in a particular place, the department of the Loire in southeastern France. To establish this geographic locale of the story, a description, tailored to our needs, is a first requirement of this account. The department itself is a construction of the French nation at its most self-conscious, formed in 1793 when the *Représentants en mission* of the Convention provisionally divided the department of Rhône-et-Loire into two separate departments, the Rhône and the Loire. This latter department, the western half of the old *généralité* of Lyon, was shaped as a rough rectangle, standing on its short side. It formed a geographic unit, bounded on three sides by mountains, with the Loire river running down its center. Only in the north was the department open to its neighbor; there, the Plaine du Roannais opened out into the Saône-et-Loire.[18]

For the *conventionnels* and most subsequent observers, the new department was dominated by its three principal cities. In the south, the industrial city of Saint-Etienne was the hub of a nascent industrial center that extended some twenty kilometers along a valley. In the north the principal city was Roanne, notable early in the century as a port on the river Loire, and later a center of cotton textile production. The middle part of the department was under the sway of Montbrison, an administrative

18 On the formation of the department and the revolutionary period in general, see E. Brossard, *Histoire du département de la Loire pendant la Révolution française, 1789–1799* (Paris: H. Champion, 1904–1907); and Colin Lucas, *The Structure of the Terror* (Oxford University Press, 1973). Much general information on the department can be found in Joseph Duplessy, *Annuaire du département de la Loire* (Montbrison: Cheminal, 1818), from which many later *Annuaires* copied. The linguistic characteristics of the department are described in Pierre Gardette, "Carte linguistique du Forez," *Bulletin de la Diana* (1943), 269–281.

town that had been the seat of the province of Forez under the ancien régime, became the capital of the new department, and was the home of an administrative and landowning bourgeoisie. Each of these cities headed an arrondissement of the new department, administrative units that corresponded, very roughly, to the economic regions of the principal cities.

Beyond these three administrative cities and a few other market towns, however, the department was rural, and against the uniformity of the administrative description we might place descriptions of topographical and linguistic diversity. There were a number of different regions formed by distinct geographical features. The south was marked by mountains and valleys. The Monts du Pilat ran along the southern border of the department. To their north lay first the valley around Saint-Etienne and then a hilly region that only gradually gave way, near a town called Saint-Galmier, to the narrow Plaine du Forez in the center. To the southwest of the Plaine was a plateau known as the Haut-Forez, and to its east and west rose mountains: the Monts du Lyonnais (known as the Monts du Matin) to the east; the Monts du Forez (or Monts du Soir) to the west. About two-thirds up the department's length, the northern edge of the Plaine was broken by a low range of hills, the Seuill de Neulize. North of these was the Plaine du Roannais, open to the north but bounded on the east by the Monts du Beaujolais and on the west by the Monts de la Madeleine. The Loire was therefore a department of varied geographical features, marked by mountains, plains, and hills.

It was also a department of linguistic contrasts. North of the Seuill de Neulize, northern French was spoken, and a Parisian would have had little difficulty understanding the inhabitants. South of this dividing line, however, the patois was a combination of northern French and southern dialect that increasingly led into an area in the southwest, in the Monts du Pilat and the Haut-Forez, where the patios was distinctively Provençal. The Loire lay astride the cultural division of France, therefore, between North and South, and both language and culture reflected this division.

III

The Loire was not, for all of its characteristics that easily slide into pastoral descriptions of peaceful countrysides, a distinctive place in the French nation of the the past several centuries; it was, simply put, a part of the landscape, physical and cultural, of that community under construction called France. In this setting, during the period between the Second Republic and the First World War, and especially in the first decades of the Third Republic, the country dwellers of the Loire experienced changes in their way of life that frequently made them appear to be participants in urban French "civilization." Many of them married at an earlier age, had fewer children, and lived in smaller households with fewer kin than their parents or grandparents. They learned to read and write, stopped listening to their parish priests, and even began to vote for republicans. There was nothing "local" about this; they were, of course, joined by many other country people throughout France.

There is no doubt that in this process many of the most powerful resources lay in the hands of French civilization. The most important institutions in the lives of the "peasants" in the Loire were arranged on the side of French, not rural culture: the Church, priests, schools, schoolteachers, police, the state. While French country dwellers have certainly been unruly at times, I know of few instances of open resistance to these institutions in the nineteenth-century Loire. But even in acknowledging that country dwellers were the weaker of the parties in the continual negotiation of their identities, we must not assume as a static given the hegemony of French culture, or overlook the ability of rural people to converse in numerous ways within the discourses of French civilization.[19] By their own means, in a continuous process, country dwellers in the Loire negotiated the meaning of the category in which France placed them. Because "peasant" was a part of French culture, these negotiations forced changes in the identity of the French nation. In paying attention to this conversation, we may hear not only a new history of country dwellers and the places they lived, but also gain a better understanding of France.

19 See, for various perspectives on this approach: Susan Carol Rogers, *Shaping Modern Times in Rural France* (Princeton, N.J.: Princeton University Press, 1991); Suzanne Desan, "Redefining Revolutionary Liberty: The Rhetoric of Religious Revival during the French Revolution," *Journal of Modern History* 60 (1988), 1–27; Ford, *Creating the Nation;* Sahlins, *Boundaries;* Harriet G. Rosenberg, *A Negotiated World: Three Centuries of Change in a French Alpine Community* (University of Toronto Press, 1988); Ranajit Guha and Gayatri Chakravorty Spivak, eds., *Selected Subaltern Studies* (New York: Oxford University Press, 1988); Eugene D. Genovese, *Roll, Jordan, Roll* (New York: Random House, 1972); James C. Scott, *Weapons of the Weak: Everyday Forms of Peasant Resistance* (New Haven, Conn.: Yale University Press, 1985); and idem, *Domination and the Arts of Resistance* (New Haven, Conn.: Yale University Press, 1990).

2

The French nation and its peasants

I

The question of membership arises continually in national histories. Imagining the French community has meant determining both who would be included in the nation and what form that inclusion would take, from the centralized monarchy to the gradual incorporation of "the people" into the nation during the nineteenth century, and the continued refusal of some parts of the French national territory, such as Brittany, to accept their place in the French nation.[1] It has also meant a variety of ways of imagining the place of country dwellers in the nation.[2] This national component of the history of French "peasants" has taken the form of different representations of country dwellers, constructions that can be found in multiple places in French national culture, describing the

1 Benedict Anderson, *Imagined Communities*, 2d ed. (New York: Verson, 1991); Liah Greenfeld, *Nationalism: Five Roads to Modernity* (Cambridge, Mass: Harvard University Press, 1992), ch. 2; Eric Hobsbawm, *Nations and Nationalism since 1780* (Cambridge University Press, 1990), esp. ch. 1; *Echoes of the Marseillaise: Two Centuries Look Back on the French Revolution* (New Brunswick, N.J.: Rutgers University Press, 1990); Rogers Brubaker, *Citizenship and Nationhood in France and Germany* (Cambridge, Mass.: Harvard University Press, 1992), chs. 2, 5, 7; Eugen Weber, *Peasants into Frenchmen* (Stanford, Calif.: Stanford University Press, 1975); Jack E. Reece, *The Bretons Against France: Ethnic Minority Nationalism in 20th-Century Brittany* (Chapel Hill: University of North Carolina Press, 1977); Maryon McDonald, *We Are Not French! Language, Culture and Identity in Brittany* (New York: Routledge, 1989); Caroline Ford, *Creating the Nation in Provincial France* (Princeton, N.J.: Princeton University Press, 1993); Peter Sahlins, *Boundaries: The Making of France and Spain in the Pyrenees* (Berkeley and Los Angeles: University of California Press, 1989); Anthony P. Cohen, *The Symbolic Construction of Community* (New York: Tavistock, 1985); and Maurice Agulhon, "Conscience nationale et conscience régionale en France de 1815 à nos jours," in *Histoire Vagabonde* (Paris: Gallimard, 1983), vol. 2: 144–174.
2 Pierre Barral, "Note historique sur l'emploi du term 'paysan,'" *Etudes Rurales* 21 (1966), 72–80; and Susan Carol Rogers, "Good To Think: The 'Peasant' in Contemporary France," *Anthropological Quarterly* 60 (1987), 56–63.

economic, social, political, and religious behaviors expected of "peasants." There is no straightforward chronology of these constructions, for they were inherently unstable and contradictory, conceiving of country dwellers as a group apart from the nation, yet endowed with important national values. In subsequent chapters, as we take up different places of contact between French and rural cultures, we will need to consider the ways in which the French discourse about the countryside created these particular characteristics of the "peasant." This chapter, however, will survey the stories that have been told about country dwellers in novels, histories, and visual representations. This is not a complete survey; its purpose is rather to highlight the contradictory images made available as these cultural forms developed a series of pictures, characters, and stories that, like other forms of discourse, both facilitated discussion of the countryside and limited the frame within which that discussion could take place and the voices that could be heard. Their representations of country dwellers portrayed a group that was usually passive, though almost always male. Their closeness to nature made them a potential source of virtue, but when aroused to action they quickly became irrational and lost whatever characteristics of "civilization" they possessed. These representations of "peasants" reveal the inability of French culture to maintain a coherent, unified identity for country dwellers as a part of the nation. These instabilities and fractures required the continual recreation of the French construction of "peasants," a process in which country dwellers themselves could participate.

Even if Jean-Jacques Rousseau could write that "it is the rural people who make the nation," the perception of the countryside as a place different from the city, and of country dwellers as a distinct group, was a widespread literary theme during the ancien régime. This pastoral form emphasized rural simplicity, nature, virtuous heroes, and love of a small *patrie*,[3] and the sense of difference persisted through the revolutionary decade and into the nineteenth century. The distinction between urban and rural, "French" and "peasant," however, produced sharply different and contested versions of the "peasant" to be incorporated into the French nation.

One of the most striking demonstrations of the construction of the French nation and the residents of the countryside as separate groups is found in an inquiry on the use of the French language launched in the early 1790s by Abbé Grégoire. The *abbé* intended not only to discover

3 Rousseau quoted in Maurice Cranston, "The Sovereignty of the Nation," in Colin Lucas, ed., *The French Revolution and the Creation of Modern Political Culture* (New York: Pergamon, 1988), vol. 2: 103; see also Paul Vernois, *Le Roman rustique de George Sand à Ramuz* (Paris: Nizet, 1962), 23–25; and Lynn Hunt, *The Family Romance of the French Revolution* (Berkeley and Los Angeles: University of California Press, 1991), 86.

the uses of patois but also to develop a policy that would destroy those local forms of language. His work was thus a part of a nationalizing program in which the nation represented a common unity against a particularism seen as rampant under the ancien régime, and that the Revolution sought to eliminate.[4]

In the responses to Grégoire's inquiry, patois and the French language stand for the countryside and French civilization respectively. Patois was not only speech but also a primitive, passive, and irrational cultural place where nature could be read in the inhabitants. Knowledge, history, and prose, the "discourse of action," were in French. Rural "morals" contrasted with urban opinions, artifice, and industry, but these morals were often rough and crude, like the patois.[5] The difference between the French language and local patois was therefore clearly marked, and membership in the French nation meant use of the French language. Patois was a trace of something that no longer had a place in "France," and the destruction of patois was the necessary price of admission into the French nation. The association of patois with nature suggests that patriotic, rational French culture is only the result of an effort that "at its limit, is a struggle to the death."[6]

In the responses to the inquiry, therefore, there is a shift from language to participation in or exclusion from national identity. There were, however, contradictions in this nationalizing agenda. There was not only an opposition between city and countryside, national and local, but also a desire to bring these apparent opposites together in some way. Dominique Villar, a botanist and military doctor, spoke, for example, of "two peoples" that the Revolution should "reconcile and rally."[7] But the way of making the countryside "a part" of the French nation was not at all clear. It proved impossible to bring the countryside as it existed into the discourse of the Revolution,[8] and the *abbé's* conclusion was that the countryside had to be changed. By 1794, when he produced his final report to the Convention, he thought of language as the force that would create a French nation.[9]

The inquiry of Abbé Grégoire, in its disdain for rural culture and its

---

4 See Hobsbawm, *Nations and Nationalism*, 20.
5 Michel de Certeau, Dominique Julia, and Jacques Revel, *Une Politique de la langue* (Paris: Gallimard, 1975), 147–148, 116, 80, 223. See also R. D. Grillo, *Dominant Languages: Language and Hierarchy in Britain and France* (Cambridge University Press, 1989); R. Balibar, *Les Français fictifs* (Paris: Hachette, 1974); R. Balibar and D. Laporte, *Le Français national: politique et pratique de la langue nationale sous la Révolution* (Paris: Hachette, 1974); and Peter Burke and Roy Porter, eds., *The Social History of Language* (Cambridge University Press, 1987).
6 Certeau, *Une Politique*, 61, 57, 104–105.   7 Ibid., 151–153.   8 Ibid., 156–157.
9 Ibid., 161–164. See also Patrice Higonnet, "The Politics of Linguistic Terrorism and Grammatical Hegemony during the French Revolution," *Social History* 5 (1980), 41–69.

attempts to efface the most obvious marker of that culture, patois, suggests the importance in the ancien régime and the revolutionary era of distancing urban, French culture from that of the countryside. This disdain would be echoed by many other participants in the French discourse about the countryside. Napoleonic prefects drew similar portraits of the countryside and its inhabitants in their inquiries, and novelists such as Stendhal, in *Le Rouge et le noir* (1830), found it easy to portray "peasants" as avaricious and brutal, effective counterparts to members of other social groups such as Madame de Rênal.[10]

But this view of country dwellers coexisted with a more generous one whose presence suggests the ambiguity of French culture in this area. The novelist Rétif de la Bretonne's *La Vie de mon père* describes the novelist's father as a hardworking man who made his way in the world in spite of its dangers and the poor example shown him by his own father. The characterization of Rétif's father, however, is made within the framwork of an image of most country dwellers that, like the one created by the respondents to Abbé Grégoire's inquiry, endowed "peasants" with an unchanging set of attitudes and tastes, whether the subject was wine, behavior, or types of argument.[11] "Peasant" therefore became a timeless, fixed category filled with specific virtues, vices, emotions, and aims embodied above all by men. In this context Rétif employs two techniques to distinguish his own family from its neighbors, and to emphasize the characterization of most "peasants." His own mother, virtually the only female character to be developed to any extent, is portrayed as a model even in her submission to his father. At the same time, the father portrayed by Rétif provides the inverse of his version of country dwellers. While Edme, the novelist's father, is recognized as a model son and man, "the just man," "the honest man" in his village, he stands in implicit contrast to other country dwellers, who are "greedy."[12] The author thus confirms the stereotype of the grasping, avaricious peasant even as he presents the alternative represented by his father.

Much of this characterization portrays the city as lax, dangerous, and immoral, while the countryside – at least in the Rétif household – remains upright, just, and with authority located in the father.[13] But the countryside is not a monolithic place, and its differences are hierarchically graded depending on their closeness to urban French culture: the patois of Rétif's village is "soft and musical" because of the village's association

---

10 Marie-Noelle Bourguet, *Déchiffrer la France: la Statistique départementale à l'époque napoléonienne* (Paris: Archives contemporaines, 1988); Stendhal, *Le Rouge et le noir* (Paris: Le François, 1946), 15–27.

11 Nicolas Rétif de la Bretonne, *La Vie de mon père* (Paris: Garnier, 1981), 130, 32, 127.

12 Ibid., esp. 55–79.　　13 Ibid., 108, 145–146.

with French national culture through language, in contrast to that of another village, where the language is dull, coarse, and incoherent.[14] And the virtuous Edme does not turn his back on urban France: he never regrets his own stay there, and he hopes that his children will settle in Paris, a great city of equality, an "ever-open book" always available to the willing reader.[15]

Rétif's glorification of his father and the countryside marked an important aspect of the late-eighteenth and early nineteenth-century discourse about the countryside and its inhabitants. Even as they confirmed the negative views implicit in Abbé Grégoire's inquiry, Rétif and other participants in this discourse set up the countryside as the repository of positive values, and drew on pastoral images of the countryside that found strong resonance in French culture at this time. In the Salon of 1798, for example, a painting by Francois-André Vincent entitled *Agriculture* depicted a bourgeois family watching as their son received a lesson in plowing from a peasant; the plowman was portrayed as a High Renaissance figure, even to the extent that his hand, pointed toward a pair of oxen, seems directly modeled on that of God in Michelangelo's Sistine Chapel ceiling. French paintings of the 1820s followed the same pattern, depicting peasants as "devout and joyous" presiding "benignly over a landscape."[16]

This approach continued throughout the nineteenth century, forming one important strand in the French construction of the countryside. There were few intrusions by markets, machinery, or politics, and novelists and painters could use rural subjects to evoke a timeless, "gentle, pastoral age."[17] This pastoral version of the countryside found its most direct expression in the rural novels of George Sand, who turned the countryside into both a refuge and a source of beauty. "The simplest and most naive peasant," she wrote in 1849, "is still an artist; and I even believe that their art is superior to ours. . . . The pastoral life is a per-

---

14 Ibid., 52–53. See also Grillo, *Dominant Languages*, chs. 8–11.
15 Rétif de la Bretonne, *La Vie de mon père*, 153.
16 Richard R. Brettell and Caroline B. Brettell, *Painters and Peasants in the Nineteenth Century* (New York: Rizzoli, 1983), 75, 17; and Raymond Grew, "Picturing the People: Images of the Lower Orders in Nineteenth-Century French Art," *Journal of Interdisciplinary History* 17 (1986), 203–231. Malcolm C. Cook, "Politics in the Fiction of the French Revolution, 1789–1794," *Studies on Voltaire and the Eighteenth Century* 201 (1982), esp. 290–310, notes the way in which the belief by physiocrats in the natural law became, in fiction, a belief in the virtue of the peasantry and led to the use of a pastoral myth and devotion to the Republic in the work of authors such as Florian and François Guillaume Ducray-Duminil.
17 Vernois, *Le Roman rustique*, 22, 37, 119, 132–133, 135, 138, 104; Jean Bouret, *The Barbizon School and 19th Century French Landscape Painting* (Greenwich, Conn.: New York Graphic Society, 1973).

fumed Eden where souls tormented and tossed by the tumult of the world can seek refuge."[18]

These values made the idealized "peasant" a bedrock of the French nation. But behind them lurked the uncivilized savage, always threatening to escape, and this tradition marginalized the countryside from the important events of the nation. A refuge by its very nature could not share in those events, but instead was a place in which full participants in the work of the nation could restore themselves before returning to the fray. The countryside also remained timeless: any history would cause it to lose its principal characteristics. For both Abbé Grégoire and the pastoralists, therefore, rural France could not become a full-fledged part of the nation without losing its essential character.

I I

The middle of the nineteenth century brought the most famous description of French peasants, Marx's characterization of them as "potatoes in a sack."[19] But the decades on either side of 1848 are particularly rich in representations of the countryside and its inhabitants, and these underscore both the instability of these images and the power of forms such as the pastoral to contain possible threats from country dwellers. Nowhere are these contradictory constructions more apparent than in the paintings of Gustave Courbet and Jean-François Millet. While Millet went on to paint the peaceful, religious *Angelus* (1858–59), his work in the years immediately after the 1848 revolution portrayed a savage "peasant" to be feared. The critic Théophile Gautier described *The Winnower* (1848) as "rugged, ferocious, bristling, and crude." *Haymakers Resting* (1849) uses a pastoral form to depict bitter and silent anger. And in a first version of *The Sower*, painted a year before the version that was displayed in the Salon of 1851, he described "an image of complete brutality." The second version of this painting similarly represented the savagery of the country dwellers, but in a more restrained, static way. The figure in *The Sower* could not break through the constraints of the pastoral genre that safely placed "peasants" on the margins of French culture.[20]

18 George Sand, "Avant-Propos" to *François le Champi* (Oxford University Press [Clarendon Press], 1910), 8, 9. See also Vernois, *Le Roman rustique*, 31–41. The characters in Sand's novels do not, however, always live up to this ideal.
19 Karl Marx, "The Eighteenth Brumaire of Louis Bonaparte," in *Surveys from Exile: Political Writings* (New York: Vintage, 1974), vol. 2: 239. See also David Mitrany, *Marx Against the Peasant* (Chapel Hill: University of North Carolina Press, 1951). Michael Duggett, "Marx on Peasants," *Journal of Peasant Studies* 2 (1975), 159–182, attempts to moderate Mitrany's view by stressing Marx's ambivalence toward peasants.
20 T. J. Clark, *The Absolute Bourgeois: Artists and Politics in France, 1848–1851* (London:

As T. J. Clark remarks, "When Courbet hangs in the next room, even *The Sower* is reassuring,"[21] and Courbet's paintings from Ornans in the Second Republic and early Second Empire sharply contrast with the unity and calm of the pastoral construction of the countryside. *The Stone-breakers* (1849) portrayed the harshness and uselessness of the physical labor carried on in the countryside: "labour gone to waste, and men turned stiff and wooden by routine." *Burial at Ornans* (1850) displays a rural community at odds with the pastoral image: the "participants" in the funeral ritual are distracted, distinct from each other. This is not much of a community, nor are its members particularly religious even though they are in the middle of a religious ceremony. Courbet's version of *Peasants of Flagey Returning from the Fair* (1850), a traditional pastoral scene, breaks with the usual picturesque version of the story. His country dwellers, therefore, refute the pastoral image at virtually every point: they engage in brutish physical labor of little redeeming value; they are not part of a unified community, nor are they religious; and they are directly linked to the nineteenth-century intrusion of capitalism into the country-side.[22]

Courbet's characterization of country dwellers found only weak imitations in the novels and histories of the middle of the century. There was some interest in the harshness of rural life, but a pastoral idealization of the countryside was an almost universal backdrop that controlled descriptions of country dwellers. When Jules Michelet wrote *Le Peuple* in 1845, for example, he began his discussion of the different kinds of bondage in French society with a section on the peasantry. For Michelet this was the touchstone of that "living brotherhood" France, and the touchstone of the peasantry was the land of France. The tie between the people and the French nation, therefore, began in the soil of the country. It was a relationship that led Michelet to metaphors such as friendship, mistress, and marriage, which make clear that he is speaking about the "brother-hood" of France.[23] From this fundamental relationship, patriotism and the love of France is generalized and ennobled to extend from the local society of the countryside to the nation as a whole. Small rural land-

Thames & Hudson, 1973), 72–98, esp. 74, 78, 93–94. Robert L. Herbert, "City vs. Country: The Rural Image in French Painting," *Artforum* 8 (1970), 44–55, stresses the emphasis of Millet and later nineteenth-century painters on the timelessness of the peasantry and its role as a subject of anti-industrial and antiurban sentiments.

21 Clark, *Absolute Bourgeois*, 96.

22 T. J. Clark, *Image of the People: Gustave Courbet and the Second French Republic, 1848–1851* (Greenwich, Conn.: New York Graphic Society, 1973), 78–85. See also Michael Fried, *Courbet's Realism* (University of Chicago Press, 1990), esp. 254–263.

23 Jules Michelet, *The People*, trans. by John P. McKay (Urbana: University of Illinois Press, 1973), 25, 26, 157.

owners were the "heart of the people," endowed with morality, sobriety, and thrift.[24]

Michelet does not ignore conditions in the countryside, pointing to the contemporary crisis of rural society. But the limits of his representation of country dwellers emerge in the trap he sets for them. Michelet's peasants turn inward, isolating themselves from the urban world. Michelet understands that this isolation compounds the problems of the country dweller: "It prevents him from getting along with the other peasants. . . . On the other hand, the townsman has no desire to approach this fierce-looking man; he is almost afraid of him."[25] Michelet turned away from the obvious escape route, migration from the countryside to work in the cities, since it meant leaving the soil. Peasants can only be a separate group, busy at the "holy work of France: the marriage of man and the land," a group against which the moral downfall of the rest of France may be judged. They are not participants in the history of the country.[26]

The story of rural history was much more in the foreground for Michelet in his *Histoire de la Révolution française* (1847–53). This history is primarily about the events in Paris and the revolutionary assemblies, but the sections concerned with 1793 also include the uprising in the West known as the Vendée. The people who provide the Republic's soldiers in this conflict are heroes. Against them are ranged "great masses" of "unhappy, blind and ignorant people," a "barbarian army" of "brigands" and "savages," a "turbulence," a "blind and frenzied mass." The peasants of the West are "ignorant, intelligent and heroic," but under clerical influence, following their habits and more like animals than heroes of the Parisian revolution such as Danton and Desmoulins: the metaphor of a wounded, cornered stag ready to turn and fight accomplishes the slide toward instinctual animal behavior.[27]

For Michelet, therefore, the war in the West was between the heroic Blues, with their individual leaders, and the faceless, virtually incomprehensible "peasants" of the West. And whereas in Paris developments are rapid and complex, in the countryside there is virtually no development: Vendéens are not converted to the Republic; they, along with their Blue neighbors, are simply destroyed by the civil war. "Peasant" in the West, therefore, is a static category, brought into a history of France but without its own history.

The creation of such "peasant" identities in a genre like history, which with Michelet was beginning its claim to represent the truth, was a power-

24 Ibid., 83, 89.   25 Ibid., 32–33.   26 Ibid., 36.

27 Jules Michelet, *Histoire de la Révolution française* (Paris: Gallimard, 1952), vol. 2: 608, 450, 448, 447, 458, 454, 607, 459, 449, 452, 732, 583. See also Patrick Hutton, "The Role of Memory in the Historiography of the French Revolution," *History and Theory* 30 (1991), 60–62.

ful contributor to the discussion of the countryside in French culture. Country dwellers are marginalized at around the same time in fiction, another form staking its claims to a version of truthfulness.[28] "Peasant" characters, such as Julien Sorel in Stendhal's *Le Rouge et le noir* (1830) or Fréderic Moreau in Flaubert's *L'Education sentimentale* (1869), usually leave the countryside. It also served as the setting for stories about rural notables, as in *Madame Bovary* (1857). This is also the case in the fictional works of this period most directly concerned with the countryside, those of Honoré de Balzac. His "peasants" are separate from the French nation. In *Les Chouans* (1827), the whole of Brittany is an immobile island in France, "surrounded by enlightenment whose beneficient warmth never penetrates it; the country is like some frozen piece of coal that lies dim and black in the heart of a blazing fire."[29] In *Les Paysans* (1844, 1855) they live in their own world, one filled with strong kinship ties, passions, and its own institutions that the representatives of French culture cannot penetrate. The countryside and its residents are therefore vaguely threatening to civilized Frenchmen. The journalist Blondet, vacationing in the countryside, writes, "Wherever you may be in the country, sure though you feel that you are quite alone, you are the focus of attention of two eyes under a cotton cap."[30]

Balzac's peasants were not only unenlightened, they were barely human. At best they acted out of blind loyalty to religion or their social betters, at worst out of animal instinct or ingrained cupidity. The troop whose march opens *Les Chouans* is barely distinguishable from animals. The Chouan peasant Marche-à-Terre is compared by republican officers "first to one of the cattle browsing in the pastureland below, next to an American Indian, and lastly to a native of the Cape of Good Hope," and the republican commander refers to him as an animal. Even his lover Francine sees Marche-à-Terre as a "fair-sized bear." The *gars* in general are "savages" and "brutes."[31] The country dwellers in *Les Paysans* slide from difference to irrationality to immorality to subhuman status. Their passion for gleaning, for example, is "inexplicable" as they will leave higher-paid work to gather stray ears of grain. "If a daughter is seduced, they only invoke morality if the seducer is rich and can be frightened," and "the peasant has only cravings." They are "a hot-headed race" whose principal natural inclination is selfishness. Seeing Fourchon, the archetypical peasant in the novel, Blondet is struck by the combination of sloth

28 On Michelet, see Linda Orr, *Headless History* (Ithaca, N.Y.: Cornell University Press, 1990); on realist fiction, see Richard Terdiman, *The Dialetics of Isolation* (New Haven, Conn.: Yale University Press, 1976).
29 Honoré de Balzac, *Les Chouans* in *La Comédie humaine* (Paris: Seuil, 1966), vol. 5: 633.
30 Honoré de Balzac, *Les Paysans* in *La Comédie humaine* (Paris: Seuil, 1966), vol. 6: 10.
31 Balzac, *Les Chouans*, 628, 632, 674, 683, 634, 653, 686, 707.

and cunning in his countenance, and is led to wonder "Is that like me? We have only our shape in common." In Balzac's rendering, even the peasants know they are distinct from the civilized French: Fourchon explains his ability to discover otters by saying, "We peasants are such stupid animals ourselves, we come eventually to understand the animals."[32]

French civilization, and the French nation, becomes defined as the counter to the savagery of the countryside. The stoically admirable characters in *Les Paysans*, especially the gamekeeper Michaud, drew their strength from their service in the army: they were certainly outsiders to rural society, but their origin, the Napoleonic army, made them different from other French men and women, such as Blondet or the vacuous countess. And if the defrocked Benedictine Rigou seems to have turned the ideals of the Revolution upside down in his pursuit of money and power, there is also a character such as the old Jacobin, Jean-François Niseron, whose "sublime" relationship to France made him "a part of France itself."[33] But the peasantry remains outside of this elevating experience: "the peasant will always be the peasant," says Fourchon, and that is how it turns out.[34]

In these images from the middle decades of the nineteenth century the countryside could still be a place to find respite from urban cares, as Balzac's Blondet did in *Les Paysans*. Yet while an opaque screen separates the French observer from his subjects, there is also apparent a recognition of the linkage of the two civilizations. Just as the universal manhood suffrage of the Second Republic and Second Empire incorporated male country dwellers into the political nation, the middle of the nineteenth century saw them incorporated in French culture's version of the nation. The cultural work of these representations was to control country dwellers by placing them at the periphery, as ahistorical observers rather than participants in the nation. But this task was unevenly accomplished. It could take the restful and reassuring form of the strong rural vote for Louis Napoleon or Millet's *Angelus*, but it could also mean the threatening ambiguity of the rural response to the coup d'état of 1851 or the images in *The Winnower* or *The Haymakers Resting*.

III

The unsettled incorporation of country dwellers into French culture evident at midcentury may be read as a reflection of the profound ambiguities involved in the construction of a national culture that not only included threatening groups such as workers, women, and "peasants,"

32 Balzac, *Les Paysans*, 24, 111, 24, 15, 106, 24, 17, 20, 32, 18.
33 Ibid., 73–74.   34 Ibid., 27.

but also limited their ability to play active roles in the life of the nation. By the last decades of the nineteenth century, provisional resolutions of these paradoxes were being essayed, in the form, for example, of the republican experiment with a system of parliamentary government, the crystallization of a social structure based on class, and the creation of separate gendered spheres. That such constructions were necessary, however, should not lead us to conclude that the ambiguities of French culture's versions of these groups disappeared; rather, they must be viewed as ongoing attempts to resolve persistent cultural contradictions.

In this context, countrydwellers continued to bear the images that marked them earlier in the century. The country dwellers in Hippolyte Taine's *Origines de la France contemporaine* (1877), for example, seem much like Balzac's peasants: the violence of the Midi was such that "one would imagine oneself in a war with barbarians." The distance between French civilization and "peasant" civilization is marked both in terms of the kinds of metaphors that seem apt to Taine and in the possibility of "peasants" moving into French civilization. The forced surrender of produce under the Terror brought country dwellers to the situation of "fellahs"; their condition under the Jacobins was that of "laborers in a Mussulman country." As with Balzac's Chouans, Taine's peasants move imperceptibly toward being animals: their problems make them conceive of themselves as part of "a vast herd . . . everywhere ill used, starved, and fleeced." Only an "acquired self-control, reflection, and culture which interposes between belief and action the solicitude for social interests, the observance of forms and respect for the law" can restrain this herd of savages. Taine was writing in 1877 of the 1790s, but he echoed the respondents to Abbé Grégoire.[35]

Popular fiction during the Second Empire and early Third Republic also persisted in painting a picture of avaricious, cynical, immoral, and unpatriotic country dwellers.[36] Two of the major rural novels of the late nineteenth century, Emile Zola's *La Terre* (1887) and René Bazin's *La Terre qui meurt* (1898), continued the sharp distinction between civilized France and savage peasant, with the rural actors driven to seemingly unreasonable actions by their "peasant" instincts. But at the end of the nineteenth century, images of the "peasant" that pressed against this long-standing type, by emphasizing "the peasant" as a source of national strength, also emerged.

The country dwellers in Zola's *La Terre* are not immediately distin-

35 Hippolyte Taine, *Les Origines de la France contemporaine* (Paris: Hachette, 1921–1938), vol. 4: 253; vol. 8: 253, 285; vol. 3: 13; vol. 4: 83.

36 Guy Robert, *La Terre d'Emile Zola* (Paris: Belles lettres, 1952), 67–106; see, for example, Guy de Maupassant, "Histoire d'une fille de ferme" in *Oeuvres complètes* (Paris: L'Edition d'Art H. Piazza, 1968), vol. 1 117–139.

guishable from earlier characterization. The schoolmaster considers his pupils "brutes,"[37] and the principal characters, the members of the Fouan family, are driven to their destiny by their natures. The land was the principal focus of that "peasant" nature, and if, like Millet, Zola took pains to show country dwellers actually cultivating the soil, it remained a source of prototypical "peasant" characteristics: both men and women are lusty, calculating, greedy, avaricious, and suspicious.[38] This theme is established early in the novel through the description of old Fouan's feelings as he divides his land among his three children.[39] Various characters subsequently display their "peasant" qualities in their sly, calculating, and plodding pursuit of even the smallest pieces of land. While these characteristics are applied to a social category, they easily become essential aspects of country dwellers. A sexual metaphor is often used. As with Michelet, the metaphor not only makes the relationship to the land the result of an instinctual drive, it also ensures that "peasant" is understood as "male." And the essentialist character of "peasant" provides the dénouement of the novel, as Jean Macquart – who, born in a town, can never become a "real peasant" – is cast aside by his dying wife through her failure to execute the will that would allow him to continue working her land. Instead, her land reverts to her sister and cousin – blood relatives and true "peasants" – who had persecuted her throughout the novel.[40]

The connection between these country dwellers and the French nation is minimal. The memory of the Revolution is either the source of anger, as in the Fouan family's lingering complaint about the sale of national lands, or marginalized in the figure of Fouan's son Jesus Christ, a drunk who occasionally rants about the ideals of 1789 and 1848. National politics is outside of their lives, reduced to petty rivalries within the village. The conscription lottery, held in the shadow of the oncoming Franco-Prussian war, is far from a chance to serve in the glorious armies of France: military service is worse than cholera. Even the French flag is cast aside by Delphin, who drew an unlucky number, with the comment, "I've had enough of that bloody rag. It brought me nothing but bad luck," a sentiment parents of conscripts echo. The only "patriot" in the novel is the outsider, Jean, with his teary-eyed memories of the Italian war and his decision to reenlist in 1870, incomprehensible to the good "citizens" of Rognes. In the end, he proves that he is not a "peasant": unable to till the land of France, he was still willing to defend it.[41]

René Bazin's *La Terre qui meurt*, set in Brittany, also draws on the stock portrait of French country dwellers. The emphasis on the land as

37 Emile Zola, *La Terre* in *Oeuvres complètes* (Paris: Fasquelle, 1967), vol. 5: 797.
38 See Vernois, *Le Roman rustique*, 118; and Robert, *La Terre*, 67.
39 Zola, *La Terre*, 774.   40 Ibid., 777, 834, 905, 934, 966, 1078.   41 Ibid., 1100, 1143.

the immutable basis of society is there,[42] and the love of Toussaint Lumineau for the *métairie* that his family had worked for generations is reminiscent of Michelet's description of the bond between the peasant and the land of France.[43] There is a softening of earlier, harsh attitudes toward women, but the principal characters are almost all men. There is also mistrust of outsiders, even those from other parts of Brittany; powerlessness against "men from the city, *fonctionnaires*, administrative officers, against all the immense unknown that extended around the parish"; and the urban characterization of the country dweller as at best out of his element in the city, but more often a "savage."[44] These standard parts of the character of "peasant" in modern French culture are used by Bazin less to condemn the country dweller than to evoke sympathy for his plight.

These qualities also become the basis for tragedy. To some extent this reduces social problems to the psychological struggles of the characters, as Paul Vernois has suggested, but these are still distinctively "peasant" characters.[45] For Toussaint's crippled eldest son Mathurin, the love of the land becomes a fatal flaw: he envies those who would take his "rightful" place as the heir of the farm, and his drive to prove his worthiness to succeed his father in spite of his injuries leads to his death. Toussaint's dreams are also broken by the same kind of external factors that recent historians have noted as undermining "peasant" society. His son François lacks Toussaint's love for the land and prefers the easier life of the city; Andre, the joy of his father when he returns from the army and shows his ability and devotion to the work of the peasant, falls under the attractive spell of larger, more productive farms in the New World. It is this Breton family's involvement in the ongoing history of France, a history that describes the end of the French peasantry, that generates their problems. In a reversal of roles that underscores the powerlessness of this family, its future is redeemed only through the actions of the youngest daughter.

While Bazin himself could draw "peasant" characters who lacked civilization, his sympathetic portrayal of Toussaint, so different from Zola's old Fouan, suggests a different aspect of the discourse of French culture about the countryside, one that placed traditional pastoral versions in a new national context. This construction is even more apparent in the developing republican historiography of the Revolution and in other novelistic accounts of the countryside and its residents, yet these also demonstrate the difficulty of escaping the traditional story about "peasants." In the historical works of Alphonse Aulard, Albert Mathiez, and Jean Jaurès

---

42 René Bazin, *La Terre qui meurt* (Paris: Calmann-Lévy, 1987), 208.
43 See, for example, the description on pp. 31–32 of Toussaint's feelings about his farm.
44 Ibid., 50–53, 82, 226, 88.   45 Vernois, *Le Roman rustique*, 291.

there is a concern to describe the Revolution as both the triumph of the Republic and as the work of "the people." They therefore sought to bring the "peasantry" of the late eighteenth century into the story of the development of the French nation.[46] At the same time novelists such as Emile Guillaumin and Eugene Le Roy took a more favorable view of country dwellers than did Zola or even Bazin. All of these accounts attempted to incorporate "peasants" into the French nation; yet they still encountered the limits imposed by the French narrative that provided characterization, action, and often dramatic resolution in the long-standing terms that consigned country dwellers to either extinction or the periphery of the French nation.

Aulard's most popular attempt at the history of the Revolution was his *Histoire politique de la Révolution francaise*. He describes an ancien régime in which there were significant differences between the educated "Frenchman" and the illiterate "peasant." "Peasants" were not only ignorant, they were apolitical: "The rural mass ignores, suffers and keeps quiet, practically everywhere."[47] The Revolution, in Aulard's telling, becomes the foundational moment of the French nation, with the notion of "citizen" defining membership in the nation. But in this history of France, "peasants" appear only briefly, not in the story of the great events of the foundation of republican France, but either as happy supporters of the decree of August 1792 that ended feudal restrictions on landownership or, in the Vendée, as a group bound to their own small part of France and willing to follow refractory priests in stabbing the Republic in the back.[48] A contemporary of Aulard, Albert Mathiez produced a more radical version of the Revolution, one that highlighted the achievements of the Terror and its leader, Maximilien Robespierre. Mathiez's Revolution was urban, Parisian, and encapsulated in Robespierre, and his country dwellers are distinct from the revolutionaries who surround Robespierre. "Peasants," he announces in the first chapter of his *Révolution francaise*, written just after the First World War, "were the beasts of burden" of the ancien régime, a metaphor that had already occurred to many Frenchmen. These peasants were passive: incapable of changing the social order, they could be influenced by their priest and lawyer, as in the Vendée.[49] Firmly committed only to their religion and village, not under-

46 See William Keylor, *Academy and Community: The Foundation of the French Historical Profession* (Cambridge, Mass.: Harvard University Press, 1975); Hutton, "Role of Memory," 62–65; and Fritz Ringer, *Fields of Knowledge* (Cambridge University Press, 1992), esp. 174–175; 265–282.

47 Alphonse Aulard, *Histoire politique de la Révolution française*, 5th ed. (Paris: Colin, 1913), 16, 19, 25, 29.

48 Ibid., 260, 375–77.

49 Albert Mathiez, *La Révolution française* (Paris: Colin, 1978), 26–27.

standing the great events of the day but appreciating them when they are economically useful, Aulard and Mathiez's "peasants" are useful figures against which they can place the great men who were precursors of the Third Republic.

The *Histoire socialiste* of Jean Jaurès also emphasized the identity between the nation and the revolutionary movement, especially the Convention, and the way in which "peasants" were distinct from that revolutionary movement. The limits of this historiographic discourse about country dwellers are evident in Jaurès's history precisely because he was so committed to including "the people" in his account. The Revolution was, for Jaurès, the even that created democracy and capitalism, bringing the bourgeoisie to power and preparing the way for the eventual triumph of socialism.[50] There was a distinctly urban tinge to this scheme of French history: the Revolution "consecrated the definitive unity of Paris and France." The Convention was a "national force" that, combined with the Commune of Paris in 1793–94, was France.[51] Jaurès therefore tells a story concerned with national development, with the Revolution again as the founding event of the French nation. In this national story, however, country dwellers still played a marginal role, and his attempts to make them active participants in the Revolution's events remained incomplete. He describes their suffering under the ancien régime; an entire section at the beginning of the volume on the Legislative Assembly is devoted to the "peasant movement." And the pressure of country dwellers on the assemblies in 1789 and 1792 is given a significant place in Jaurès's explanation of the abolition of feudalism.[52] But even country dwellers who supported the Revolution are not given the same kind of active participation in events as the Parisian actors. Their actions are in response to "liberty that came from Paris" and Jaurès suggests that country dwellers understood that once the Revolution was under way, they had to take care of themselves. By 1792, the "peasant" stood "deceived and bitter," as the Revolution had failed to fulfill its promise.[53]

The Revolution's deception of country dwellers did not, however, lead Jaurès to condemn it. Rather, he himself excluded rural opponents of the Revolution, such as those in the Vendée, from the national community. They "excommunicated themselves" from the Revolution: the Vendée was a product of "peasant egoism," and the "fanaticism" and "egoism" of the peasants led them to accept the benefits of the Revolution but repudiate its costs.[54] The "peasant" was therefore often separated from the

50 Jean Jaurès, *Histoire socialiste* (Paris: Jules Rouff et Cie, 1900–1902), vol. 1: 3.
51 Ibid., vol. 1: 108; vol. 4: 1620, 1001.
52 Ibid., vol. 1: 18; vol. 2: 757–791; vol. 1: 282–286; vol. 2: 759, 1300.
53 Ibid., vol. 1: 18; 199; 229–230; vol. 2: 776.
54 Ibid., vol. 4: 1631; vol. 1: 646; vol. 4: 1142–1162.

nation by his rejection of the Revolution. But Jaurès also distinguished "peasants" through a characterization that is already familiar in its emphasis on instinct rather than reason. The rural rebellion in 1789 broke out suddenly, "like a spring expanding." Their "anger" is often invoked as an explanation for their actions. They sought to destroy feudalism because of "an irrepressible instinct," and although Jaurès criticizes Taine for giving a "false air of unchained bestiality to peasant subtlety," he himself is soon writing of "instinctive and savage violence." The country dweller is less than human: a cold-blooded murderer, he seeks out the bourgeois he hates and kills him.[55] In spite, therefore, of Jaurès's desire to include country dwellers in the story of the French nation, he was unable to write about them as he did the city dwellers who defined that nation.

Fictitious "peasants" at the turn of the century also acquired some of the trappings of Frenchness as the pastoral image of the countryside was revitalized and transformed. The city was seen as itself threatening, and those who knew the countryside were better off there than in the city. There were no longer the identifications between the city as civilized and the countryside as savage; instead, although the divisions between the two social and cultural places remained strong, they were both perceived as threatening, and safety lay with one's own family.

This is apparent in Emile Guillaumin's account of a visit by his nephew Georges and Georges's wife in his autobiographical novel *La Vie d'un simple* (1904).[56] Georges and his wife were relatives, but they were also Parisians, and the description makes apparent that two different civilizations were in contact. Guillaumin seems to realize this; he is very conscious of how ridiculous his guests' questions about rural life are, and has no desire to embarrass himself by asking such questions about city life. What is striking about this description of the relationship between Parisians and "peasants" is how little there was in common. Townspeople had no idea of the sufferings of the country dweller, who had no idea of the conditions of workers in the towns. Kinship was the only apparent tie between the families of Georges and Emile. But the two families are defined through their relationship of difference: Parisians are not like peasants, peasants are not like Parisians, and trying to be the other could only lead to embarrassment.

"Peasants" were still above all local, and dangers came from outsiders, both rural and urban. "Now in our remote country parts," Guillaumin writes, ". . . the world beyond our district, beyond known distances, seemed full of mystery and danger and peopled by savages."[57] While this

55 Ibid., vol. 1: 272; 229–230; vol. 2: 776; 1076, 1078; vol. 4: 1151.
56 Emile Guillaumin, *The Life of a Simple Man*, trans. by Margaret Crosland (Hanover, N.H.: University Press of New England, 1983).
57 Ibid., 29.

might be seen as a parody of French views of country dwellers by this young author, this approach pervades his writing in this book. One of the most powerful incidents occurs when the young Tiennon accompanies his father to the market, and it portrays the mystery of the outside world. The town itself appears somber, the tower of the church "darkened naturally by the passage of the centuries," but even darker under the gray sky in the evening mist. The atmosphere is "gloomy." He is left in the town square while his father drinks in the tavern, and the waning day becomes a metaphor for the growing fears of the young boy: "At four o'clock darkness fell: it came down from the great sky low and black; it rose from the ground with the floating mist which suddenly thickened."[58]

The relationship of this local society to the French nation is slim at best. Language continues to serve as a cultural marker; Charles learns better French while in the army, and when he returns he attempts to keep speaking it. "I don't see why," he argues, "because we are peasants, we should talk nonsense." His sister, however, points out to him the true nonsense: "It would be funny if we began to talk like the lady at the chateau." Little by little, Charles returns to the language of his upbringing.[59] Military service appears as a threat from the outside, not as a source of glory, as it was for Michelet. But it also is not the disruptive force that it is in Zola or Bazin's novels. National events are also distant and remote, even as the French political system becomes more participatory under the Second Empire and the Third Republic: republican politics are personified in Doctor Fauconnet, the son of the owner of a farm Tiennon's family had worked.[60]

Guillaumin, therefore, found a calm in the countryside through a return to the ahistorical and marginalized position that earlier pastoral visions had given "peasants." It was a strategy that, while it attenuated the tendency to view country dwellers as subhuman, reinforced the same habit by reconstructing in new ways the passivity of "peasants" and the tendency to efface rural women from the story. This strategy is even more visible in Eugène Le Roy's *Jacquou le Croquant* (1899). The countryside is portrayed as a mysterious, empty place. The novel opens with the child Jacquou riding home from Christmas mass with his mother in an unearthly setting: "The deserted countryside was all white; the hills seemed

---

58 Ibid., 21, 23. *La Vie d'un simple*, because it was written by a "peasant," might be taken as an attempt to alter the discourse about peasants, just as, from different origins, was Jaurès's attempt to change their role in the Revolution. This passage in particular, however, suggests how this discourse could limit, if not eliminate, such attempts. See Richard Terdiman, *Discourse/Counter-Discourse: The Theory and Practice of Symbolic Resistance in Nineteenth-Century France* (Ithaca, N.Y.: Cornell University Press, 1985).

59 Guillaumin, *La Vie d'un simple*, 58–60, 144–145.

60 Ibid., 13, 75, 132–134, 172, 114–115, 189–190.

covered with a great sad shroud, like those placed on the caskets of dead paupers. . . . A deathly silence hung over the desolated earth."⁶¹ Places are often described as "deserted," and it seems as if "one hardly ever sees anyone in the forest."⁶² The countryside also has an ethical quality: the occupation of cultivator is, Jacquou is advised, the highest peasant calling, and the (rural) poor who suffer in this world will be rewarded in the next.⁶³

Country dwellers in Jacquou's story have only a limited ability to act on their own behalf. In their relationship with the countryside as a natural setting, they have surprising skills of survival in potentially dangerous circumstances. In the opening scene, Jacquou and his mother are threatened by a wolf, which his mother scares away, safely negotiating that pitfall of the countryside. Jacquou's father patches together a living from a myriad of sources, and his mother picks up the custom with similar ingenuity after the father's imprisonment. Jacquou quickly becomes at home in the most forbidding part of the countryside, the forest, where his skills enable him to carry out vengeance on the Comte de Nansac.

Whereas the countryside is empty, the city, in contrast, is complicated, full physically and emotionally. The description of Périgueux, where Jacquou's father is tried, goes on for pages, describing a dense array of houses, physical shapes, and colors, "a crowd of houses . . . in disorder."⁶⁴ In this setting, country dwellers lose their cleverness. As Jacquou and his mother set out for Périgueux, they are aware that they are not dressed for the city; once there, Jacquou realizes that people look at them with curiosity, "knowing from our air and our dress that we have come from one of the most savage parts of Périgord."⁶⁵

"Peasants" are also passive when faced with their poverty and with the injustices that rural society, especially its feudal vestiges, visits upon them. But while *Jacquou le Croquant* creates an image of the countryside that is relatively empty, calm, and peaceful, one of the most striking aspects of its storytelling is the way in which agency develops among country dwellers. Jacquou is not a passive subject of the orders and abuses of the Nansac family. As a child he swears an oath of vengeance against the Count; he burns the Count's forest; and he and the other country dwellers burn the chateau. This development of Jacquou's agency takes place within a story in which "peasants" are as usual defined in part by their submissiveness. But because "peasants" are passive, Jacquou is obviously unusual: the Comte de Nansac, it is said, would have continued to dominate and oppress the "peasants" for a long time if Jacquou had not arrived on the scene to organize the chateau burning.⁶⁶ By the end of the novel (with Jacquou eighty years of age), however, his willingness to take

61 Eugène Le Roy, *Jacquou le croquant* (Paris: Calmann-Levy, 1946), 12.
62 Ibid., 213.   63 Ibid., 134.   64 Ibid., 62–63.   65 Ibid., 52, 72.
66 Ibid., 321.

action to redress grievances has spread: by the early Third Republic, country dwellers no longer respond to tyranny by saying, "There is no justice for the poor!"[67]

IV

The late-nineteenth and early twentieth-century description of country dwellers had some elements that were significantly different from previous versions. Yet all of these works seem to draw on the same collection of possible "peasants," even though novelists and historians might put the parts together in their own ways. With the turn of the century, country dwellers had been "placed" in modern French culture. But this positioning neither made them "French" nor resolved the ambiguities of the French version of "peasants." Twentieth-century versions of the "peasant" show a curious blend of familiarity and contempt overlaid by a thorough conviction that, while distinctive, "peasants" were now a part of the French nation. This did not mean that the countryside took an equivalent place with urban France; rather, its place in the nation came from its subordinate relationship to the city.[68] While it was difficult for anyone to imagine a "peasant' history of France, one in which country dwellers retained their distinctiveness, yet also shared in the developments that had clearly marked urban France during the century since the Revolution, they did begin to attract attention. The *poilus* of the First World War demonstrated that country dwellers were participants in events of national significance.[69] They also became the subjects of academic study after the First World War, both in historical studies and in the development of folklore as a discipline. Georges Lefebvre's *Paysans du Nord*, the first major study of the contribution of the peasantry to the Revolution, appeared in 1924, and his *Quatre-vingt-neuf*, written for the sesquicentenary of the Revolution in 1939, provided a place in the revolutionary story for country dwellers that, even if placing them away from the most significant action, was nonetheless vital.[70] The Musée des arts et traditions populaires, founded in 1937, was the result of growing eth-

---

67 Ibid., 329.
68 Maurice Agulhon, "L'Ebranlement, 1800–1914" in *Histoire de la France rurale* (Paris: Seuil, 1976), vol. 3: 529. See also Nancy Fitch, "Mass Culture, Mass Parliamentary Politics, and Modern Anti-Semitism: The Dreyfus Affair in Rural France," *American Historical Review* 97 (1992), 55–95.
69 See, for example, the novels by E. Pérochon, *La Parcelle 32* (1922) and *Les Gardiennes* (1924), discussed in Vernois, *Le Roman rustique*, 284.
70 Lefebvre was unable to find a commercial publisher for his *thèse* when it first appeared; it was finally made widely available in the year he died. Georges Lefebvre, *Les Paysans du Nord pendant la Révolution française* (Bari: Laterza, 1959); idem, *The Coming of the French Revolution* (Trans. by R. R. Palmer; Princeton, N.J.: Princeton University Press, 1947).

nographic interest in France's rural civilizations. Especially under the Vichy regime, folklore studies focused on rural cultural practices and were easily subsumed under the *Etat Français's* interest in an ahistorical, essentialist traditionalism that would regenerate the nation. Vichy's motto, "La terre, elle ne ment pas" [the land does not lie] sums up this regime's version of country dwellers and their culture, the foundation of its claim to legitimacy; yet it also recalls earlier views of French "peasants."[71]

Since the First World War, the French countryside has continued to be a place in which pastoral values may be found. But it is too closely linked to French culture to have the pristine qualities that George Sand discovered. The result has been a profoundly confused construction of the countryside. As the historical vision of country dwellers began to give them a share in national developments, the story turned out to be one in which they disappeared as a distinct group. Charles Seignobos, in the volume of Ernest Lavisse's *Histoire de France contemporaine* dealing with the Third Republic, described the disappearance of rural culture as market agriculture developed, yet emphasized that this was a consequence not of the actions of "peasants" but of the urban French. Since World War II, this has become the canonical version of rural history.[72]

In a more popular medium, Jean Renoir's classic film *La Regle du jeu* (1939), primarily set in the countryside at the Chateau de la Colinière, deals with the same ambiguities. There is an initial assertion of urban control over the countryside and the peasantry, as the marquis orders his gamekeeper, Schumacher, to kill the rabbits overrunning his lands, and beaters flush game for the shooting party. It is a "society organized for the systematic destruction of nature."[73] The contrast between the wealthy urban French who visit the chateau for a lengthy holiday, and the "peasants," Schumacher and the poacher Marceau, for whom survival is a daily struggle, continues the long-standing theme in French culture of the

---

71 The Vichy regime did, of course, aim at a reorganization of the countryside even while calling for a return to "peasant" farming. See: Herman Lebovics, *True France: The Wars over Cultural Identity, 1900–1945* (Ithaca, N.Y.: Cornell University Press, 1992), 135–188; Christian Faure, *Le Projet culturel de Vichy: folklore et révolution nationale, 1940–1944* (Lyon: Presses Universitaires de Lyon, 1989); and idem, "Le film documentaire sous Vichy: une promotion du terroir," *Ethnologie Française* 18 (1988), 283–290; Robert O. Paxton, *Vichy France: Old Guard and New Order, 1940–1944* (New York: Knopf, 1972), 206–209; and Pierre Barral, *Les Agrariens français de Méline à Pisani* (Paris: Presses de la Fondation nationale des sciences politiques, 1968), 256–282.

72 Charles Seignobos, *L'Evolution de la Troisième république (1875–1914)* (Paris: Hachette, 1921), 434–443; Weber, *Peasants into Frenchmen;* Agulhon, "L'Ebranlement" and "Conscience nationale et conscience régionale," 149.

73 Charles William Brooks, "Jean Renoir's *The Rules of the Game,*" *French Historical Studies* 7 (1971), 281.

distinctiveness and hardness of rural life. And like Balzac's Burgundian peasants, Marceau and Schumacher have their own civilization, dimly glimpsed through Marceau's descriptions of his life as a poacher. Accompanying this is a mutual understanding and solidarity that sets them apart from the urban French.

Throughout the film, the chateau exists as an urban island in the middle of the countryside. The boundary between the two spaces is as significant a rule of the game as the ones that govern the relations between the urban characters, and crossing the boundary is one of the principal themes of the film. The marquis's guests easily pass between the chateau and the surrounding countryside without losing their French culture, nor with serious consequences. They are, in the long-standing pastoral tradition, on vacation in the countryside, finding refuge from their cares. But the situation is different for country dwellers: the chateau is off-limits to them, but it is also their goal. When Schumacher crosses the boundary, he is discovered and ordered to leave. As Charles Brooks remarked, his "uncontrolled rural passion and rustic chivalry in the chateau of society show nothing so much as a lack of breeding."[74] Marceau, however, is the true "peasant" aspiring to be a Frenchman. When the marquis offers him a job trapping rabbits, he asks if he may work in the chateau instead. Once admitted to the chateau, he finds himself forced to learn unfamiliar ways, and his first attempt, shining shoes, ends in farce. Eventually, however, Marceau achieves near entry into French civilization, and this has more tragic consequences. He and the marquis exchange, as virtual equals, pleasantries and advice about women during a party in the chateau. But Marceau's advances toward Lisette, Schumacher's wife, have drawn Schumacher into the chateau, and "lack of breeding" shows. Marceau and Schumacher disrupt the party and, ultimately, kill Andre Jurieu, the hero of the French nation. While Schumacher and Marceau understood each other – Marceau really was trying to seduce Lisette – they were badly fooled by the mysteries of urban France, mistaking the Marquise Christine for Lisette and Andre for Christine's longtime friend Octave.

The downfall for both Schumacher and Marceau returns them to their places in the countryside; Schumacher is restored to his position as gamekeeper while Marceau returns to poaching. A final scene, as Marceau and Octave leave the chateau, contrasts their different places in the nation. Marceau will go back into the woods to make a living. Octave, having lost his close friend Andre and his lifelong love, Christine, will return to Paris. And when Marceau suggests that perhaps they will meet again, Octave, wiser at least in this rule of the game of French culture, suggests

---

74 Ibid., 279.

that this is doubtful. Anything may happen, of course, but both French and "peasant" know this would not.

La Regle du jeu underlines the distinctions in French culture between its urban representatives and the country dwellers who entered at the risk of disrupting that culture. Clearly "peasants" are a part of the French nation: Schumacher at one point refers to his service in the Great War, and they are useful as subordinates to the elite carriers of French culture. Disaster threatens everyone, however, when they cross the boundary between "peasant" and "French" cultures. Marceau's sin was not to want to enter the chateau as a servant – that had been going on for centuries – but rather in thinking that his new clothes made him the equal of his master, the marquis.

Twentieth-century versions of the "peasant" have generally recognized, as did Renoir, the necessary interrelation of "French" and "peasant" cultures, although they also maintain a strong sense of the differences between the two, and they have often seen French culture as a threat to "peasant" culture. What remains problematic, therefore, are the consequences of contact between urban France and the countryside. Georges-Henri Rivière, the director of the Musée des arts et traditions populaires from 1937 to 1967, hoped for a national culture that would synthesize rural and urban culture, even while his work supported the peasantist ideology of the Vichy regime. For someone interested in economic development, such as J.-F. Gravier, writing immediately after the Second World War in his *Paris and the French Desert*, becoming more urban was the only economic hope for the countryside. But for Pierre Jakez Hélias, urban France was a maleficent force that had destroyed his Breton culture.[75]

The ambiguity of the countryside is emphasized especially in two popular films released in the 1980s, *Jean de Florette* and *Manon des sources*, directed by Claude Berri. Based on a 1962 novel by Marcel Pagnol, *L'Eau des collines*, these films portray a countryside that is not only a source of revitalization for tired urban French men and women, but also peopled by finely etched "peasants" with many of the characteristics of the long line of fictional representations of French country dwellers. Desire for land, cupidity, cruelty, a lack of remorse, and secretiveness are dominant traits of the rural society of the period between the world wars that Berri portrays. The hunchback Jean comes from the city to take up his inher-

---

75 Lebovics, *True France*, 182; J. F. Gravier, *Paris et le désert francais*, 2d ed. (Paris: Flammarion, 1958); Pierre Jakez Hélias, *Le Cheval d'orgueil* (Paris: Plon, 1975). See also Edgar Morin, *Commune en France: La Metamorphose de Plodémet* (Paris: Fayard, 1967); Maryvonne Bodiguel, *Le Rural en question: politiques et sociologues en quête d'objet* (Paris: Harmattan, 1986); Fernand Braudel, *The Identity of France*, trans. by Sian Reynolds (New York: Harper & Row, 1988).

ited farm, bringing with him an enthusiasm for the countryside; he wishes to "cultivate the authentic." But he also brings his urban ways: he himself was a tax collector; his wife, an opera singer, is a curiosity to the villagers; his silently observing daughter is incongruously named after an opera. Above all, he brings his belief in modern agricultural methods. As the son of a woman who married outside the village, and as a hunchback, he arouses suspicions and enmity worthy of characters in Zola, Balzac, and Bazin, and the calculating César Soubeyran and his nephew Ugolin are masterful variations on the old theme of greedy, conniving, and often ill-starred peasants. Ugolin, rebuffed and humiliated by Manon, accepts his destiny and hangs himself, while César seems to will his own death after learning the tragic secret of the story, that Jean was his own son.

But it is Manon, the daughter of the hunchback and virtually the only female character of consequence in either film, who is most interesting in these films. She passes – easily, it appears – back and forth between peasant and French civilizations. She sits uneasily in the countryside in the first half of the story, silently watching her father lose his civilized veneer and become increasingly driven, eventually to his death, in his search for water. Even as Jean unpacks the agricultural tools that he hopes will make him happy, Manon pulls a schoolbag from the wagon. And at the end of the first film, our last view of her is running away from César and Ugolin after she has discovered that their cruelty killed her father.

Manon's screams echo the birds that periodically swoop across the rough Provence landscape, and at the beginning of the second film Manon is not only an adult but seemingly at one with the countryside, a goatherd who bathes nude without shame, unaware of the watching Ugolin. She is even described – by the villagers, no less – as "a savage." Soon, however, she has befriended the young schoolteacher, the representative of the French nation in the village. In the course of the film, she uses "peasant" guile to wreak revenge on the entire village. In the end, with little difficulty, she again becomes French, enclosed in the walled schoolhouse after her marriage to the *instituteur* and renouncing whatever "peasant" qualities she may have shown earlier in the film. The victors are not only the Manon who has resumed her place in French civilization, but also that civilization itself.

Manon demonstrates the ambiguity of the distinctions implicit in the French construction of the "peasant" and the play of "French" and "peasant" cultures against each other. However permeable the boundaries between these cultures were, and whatever the beauty and values transplants like Manon may find in rural culture, "peasants" are subordinated to French culture. Manon ultimately finds redemption not in returning to the countryside, as her father tried to do, but in taking up her place in French culture, a position her father's tragic death and the need to revenge that death – itself a "peasant" imperative – delayed. Jean sought "the authentic" in the countryside; French culture, however, insisted on the incompatibility between itself and the countryside, and on the higher value of urban civilization.

The films of the late twentieth century are the latest versions of "peasants" that have made up the French discourse about the countryside. This chapter has only sampled those stories as they have been told over the past several centuries, and we will encounter more of them. The relative truth or falsity of these various accounts is beside the point, and it is a mistake to assume that the stories that French culture has told about the countryside are the only ones possible. As Ernest Renan noted in 1882, "Forgetting, and even historical error, is an essential factor in the creation of a nation."[76] These texts and others like them have constructed rural France, but their lapses of memory and errors forced a continuous reconstruction of the incorporation of the country dweller into the French nation. The creation of the linkage between "French" and "peasant" has been manifestly unequal, and has made it difficult for country dwellers to describe themselves. But imagining their side of this process of cultural contact in the countryside, we will see, casts French history in a different light.

76 Ernest Renan, "Qu'est-ce qu'une nation?" *Oeuvres complètes* (Paris: Calmann-Levy, 1947), vol. 1: 891.

3

The landscape in the
early nineteenth century

I

Even if we must guard against recounting rural history as a part of the discourse about "peasants becoming French," stories must have beginnings, and for this one the place to begin is the end of the eighteenth and the first half of the nineteenth century. As we have already seen, perceptions of the countryside at this time emphasized its difference and isolation from "French" civilization, a perception found not only in linguistic inquiries such as that of Abbé Grégoire but in a number of other places in French culture. Students of the economy, mercantilist and physiocrat, and early demographers such as Messance and Moheau, focused on drawing distinctions between cities and the countryside even if this meant overlooking differences within the latter.[1] Departmental inquiries launched under the Consulate and Empire consolidated this distinction between the French nation, represented by the state and departmental notables, and peasants – a distinction epitomized in the Year 9 by the prefect of the Ardèche as he described well-educated (*bien élevé*) city dwellers and ignorant or fanatical *campagnards*.[2] Indeed, the notion of country dwellers separated from the rest of the country is one of the most persistent aspects of the discourse about the countryside and its residents.

This separation provides a seemingly natural starting point for histories, an isolated countryside. But the countryside was neither timeless nor static prior to the nineteenth century, nor was it isolated from French civilization. Indeed, implicit even in late-eighteenth-century notions of

1 Steven L. Kaplan, *Bread, Politics and Political Economy in the Reign of Louis XV* (The Hague: Martinus Nijhoff, 1976), vol. 1: 31–32; Moheau, *Recherches et considérations sur la population de la France* (Paris: Geuthner, 1912), 58–59; L. Messance, *Recherches sur la population des généralités d'Auvergne, de Lyon, de Rouen et de quelques provinces et villes du royaume* (Paris, n.p., 1766).
2 Marie-Noelle Bourguet, *Déchiffrer la France* (Paris: Archives contemporaines, 1988), esp. 123, 208, 295.

the countryside as different is that they were linked to the rest of society by a market for agricultural goods, by streams of migration that brought country dwellers into the cities, or, as was increasingly the case in official *Enquêtes*, by a state that aimed, by its actions, to bring a disparate peasantry into a unified nation. Such notions were also a part of the construction of rural France as a place that had to be "acted upon" to bring it into the nation, in the same way that, as we have seen, Abbé Grégoire wished to accomplish this linguistically. This chapter and the next will examine this perception of the countryside in economic, social, and demographic terms.

It is important at the outset to place the connections between France and its countryside in the context of rural life. Any activity required reference to sites such as the physical landscape, the family, and the community, and one of the ways the country dwellers of the Loire formed their identities was by making these references. But the meaning of these sites in rural culture depended as well on the French discourse about the countryside and the version of "peasant" it constructed. Rural culture could be illustrated by a close reading of any rural activity, from cultivating fields to resisting the Napoleonic draft. But a marriage will do. When Claude Chorain and Marie-Philomène Boudarel wed in the village of Marlhes in the Loire in 1867, the sacristan, Jean Chatelain, recorded the ceremony, creating a detailed ethnographic document.[3] There was nothing exceptional about the marriage ceremony. But we can read its details to learn about rural culture. The actors involved, their roles, the scenes in which they acted, and the props that they used, all tell us about the way these people construed themselves and the world around them.

The most obvious actors were the members of the two families being joined by the marriage. Active participation was generally limited to family members and, while the community did take part, it is clear that from courtship through the wedding to the last part of the ceremonies, a visit to family graves, marriage was a family affair. The family group was, however, limited in scope. It consisted only of immediate kin: the parents of the couple and their siblings. This was expanded somewhat in the wedding procession and the guest list for the wedding meal to include extended kin, but their role was limited. Marriage established a separate entity, and the members of this limited group participated in the wedding ceremony of their children. The ceremony also distinguished in status between the two families. The bride and her father led the procession to the church, and the wedding meal took place at the farm of the bride's

---

3 The account was published by the folklorist Victor Smith as "Un Mariage dans le Haut-Forez en 1873," *Romania* 9 (1880), 547–570. See also Paul Fortier-Beaulieu, *Mariages et noces compagnards* (Paris: G. P. Maisonneuve, 1937); and Arnold Van Gennep, *Le Folklore de l'Auvergne et du Velay* (Paris: G. P. Maisonneuve, 1942).

parents. At the church the father of the bride transferred authority over her to the groom, not to the family of the groom.

The marriage ceremony also published the relationship to the village. The public aspect of the ceremony is first of all evident in its deployment of space, a use that demonstrated clear geographic limits to the social and cultural groups to which the bride and groom belonged. The custom of erecting barricades on the road to the church, usually just outside the bourg, by the village youth in the case of exogenous marriages suggests that marriage was a community affair and that the community was geographically bounded. Its topography was, however, structured, with some areas more private or familial, while others belonged to the larger community. The movements of the wedding party on the day of the wedding clearly indicate this: the wedding procession began at the house of the bride's family, but gradually moved across public roads past the dwellings of many of the village community's members to the parish church located in the bourg. In some places the civil ceremony was considered only a legal necessity – in the Loire, for example, the phrase used was "*on va s'enregistrer*" – and the principal marriage ceremony was the religious one, in the church. In less devout areas the two ceremonies were more balanced. In both instances the marriage moved from the privatized domain of the family house to the public space of the bourg, the *place* (square), and a public building, whether church or *mairie*.

In the church ceremony itself, the public proclamation of the marriage predominated. The ritual of the Catholic Church included a public call for any member of the congregation who knew a reason why the marriage should not take place to intervene. The nuptial blessing meant the confirmation of the union by one of the most powerful public institutions in the village. Beyond this, the ceremony often included a public statement by the father of the bride that was an accounting of his conduct as a parent. After the ceremony, candies or *sous* were tossed from the church steps to the youth of the village, and the male members of the wedding party repaired to a local café. The procession finally returned to the farmhouse of the bride's family for a wedding meal that returned the ceremony to the private space of the family. With few exceptions, such as the *balendraud* who had helped to arrange the match, only family members attended this meal.

Community participation reflected a division in the village between irresponsible, unmarried youths and married adults. The participation of the village youth began with a celebration of the end of the youth of the groom, but the principal youth activity occurred without him, in an attempt the night before the wedding to capture the bride from her family. The theft of chickens during this night was a reversal of usual norms, allowing the youth to carry out activities that in normal circumstances would be considered unlawful. While these chickens eventually became a part of the marriage celebration itself (in some places they were carried in the procession to the church), the way in which they were obtained could only be approved in extraordinary circumstances. The purpose of the theft, however, was to emphasize the community's interest in marriage: chickens were a symbol of fertility, and their use in the marriage ceremony showed the need by the community to reproduce itself into the next generation. The day of the wedding the village youth acted as enforcers of village rules: they built barricades on the road to the church in the case of exogenous marriages and punished second marriages through charivaris. To some extent these practices reflected the recognition by the community of the youth as a separate group that should be compensated for loss, and that did not have to play by the same rules as others. Their privileged status also allowed them to take actions, such as theft, that more responsible members should disapprove, but that were in the overall interest of the community. More than that, such practices explicitly showed the existence of a community actively interested in the marriage. The participation of the more responsible members of the community, those already married, was minimal, perhaps extending no further than witnessing the church ceremony and wishing the new couple well on the church steps. But their interest in the marriage was made apparent in ways that showed the community's generosity and sense of the significance of the event.

Throughout the ceremonies, food and drink acted as instruments of communication. The most obvious use of food is the wedding meal that celebrated the marriage, but this was only one in a series of meals that occurred at each stage of courtship and marriage. During courtship, a common dinner of the two families at the home of the groom's parents signaled acceptance of the match. The burial of the life of the youth was marked by the consumption of food and drink; the chickens were stolen; each of the male members of the wedding party purchased a round of drinks after the church ceremony; tables of food were set out by farmers along the road back to the farm of the bride's parents as a gift from the community to the wedding party; farcical salads of onions, weeds, or paper were given at the wedding meal to unmarried brothers and sisters of the couple; the couple was given bad-tasting soup or black bread; and most gifts to them were of food or drink. The Sunday after the wedding was the occasion for another meal, following Mass and visits to family graves. At every key point in the ceremonies, and especially when the local community participated, food, drink, or both were involved.

The meals involved in the wedding ceremony solemnized the ceremony in terms readily understandable in village culture. This reflected the agrarian nature of the village economy and the closeness of rural culture to its principal product, food. But there was more to it than just accessibility.

Giving food in the quantity and quality expected involved great sacrifice, signifying the generosity of families and the community. As the dear product of household labor, it was a sign of approval when given by heads of household in the *tables d'honneur* along the road, thus showing "responsible" opinion. Poor-quality food communicated warnings of future pain or disapproval for dishonorable behavior such as celibacy. Giving a gift was also a guarantee that a gift would be returned, implying a continuing relationship between giver and recipient, and suggests the way that the village community was reinforced by these kinds of practices. Finally, the consumption of food and drink was an occasion of sociability, formalizing and raising the significance of social interaction.[4]

The wedding ceremony is described to us by folklorists, and it would be surprising if it always occured as peacefully as they saw it; we might speculate about each of these parts of the ceremony when one or both families were unhappy about the match. It is also a rare account of rural life that privileges the countryside and its residents, while effacing the larger French nation. As such, it emphasizes the isolation of the countryside both in its form as folklore and in its contents. Nonetheless, even this sanitized version captures in still life a series of characteristics of rural society and culture. We might employ a spatial metaphor to think about these characteristics: they were sites in which the family members who made up the wedding party, and the other people that they met along the way, lived and found their identities. We need to explore these sites further to understand their world and its linkages to French culture.

II

The marriage ceremony describes a physical landscape covered by a series of cultural markers: country dwellers interacted constantly with a countryside shaped by roads, buildings, and settlements that were endowed with meaning. These settlement patterns varied across the country, from the *bocage* of the West, to the open fields of the Ile-de-France and North, to the large central settlements and irregular fields of the Midi.[5] These markers were only dimly visible to representatives of French culture, who struggled to visualize and describe this countryside: firm knowledge was

4 See Marcel Mauss, *The Gift*, trans. by Ian Cunnison (New York: Free Press, 1954), 31. This "gift economy" suggests the "moral economy" described by E. P. Thompson in "The Moral Economy of the English Crowd in the Eighteenth Century," *Past and Present* 50 (1971), 71–136. For a discussion of the cultural significance of food and meals, see Mary Douglas, "Deciphering a Meal" in her *Implicit Meanings: Essays in Anthropology* (London: Routledge & Kegan Paul, 1975), 249–275.
5 Marc Bloch, *Caractères originaux de l'histoire rurale française* (Oslo: H. Aschehough, 1931); and Robert Specklin, "L'Achévement des paysages agraires" in Georges Duby, ed., *Histoire de la France rurale* (Paris: Seuil, 1976), vol. 3: 255–277.

Cantons of the department of the Loire

11 Bourg-Argental	27 St-Georges-en-Couzan
12 Le Chambon	28 St-Jean-Soleymieux
13 Pélussin	29 St-Rambert
14 Rive-de-Gier	31 Belmont
15 St-Chamond	32 Charlieu
16 St-Etienne	33 Néronde
17 St-Genest-Malifaux	34 La Pacaudière
18 St-Héand	35 Perreux
21 Boën	36 Roanne
22 Feurs	37 St-Haon-le-Châtel
23 Montbrison	38 St-Just-en-Chevalet
24 Noirétable	39 St-Symphorien-en-Laye
25 St-Bonnet-le-Château	40 St-Germain-Laval
26 St-Galmier	

Figure 3.1   Cantons of the Department of the Loire.

hard to find and informants even scarcer. Their attempts produced some-what contradictory results, but nevertheless contributed to the construction of French versions of the rural parts of the national territory.

A first place in which these constructions of the landscape appear is in maps drawn by civil authorities. Maps of the rural department of the Loire show a territory marked by occasional central settlements and scattered hamlets.[6] (See Figure 3.1 for cantons and principal cities of the

6 I am using the term *commune* here to refer to the administrative unit imposed on the

department.) The central settlements were usually larger than the hamlets and were strung along what passed for a main road connecting the village and hamlets with more important settlements. These might be the *chef-lieu* of the canton, a principal city such as Roanne, Montbrison, or Saint-Etienne, or a city beyond the department: Clermont-Ferrand to the west, Lyon to the east, Paris to the north. With between 10 and 25 percent of a commune's population usually residing in the bourg, the density of the principal settlement varied, but even in the smallest villages the patterning of buildings is apparent. A plan of the communes of Vendange (*sic*), Neulise (canton of Saint-Symphorien-de-lay), Pinay, and Saint-Jodard (canton of Néronde) in the Plaine du Forez, for example, shows central settlements of ten to thirty buildings lining the main road.[7] In the case of Neulise, a large commune with more than two thousand residents in 1841, the central road was the Rue Royale between Roanne and Lyon, and the village was a large settlement of some thirty buildings that one can imagine bustling with activity on most days. In smaller villages such as Vendanges, with only five hundred residents in the entire commune, the road was a local one connecting to the Rue Royale, and only a dozen buildings made up the village. The same pattern is visible in Saint-André-d'Apchon (canton of Saint-Haon-le-Châtel) in the Monts du Beaujolais in the northeastern part of the department, where some eighteen buildings lined the several roads that intersected in the village, and in Villemontais (canton of Roanne).[8] Farther south, in the Monts du Pilat, the large villages of Saint-Genest-Malifaux and Marlhes surrounded the intersections of local roads and the principal road from Saint-Etienne south into the Haute-Loire.[9]

The maps focused most directly on the central settlements, and what seems to set these apart from most other places in each commune was their physical layout and the kind of buildings they contained. These made clear the primarily public nature of the bourg. The settlement was formed around a *place*, which gave the village a focus and frequently served as the site for a market or fair. Many of the buildings around this *place*, of course, were farmhouses and supporting buildings such as barns

countryside by the Law on Municipal Government of 14 December 1789, which in geographical terms included both the central settlement that gave its name to the commune as well as the numerous hamlets that dotted the countryside; *village* refers to a single contiguous settlement within the commune. For a similar use of maps, see Peter Sahlins, *Boundaries: Making France and Spain in the Pyrenees* (Berkeley and Los Angeles: University of California Press, 1989).

7 Archives départementales de la Loire (hereafter A.D.L.) 46 M 51/1, *Plan des communes de Vendange, Neulise, Pinay, et Saint-Jodard, 1838.*

8 A.D.L. 46 M 41/1, *Plan d'Arcon, Chenier, Lentigny, Saint-André-d'Apchon, Villemontais, 1839.*

9 A.D.L. 46 M 24, *Plan de formation de commune de Saint-Régis-du-Coin.*

and stables, but the most imposing and culturally significant was usually the Catholic church. Frequently, as in Vendanges, Saint-Genest, and Marlhes, the church fronted the *place* of the village; in others, such as Neulise and Saint-André, it was only a few yards away. The central bourg also contained the communal (and parish) cemetery, either next to or within easy walking distance of the *place* and church.[10] School buildings and *mairies* increasingly became fundamental parts of the central bourg's equipment, but the sacred spaces of church and cemetery consecrated the importance of religion in rural culture in the first half of the nineteenth century.

Hamlets were usually smaller than the bourg. Rarely the sites of public events, they also were less significant, at least for nineteenth-century mapmakers. Sometimes they were no more than a single farmhouse and its barn and stable, in other instances four or five farmhouses grouped together. Some hamlets were located on a communal road; others were connected to the rest of the commune only by a rude footpath. The poor state of local roads, left to the charge of communal governments, meant that hamlets could be isolated even from neighboring hamlets.[11] This isolation – which meant separation from public space – could create tensions within the commune. The hamlet of Saint-Régis-du-Coin in the canton of Saint-Genest-Malifaux, for example, had its own church and its own school for boys by midcentury, but still depended on the bourg of the commune within which it was located, Marlhes. As they lobbied the prefect for status as a separate commune in the early 1850s, the inhabitants of Saint-Régis pointed out the difficulty of communication with Marlhes as well as their sense that they were excluded from the decisions made by the commune. Such accusations surfaced frequently in petitions for separate status; whether they were true or not is less important than the sense they convey of the isolation and divided loyalties that could separate a hamlet from its neighbors.[12]

The image of the "peasant" that Balzac and others described easily resurfaces in these maps and administrative sources. It was difficult to enter and describe spaces in which rural, rather than French, culture dominated, and contemporary sources are for this reason virtually silent

---

10 On attempts during the early nineteenth century to move cemeteries away from the residences, see Thomas Kselman, *Death and the Afterlife in Modern France* (Princeton, N. J.: Princeton University Press, 1993), 166–182.

11 L.-J. Gras, *Les Routes du Forez et du Jerez* (Saint-Etienne: Théolier, 1925), 169–170.

12 A.D.L. 46 M 24, pc. # 113, *Habitans de la paroisse de Saint-Régis-du-Coin à M. le préfet de la Loire, 11 avril 1853.* See also A.D.L. 46 M 8, *Habitans d'Aboën à M. le préfet de la Loire, 20 janvier 1868,* and A.D.L. 46 M 23, *Requête à M. le préfet de la Loire, par les habitants de Verlieu sur Chavanary, pour demander l'annexation de leur section à la commune de Saint-Michel.*

about domestic places. From more recent inquiries based on physical evidence, however, it appears that the farmhouses that made up these bourgs and hamlets were spaces that were flexibly used. Usually only one or two rooms were dedicated to lodging the family. A large central room (*la maison*), dominated by a fireplace and oven, was the focus of family life, the space in which virtually all of the indoor activities of the family – food preparation, eating, socializing, and sleeping – took place. A small side room behind the fireplace, called a *bretagne*, provided additional room for storage and the preparation and storage of foods such as cheese. The houses of better-off families might have a loft above the central room for sleeping, but these do not appear to have been frequent until the late nineteenth century. Connected to this or nearby were rooms that normally functioned as a part of the farm: the stable for livestock and the connecting barn where feed was kept. Other small buildings used for pigs and chickens could sometimes be found. But these spaces did not have rigidly defined functions. Visitors might sleep in the stable or barn for a night or two, and servants probably slept there as a matter of course in some families. When the presence of kin in the household demanded, more permanent living quarters might be arranged: Andre Brésson charted a farmhouse, the Maison Roche in Saint-Didier-sur-Rochefort (canton of Noirétable), in which rooms for several aunts of the family had been constructed in the barn.[13]

The siting of the farmhouse and associated buildings reinforces an image of separation between each family and outsiders. In the low hills on the borders of the Plaine du Forez and in the mountains, the different rooms were frequently constructed in a line facing an open courtyard, but here geography served to isolate the family, as many farmhouses stood alone, away from the road. In larger hamlets, especially on the plains and in the eastern mountains bordering on the Rhône, houses built barriers between the nuclear family and its neighbors in the hamlet. In some instances, the stable and barn were placed in front of the *maison*, with a courtyard between them; in others, especially on larger farms, the buildings formed a closed or almost-closed courtyard, separating the residence from the road. Thus even within these settlements the physical evidence suggests that each family separated itself from its neighbors and from those passing by on the roadway.[14]

13 See Andre Bréasson, "Maisons paysannes des environs de Saint-Didier-sur-Rochefort," *Bulletin de la Diana*, 39 (1965), 50–68, and his more detailed "Maisons paysannes d'un coin du Forez," typescript in Archives de la Diana (January 1964), in which the Maison Roche is described.

14 Bréasson, "Maisons paysannes d'un coin du Forez"; Robert and Madeleine Bouiller, *Les Constructions traditionelles dans le département de la Loire* (Ambierle: Musée Forézienne, 1977), 7.

These patterns of settlement certainly suggest a place in which human interaction would be restricted. The bourg was a considerable distance from most farmhouses, and the small groups in which most people lived limited their immediate social contacts. A day's work for a farmer might mean a trip across the commune to visit scattered parcels of land, including a visit to the bourg, but social contacts depended on chance encounters. Women who left the hamlet only on rare occasions were even more limited in their social relations. Maps and abandoned farm buildings certainly reinforce the notion of an empty countryside, and we can understand Jacquou le Croquant's comment that "you never see anyone in the countryside." Images of isolation spring easily from these versions of the countryside.

But the countryside in the early nineteenth century was densely peopled, even if not as densely as cities were. The bourg and its *place* provided a focus for the rest of the commune; this most public space brought country dwellers together, at times in large numbers. Whether they liked it or not, the residents of hamlets needed the bourg for many necessary services. The administrative, religious, and economic structure of rural France wrote itself on a landscape given to dispersion, and made these hamlets depend upon a distant and sometimes rival settlement for basic aspects of life: registering births and deaths, celebrating Sunday Mass and weddings, burying and remembering the dead, marketing livestock and produce, and socializing outside of a narrow group of kin and neighbors. Men did have more reasons to leave the hamlet, and this distinction between the sexes is significant. But for both sexes, these were occasions on which patterns of work at their farm or field were broken. Sowing and harvesting, Sunday Mass, weddings, funerals, and village festivals take on added significance when we consider that they were not only chances to leave the localized, isolated framework of existence marked by the farmhouse and fields and enter a different social environment, but also part and parcel of rural life even if hidden by the French discourse about an "isolated" countryside.[15]

III

The ancien régime tended to lump all country dwellers together as a group distinct from those who lived in cities, a distinction that easily led to descriptions of country dwellers in terms such as "savage." Yet important segments of the French elite also recognized the importance of the countryside in the production of national wealth and in providing food for the cities. Conflict between city and countryside was endemic in

15 Ulysses Rouchon, *La Vie paysanne dans la Haute-Loire* (Le Puy: Imprimerie de la Haute-Loire, 1933), vol. 1: 12, emphasizes the "great pomp" with which peasants in this neighboring department celebrated these occasions.

eighteenth-century France, with cities condemned as places that wantonly drained the [different] countryside without regard for the suffering this caused. As Steven L. Kaplan has pointed out, this division was often between Paris and the provinces, and the grain trade was its "most visceral expression." Economic theorizing often began with the construction of a countryside. Because it was a source of the grains that would allow the manufacturing development sought by Colbertian mercantilism in the late-seventeenth and early eighteenth centuries, the state encouraged investment in agriculture as a way of increasing wealth. The countryside was also privileged by mercantilism's most vociferous and influential opponents, the physiocrats, proponents of the market who saw agriculture as the sole source of increase in a nation's wealth. But even in emphasizing agriculture, the physiocrats saw those who lived in the countryside and worked the soil as a group distinct from the classes that owned the land or who worked in manufacturing.[16]

These varied interests made the economy of the countryside a frequent concern for many in the French elite. But observers were not certain what they were looking for as they traveled through rural areas. There was a concern to categorize, but an inability to describe the substance of categories. Late-eighteenth-century analyses of the Forez, for example, often divided it into three different agricultural regions. These were the Monts du Matin (or the Monts du Lyonnais); the Monts du Soir (or the Monts du Forez); and the central Plaine du Forez.[17] This is a very schematic description of the province. But even granting it, we have to notice that the distinctions between these regions were vague. One of these observers, a M. de Montrouge, noted in 1764 that the first was marked by a "relative progress"; the second was noted for its solidity in agriculture; and the third by "the impression of *laisser-aller*" that marked its inhabitants. Montrouge's comments suggest his ambiguous perception of the countryside: these characteristics appear, to our eyes, as apples, oranges, and peaches, but presumably the comparison made sense to him.

There was also as yet no system for gathering specific information about the countryside that would flesh out these impressions.[18] But some "systematic" inquiries were taken for other purposes, such as taxation. Lists of proprietors and inhabitants compiled in 1788, for example, gave

16 Steven L. Kaplan, *Bread, Politics and Political Economy*, chs. 1–4; Charles Gide and Charles Rist, *Histoire des doctrines économiques* (Paris: Société du Recueil Sirey, 1922), 1–58; Elizabeth Fox-Genovese, *The Origins of Physiocracy* (Ithaca, N.Y.: Cornell University Press, 1976).

17 See Archives nationales (hereafter A.N.) H 1510[1], Montrouge, *Observations sur les diffautes de la culture employée dans la Plaine de Forez* (1764); François Tomas, "Géographie sociale du Forez en 1788 d'après les tableaux des 'propriétaires et habitans,'" *Bulletin de la Diana*, 39 (1965), 80–117.

18 Cf. Bourguet, *Déchiffrer la France*, ch. 1, for the descriptive character of ancien régime inquiries.

the "occupations" and tax burdens of those listed, and these suggest other ways of describing the countryside. There were a few farmers on the Plaine du Forez, working the *domaines* of young orphans, and many *grangers*, or sharecroppers. The size of their tax burden suggests that they held large *métairies*. Outside of the Plaine, however, the importance of sharecroppers and farmers declined, and in their place, as one moved into the foothills of the two mountain ranges, appeared an overwhelming number of individuals listed as *habitans*, paying relatively small sums in taxes. François Tomas, who has studied these lists carefully, speculates that these were proprietors of small parcels and day laborers. In the foothills, small towns appeared, of which Boën and Saint-Galmier were the largest. These towns were small commercial centers populated by merchants, administrators, and lawyers, the small-town bourgeoisie of the ancien régime whose services the rural population needed. Finally, above the foothills, smallholders became even more noticeable. This was especially true in the Monts du Forez, where *habitans* made up 88 percent of those listed; a substantial number of these paid relatively high taxes, suggesting a predominance of family farmers. Supplementing these in certain areas (the plateau of Saint-Bonnet-le-Chateau and the area farther north) sharecroppers were important, but in a minority. In the eastern Monts du Lyonnais, sharecropping was very rare; *habitans* made up 68 percent of those listed, and most of the rest of the inhabitants of these mountains were farmers.

The imprecision and inconsistency of the various descriptions of the countryside around the turn of the nineteenth century, even if frustrating for the historian wanting solid data, suggest how difficult it was for educated French men and women to imagine the countryside, and how easily it could take on a "fictional" quality. This became less the case as methods for describing the countryside were refined by the French administration. By midcentury administrative mechanisms were in place that provided "France" with concise information about "important" rural activities. As part of a general European movement concerned with the mathematical description of groups rather than individuals, the systematic tables of censuses and prefectoral inquiries replaced tax lists and the impressions of observers like Montrouge.[19] These forms of information

---

19 Bourguet, *Déchiffrer la France*, p. 311, points out that the data included in the *Statistique générale de la France* emphasized the unity of the nation even in the way it was collected and tabulated, at the national level, rather than being interpreted at the departmental level as had been the case under the Empire. See also H. Le Bras, "La Statistique générale de la France" in Pierre Nora, ed., *Les lieux de mémoire*, T. 2, *La nation* (Paris: Gallimard, 1986), vol. 2: 317–353; Theodore M. Porter, *The Rise of Statistical Thinking* (Princeton, N.J.: Princeton University Press, 1986); Stuart Woolf, "French Civilization and Ethnicity in the Napoleonic Empire," *Past and Present* 124 (1989), 96–120; and

held more meaning for observers of the countryside than for its residents. But they created their own version of the countryside through their focus on certain aspects of rural life, such as the size of farms, systems of land tenure, the productivity of agriculture, and the household organization, age, and occupation of the population.

The agricultural inquiries and censuses therefore brought the country-side under the control of "France" in a specific way. From the mercantilists and physiocrats of the ancien régime to the Ministry of Commerce and Agriculture of the nineteenth century, the countryside was a place that produced wealth by producing agricultural goods, not only satisfying the consumption needs of the farmer but also generating a surplus for the nation. The *Enquêtes agricoles* were also concerned with the country-side as a source of agricultural goods. Food, so rich in meanings in rural culture, was described only as a commodity.

It appears that in the middle of the nineteenth century, when the first systematic *Enquête agricole* was taken, the rural economy of the ancien régime was still largely intact in the Loire. The low proportion of religious and noble land shown in the 1788 lists of inhabitants, and the similarities between these lists and the results of the mid-nineteenth-century *Enquêtes*, suggests that property transfers during the Revolution were limited.[20] The size of the farms in which land was held was reported in the 1862 *Enquête agricole décennale*,[21] and this systematic view supports this conclusion. Figure 3.2 maps the median farm sizes in each canton for which data is available. Farms of less than five hectares predominated in the mountainous areas of the south, southwest, and northwest. Only in two areas did median farm size exceed this level: a band across the southern part of the arrondissement of Montbrison (cantons of Montbrison, Saint-Galmier and Saint-Héand) and the northwest, in the arrondissement of Roanne. The canton of Néronde, in the southeastern part of this arrondissement, also had larger farms than most of the department.

The mid-nineteenth-century inquiries are also more precise than earlier sources about the way land was held by the persons who worked it. In most of the Loire, farms were owner-occupied, and the most striking aspect of land tenure in the department is that even the areas where farms were smallest had very high percentages of the population calling them-

idem, "Statistics and the Modern State," *Comparative Studies in Society and History* 31 (1989), 588–604.

20 Compare Gilbert Garrier, "La Formation d'un complexe économico-social de type 'Rhôdanien': Champonost (1730–1822)" in Pierre Léon, *Structures économiques et problèmes sociaux du monde rural dans la France du Sud-Est* (Paris: Belles Lettres, 1966), 357–361.

21 A.N. F[11] 2705 42 (Loire), *Enquête agricole décennale, 1862.*

KEY:
1 = 0-5 hectares
2 = 5-10 hectares
3 = 10-20 hectares
X- data unavailable

Figure 3.2   Median landholding in Loire in 1862, by canton.

selves *propriétaires-cultivateurs* or *propriétaires-fermiers*. In the small-holding region around Saint-Etienne in the south, 30–50 percent of the population listed its occupation this way in 1851.[22] The cantons of Saint-Haon-le-Châtel in the northwest and Néronde in the eastern center were even higher. Much of the rest of the department was somewhat lower, with 20–30 percent *propriétaires,* and the cantons in the arrondissement of Montbrison with relatively large landholdings had even lower percentages of proprietors.

But it is also apparent that land tenure was not simple and straightforward. It was common for proprietors also to be farmers or day laborers.

22 A.D.L. 49 M 54 to 49 M 84, *Listes nominatives de recensement de 1851.*

In the canton of Charlieu in the northeast, for example, 641 proprietors in 1852 worked only their own land, but 954 worked for themselves and for others. In the canton of Montbrison, one of the areas of larger farms in the department, 400 proprietors worked only their own land, but 1,693 cultivated both for themselves and others. Further south, in the arrondissement of Saint-Etienne, cultivation of the farmer's own land was more frequent, but rented land continued to be significant: in the canton of Saint-Héand, north of Saint-Etienne, 708 proprietors worked only their own land, while 381 worked their own land and rented land from someone else in 1862. Another 366 proprietors also worked as *journaliers*. In Bourg-Argental, southeast of Saint-Etienne in the Monts du Pilat, 652 proprietors worked their own land, but 208 also rented land, and 325 worked as day laborers.[23]

For most farmers, leases were for money rent and lasted between six and nine years. But *métayage* or *grangage* (sharecropping) also existed throughout the department, even if delineating the areas in which it dominated is difficult. In the early nineteenth century, one observer noted that in the Plaine du Forez "the greater part of properties are cultivated by *colonnes* or *grangers*."[24] In the 1851 census, *métayers* appear in relatively small numbers in most of the cantons of the arrondissement of Roanne. But the *Enquêtes agricoles* taken during the nineteenth century suggest that it was more pervasive in some parts of the department, especially in the western part of the department, as proprietors supplemented their own land with fields held under sharecropping leases. Elsewhere in the department such leases were certainly known if not frequent.

The patterns of land tenure that resulted from these arrangements were quite complex. A farm worked by a family might total only five hectares but be pieced together of inherited plots of land; of land rented for a money payment from someone else, perhaps kin who had moved to the industrial city; and, in some areas, of land rented under some form of sharecropping. Even in the major regions of sharecropping and larger farms, such as the canton of Montbrison, land tenure was no simple matter: many families worked not only their own land but also land held under both money and sharecropping leases. In that part of the department the strength of *métayage* may have contributed to maintaining large farms, but it would be a mistake to see even these sharecroppers as having only one form of land tenure.

The third concern of the agricultural inquiries was production. Livestock consisted of cows, sheep, and the ever-present chickens. Cereal

23 A.D.L. 55 M 10, 11, 12, *Enquête agricole décennale, 1852;* A.N. F¹¹ 2705 42 (Loire), *Enquête agricole décennale, 1862.*
24 Joseph Duplessy, *Annuaire du Département de la Loire* (Montbrison: Cheminal, 1818), 250, n. 2.

polyculture was the rule virtually everywhere in the department, with two or three field systems rotating a mixture of wheat, rye, and oats with annual fallowing that allowed the land to recover its productivity. Average yields in the department at midcentury were 11.3 hectoliters (hl) per hectare for wheat, 16.2 hl/hectare for oats, and 9.5 hl/hectare for rye, and no area stood out as being more productive than the others.[25]

The prefectoral inquiries emphasized agricultural activities as the basis of French rural society in the Loire, and information on farm size, land tenure, and agricultural production assumed importance in the context of a discourse that placed the countryside as the producer of goods and wealth needed by the rest of the nation. In these terms, the department did not seem promising. Most of the farms in the department were so small that they could not support a family nor fully employ the labor available even in a nuclear family. In the foothills and mountains of the Loire, subsistence required a relatively large farm. Gilbert Garrier, for example, estimates that in the similar soils of the neighboring Beaujolais and Lyonnais, a farm of at least ten hectares was necessary to both support and occupy the labor of a peasant family.[26] Such farms were unusual in the Loire. The diversity of land tenure, so difficult for the *Enquête* to capture and for us to decipher, was another aspect of that particularism that distinguished the countryside from the nation. These farms were also marked by their low productivity; and if its role was to produce basic foodstuffs, the rural Loire in the early nineteenth century seemed to epitomize the timeless, intractable countryside, producing less than regions of northern France at this time.[27]

The various strands of the French discourse about the countryside could easily come together to produce an image of a place burdened by the weight of tradition, both for contemporaries and later historians.[28] Part of this process involved focusing on agriculture, but country dwellers found work where they could, as wet nurses, haulers and, most often, in manufacturing industries organized on a putting-out basis. They either subsisted entirely on this income or, more frequently, used it to complement the agricultural work of the husband and his sons. These

---

25 A.D.L. 55 M 10, 11, 12, *Enquête agricole décennale, 1852*. One hectoliter equals 2.838 bushels; one hectare equals 2.471 acres.

26 Gilbert Garrier, *Paysans du Beaujolais et du Lyonnais* (Presses Universitaires de Grenoble, 1973), vol. 1: 130–131; see also my analysis of the labor requirements of a farm in James R. Lehning, *The Peasants of Marlhes* (Chapel Hill: University of North Carolina Press, 1980), ch. 9.

27 Michel Morineau, *Les Faux-Semblants d'un démarrage économique* (Paris: Colin, 1970), 27, 29.

28 Robert Estier, "Productions agricoles et industries rurales: l'exemple du roannais textile au XIXe siècle," in P. Bairoch and A. M. Pinz, *Des Economies traditionelles aux sociétés industrielles* (Geneva: Droz, 1985), 244.

"marginal" activities disrupt the notion of an "immobile" rural economy and further complicated the countryside from the perspective of French culture. It fitted uneasily both with images of manufacturing drawn from artisanal models, and with those of the countryside as a producer of agricultural goods, and even as the administration acquired expertise in describing the countryside, these manufacturing activities tended to be ignored. Nonetheless, it is clear that more than agriculture occurred in the countryside.

While virtually every village in the Loire had some workers in rural industry, there were several areas in which it assumed great importance. The silk-weaving industry of Saint-Etienne was a major employer in the southern arrondissement of the department, and a large aureole in which country dwellers worked on simple looms to produce the ribbons that decorated the clothing worn by most French men and women extended some forty kilometers around the city. Farther to the northeast, in the canton of Néronde, the silk industries of Lyon and Tarare in the Rhône found labor. And in the north and northeast, merchants from Roanne, Lyon, and Thizy placed orders for silk and cotton goods in the countryside.[29] Only the Plaine du Forez and the western Monts du Forez did not have substantial numbers of rural textile workers.

The organization of these rural industries connected city and countryside.[30] Urban merchants or their agents placed silk or cotton thread with rural families who wove it into cloth, usually using their own looms. The merchant then purchased the finished material, completed its processing, and sold it. Women did much of the labor, as wives and daughters in land-poor families sought cash income. Pay was poor, and it was difficult for a family to survive just on the income from rural industry. Some families did this, but others used these trades as a complement to agriculture.

Mid-nineteenth-century sources certainly provided more systematic

29 On these industries, see: Louis-Jean Gras, *Histoire de la rubannerie* (Saint-Etienne: Théolier, 1906), Charles Dechelette, *L'Industrie contonnière à Roanne* (Roanne: Imprimerie Souchier, 1910); E. Pariset, *Histoire de la fabrique lyonnaise* (Lyon: A. Rey, 1901), 306–307; Pierre Cayez, *Métiers jacquards et hauts fourneaux: aux origines de l'industrie lyonnaise* (Lyon: Presses Universitaires de Lyon, 1978), 152–159; and A. N. C 956 *Enquête sur le travail agricole et industriel du 25 mai 1848.*

30 There were, of course, variations in organization across France and Europe. See Franklin F. Mendels, "Proto-Industrialization: The First Phase of the Industrialization Process," *Journal of Economic History* 32 (1972), 241–261, and idem, *Industrialization and Population Pressure in 18th-Century Flanders* (Ann Arbor, Mich.: University Microfilms International, 1977). Serge Chassagne, "La Diffusion rurale de l'industrie cotonnière en France (1750–1850)," *Revue du Nord* 240 (1979), 97–114, is a good description of the national distribution of the rural cotton industry. For descriptions of cottage work in the Loire countryside, see Lehning, *Peasants of Marlhes*, 40–43; and idem, "Nuptiality and Rural Industry: Families and Labor in the French Countryside," *Journal of Family History* 8 (1983), 333–345.

descriptions of the countryside than earlier ones. But this does not mean that, in place of ancien régime fictions, the statisticians of the nineteenth century found the "real" countryside. There no doubt was some basis for Montrouge's comments about the regions of the Forez, just as the wheat, rye, and oats counted in the *Enquêtes agricoles* were certainly grown and harvested. But this new construction imposed on rural life those aspects that had come to be seen as central to the countryside. Agriculture, marked by landholding, tenure, and production, dominated this vision; other activities were marginalized. While there were few differences within the department in these terms in the first half of the nineteenth century, these perceptions placed the countryside and its inhabitants in a story about the way they might become a part of the nation.

IV

The description of population behavior also became increasingly statistical in the first half of the nineteenth century. As with economic activities, attempts before the mid-nineteenth century to describe this behavior were halting, even if there was a gradual movement toward methods of quantitatively describing the different components of population behavior, a process that culminated in 1855 with the invention by Achille Guillard of the very term *démographie*.[31] The elaboration of a science of population meant not only that the components of population growth received attention, but also that the administration gathered systematic information on the subject. The result was the particularly mathematical perception of population that goes unquestioned today, a perception that encapsulated the various aspects of birth, death, marriage, and migration in terms of numbers of events in a population. But as was the case with the *Enquêtes agricoles'* limited vision of foodstuffs, this construction of these processes eliminated from view many of their most important components for the country dwellers who were experiencing them, turning the complicated meanings of birth, marriage, and death into simple numbers.

Descriptions of the Stephanois region in terms such as "beehive," or utilizing hearth lists,[32] are the rule for the period before the Revolution. By the middle of the nineteenth century, however, the developing science of statistics provided a language in which French administrators and oth-

---

31 See Jacques and Michel Dupâquier, *Histoire de la démographie* (Paris: Perrin, 1985), 251–261; 279–298; and Jacques Dupâquier and René Le Mée, "La Connaissance des faits démographiques de 1789 à 1914" in Jacques Dupâquier, ed., *Histoire de la population française* (Paris: Presses Universitaires de France, 1988), vol. 3: 15–61.
32 See François Tomas, "Problèmes de démographie historique: le Forez au XVIIIe siècle," *Cahiers d'Histoire* 13 (1968), 381–399.

ers could describe population behavior more precisely. For the Loire this information allows a description of a demographic ancien régime, a concatenation of fertility, nuptiality, and mortality similar to the situation typical of France prior to 1789.[33] The most obvious implication of this information is to counter the notion of an "empty" countryside. The most heavily populated region in the department (see Figure 3.3)[34] was the south, above all the urban, industrial Stephanois Valley from Rive-de-Gier through Saint-Chamond and Saint-Etienne to Le Chambon. But the concentration of population in this valley spilled over to the north and southeast, where relatively high densities were found in the predominantly rural cantons of Pélussin and Saint-Galmier. This pattern continued up the entire east side of the department, marking the Monts du Lyonnais as a second region of relatively high density. The two northeastern cantons in the department, Charlieu and Belmont, extended this region. Beginning in the southwest in the canton of Bourg-Argental, running along the western border of the department, and broken only by the urban canton of Le Chambon, was a third region more sparsely populated than the eastern mountains. Even the principal city of this area, Montbrison, *chef-lieu* of the department until 1852, was of modest size: lacking in industry, badly situated for commerce, it was a small provincial town of only 7,054 inhabitants in 1841. Finally, the central Plaine du Forez, and especially the canton of Boën, had the lowest density in the department.

Such varying population densities are another instance of the particularism of the countryside and reflect in microcosm variations across France. They can be described in demographer's terms as the result of restricted marriage, uncontrolled fertility within marriage, and high mortality, but these different components of population behavior did not fit together the same way everywhere. Fertility, nuptiality, and mortality levels, even if broadly similar, nonetheless generated different population regions across Europe by the mid-nineteenth century.[35] In the depart-

---

33 For more detailed treatment of the demographic and family history of the Loire than can be given here, see: James R. Lehning, "Nuptiality and Rural Industry"; idem, *Peasants of Marlhes;* idem, "The Decline of Marital Fertility: Evidence from a French Department, la Loire, 1851–1891," *Annales de Démographie Historique* (Paris, 1984), 201–217; idem, "Literacy and Demographic Behavior," *History of Education Quarterly* (1984), 545–559; idem, "The Timing and Prevalence of Women's Marriage in the French Department of the Loire, 1851–1891," *Journal of Family History* 13 (1988), 307–327; and idem, "Socioeconomic Change, Peasant Household Structure and Demographic Behavior in a French Department," *Journal of Family History* 19 (1992), 161–181.

34 These densities have been calculated using data drawn from *Annuaire du département de la Loire pour 1846* (Montbrison: Imprimerie du département de la Loire, 1846), 134–145; 184–193; 236–245; and the cadastral areas for each canton in A.N. F[11] 2705 42 (Loire), *Enquête agricole décennale, 1862.*

35 Susan Cotts Watkins, *From Provinces Into Nations: Demographic Integration in Western Europe, 1870–1960* (Princeton, N.J.: Princeton University Press, 1991).

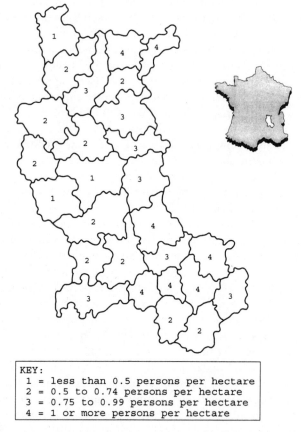

KEY:
1 = less than 0.5 persons per hectare
2 = 0.5 to 0.74 persons per hectare
3 = 0.75 to 0.99 persons per hectare
4 = 1 or more persons per hectare

Figure 3.3   Population densities in Department of the Loire, 1841.

ment of the Loire, the lowest levels of marital fertility were in the north-western corner of the department, in the cantons of Saint-Haon-le-Châtel, La Pacaudière, Roanne, and Perreux (see Figure 3.4). Two other areas also show a tendency toward lower marital fertility in 1851. Along the western border, the mountain cantons of Noiretable and Saint-Georges-en-Couzan, both located in the Monts du Forez, formed one cluster. Rive-de-Gier, in the southeast, also was low. The variations in marital fertility in the department at midcentury therefore ran from lower levels in the northwest through a region of moderate levels in the center to the higher marital fertility in the southern arrondissement. But the generally high levels at which most variation took place suggest that only in the northwest were many families limiting their fertility.

X - data unavailable

Figure 3.4 Cantonal medians of I_g (marital fertility) in Department of the Loire in 1851.

Marriage came relatively late for most Europeans in the nineteenth century for both men and women, and there were substantial proportions of men and women who did not marry.[36] The department of the Loire shared this pattern, but there was still a great deal of heterogeneity in marriage behavior in 1851 (see Figure 3.5). The lowest levels of proportions married were found in the cantons of Saint-Genest-Malifaux and Saint-Chamond in the south and Noiretable and Saint-Georges-en-Couzan in the western Monts du Forez. There were exceptionally high levels in several western cantons of the Roannais in the north (La Pacaudière and Saint-Just-en-Chevalet); throughout the rest of the department, nuptiality varied between these two extremes.

36 John Hajnal, "European Marriage Patterns in Perspective," In D. V. Glass and D. E. C. Eversely, eds., *Population in History* (London: E. Arnold, 1965), 101–146.

X - data unavailable

Figure 3.5   Cantonal medians of I_m (proportion married) in Department of the
Loire in 1851.

In contrast to the high levels of marital fertility in the Loire in 1851,
illegitimate fertility was uniformly low. This was the case even in those
cantons (Saint-Etienne, Roanne) with large urban centers, where one
would expect higher levels of illegitimacy. The rural cantons do not appear to have been exporting illegitimate births to the urban areas, nor do
those areas themselves appear to have suffered the high levels of illegitimacy typical of major urban and industrial areas in mid-nineteenth-
century France.[37]
    The natural fertility within marriage characteristic of most of the rural

37 On illegitimacy, see Edward Shorter, John Knodel, and Etienne van de Walle, "The
   Decline of Non-Marital Fertility in Europe, 1880–1940," *Population Studies* 25 (1971),
   375–393; Lehning, *Peasants of Marlhes*, 72–73; and Elinor Accampo, *Industrialization,
   Family Life, and Class Relations: Saint-Chamond, 1815–1914* (Berkeley and Los Angeles: University of California Press, 1989), 54.

X - data unavailable

Figure 3.6   Cantonal medians of I_f (overall fertility) in Department of the Loire in 1851.

Loire at midcentury meant that, even with limited nuptiality as a brake, the population was reproducing itself at high levels, and in some places overall fertility was strikingly high (see Figure 3.6). This was the case along the northeastern edge of the department, in the Monts du Beaujolais and Monts du Lyonnais, and in the more industrialized cantons of Le Chambon and Saint-Etienne. These urban areas were growing in size because of their exceptionally high birth rates.[38] Crude birth rates (CBRs)

38 See the intensive demographic analyses of Rive-de-Gier and Saint-Chamond: Michael Hanagan, "Proletarian Families and Social Protest: Production and Reproduction as Issues of Social Conflict in Nineteenth-Century France," in Steven Laurence Kaplan and Cynthia J. Koepp, eds., *Work in France: Representations, Meaning, Organization, and Practice* (Ithaca, N.Y.: Cornell University Press, 1986), 418–456, which points out the increasing fertility of miners in the mid-nineteenth century; and Accampo, *Industrialization, Family Life, and Class,* esp. ch. 2. For France as a whole, see Etienne van de

over 30 per thousand were the rule in the industrial cities: Le Chambon's stood at 35.1 in 1851, Saint-Etienne's at 38.4, and the as-yet unincorporated suburban communes of Saint-Etienne (Outre-Furens, Beaubrun, Montaux, and Valbenoite) were in the same range. High urban fertility was also the case in the north, where the textile center of Roanne had a CBR of 36.1 per thousand.

Countervailing these reproductive trends throughout the department, however, was the weight of mortality. This was relatively elevated in the Loire throughout the nineteenth century (see Figure 3.7), and it did not show much improvement in the course of the century. By 1851, the highest death rates were in the southern mountains around Saint-Etienne: this industrial center itself, however, was one of the healthiest cantons in its arrondissement, possibly because of the younger population attracted by industry. The Plaine du Forez, farther north, had lower mortality than the arrondissement of Saint-Etienne, although the cantons of Saint-Rambert, Montbrison, and Boën were only slightly below the Stephanois level. The mountains to the east and west of the Plaine were at still lower levels, and the Plaine de Roanne in the north matched these levels. Only in the cantons of Saint-Just-en-Chevalet, Saint-Symphorien-en-Laye, and Belmont did the death rate rise to the levels of the Plaine du Forez and the arrondissement of Saint-Etienne.

This description of the different components of population behavior in the Loire is certainly a rough one, although to take the relatively problematic information gathered in the nineteenth century further would create a spurious sense of exactness. It is even more difficult to describe another type of population behavior, migration, for the administration did not gather information on it. But from what can be pieced together it is apparent that few cantons in the department were able to hold onto all of their native sons and daughters in the early nineteenth century, and migration for a significant period of time was a normal part of the lives of many country dwellers. Net migration rates for the 1841–51 period show that each year a substantial number of Foreziens took to the roads, in many cases no doubt for the industrial centers of Roanne and Saint-Etienne, but also for the regional center of Lyon (see Figure 3.8). Saint-Etienne drew its immigrants from a fairly small hinterland, making the cantons immediately to the south great exporters of population.[39] Farther

Walle, "Alone in Europe: The French Fertility Decline Until 1850," in Charles Tilly, ed., *Historical Studies of Changing Fertility* (Princeton, N.J.: Princeton University Press, 1978), 257–288; and E. A. Wrigley, "The Fall of Marital Fertility in 19th-Century France: Exemplar or Exception?" *European Journal of Population* 1 (1985), 31–60; 141–177.

39 D. Tenand, "Les Origines de la classe ouvrière stéphanoise," *Diplôme d'études supérieures,* Université de Lyon II (1972), 88; Jacques Meaudre, "La poussée urbaine à Saint-Etienne, 1815–1872," *Diplôme d'études supérieures,* Université de Lyon, 1966.

X - data unavailable

Figure 3.7 Crude death rates by canton, 1851.

north and east, in the Monts du Lyonnais and Monts du Beaujolais, access to Roanne, but also to Lyon and the Rhône Valley stimulated migration out of the rural villages.[40] Lower rates of out-migration suggest that the Plaine du Forez was able to keep much of its population growth as farm labor, while in the western mountains low overall fertility reduced the pressures for emigration. In general, more commercial communes had lower rates of out-migration than others, while the communes that were isolated by language, means of communication, and transportation, and that also had high rates of population growth and limited economic possibilities, had difficulty keeping population.[41]

40 Yves Lequin, *Les Ouvriers de la région lyonnaise (1848–1914)* (Lyon: Presses Universitaires de Lyon, 1977), vol. 1: 414; Maurice Garden, *Lyon et les lyonnais au XVIIIe siècle* (Paris: Belles lettres, 1979), 648–649.

41 See also Gilbert Garrier, *Paysans du Beaujolais et du Lyonnais, 1800–1970*, vol. 1: 484; Alain Corbin, *Archaïsme et modernité en Limousin au XIXe siècle, 1845–1880* (Paris:

X - data unavailable

Figure 3.8   Net migration rates by canton, 1841–1851.

Much nineteenth-century migration was from the countryside to cities, but there was also a significant amount of movement between rural villages. A tabulation of the places of birth given in the 1872 census for several rural communes shows how important this could be. In La Fouillouse (canton of Saint-Héand), just north of Saint-Etienne, the population came from sixteen cantons of the Loire and twelve other departments. In Verrières (canton of Montbrison) in the foothills of the western Monts du Forez, thirteen cantons of the department and five other departments were represented. In Ouches (canton of Roanne), in the Roannais plain, residents came from ten cantons and seven other departments. And in Saint-Hilaire (canton of Charlieu) the population had been born

Marcel Rivière et Cie, 1975), vol. 1: 180; and André Armengaud, *Les Populations de l'Est Aquitaine au début de l'époque contemporaine* (Paris: Mouton, 1961), 158–160, 165–166.

in seven cantons and four other departments.[42] Most of this movement was over very short distances, of course: most of the nonnative population in these villages came from nearby cantons, and the Allier, the Rhône, the Saône-et-Loire, and the Haute-Loire were the usual sources of the population born outside of the Loire. But these examples serve to underline the point that a significant number of nineteenth-century migrants did not end up in industrial cities such as Roanne and Saint-Etienne, even if they may have left their homes with such destinations in mind.

Temporary and seasonal migration were also important aspects of population movement in the Loire in the first half of the nineteenth century. The department was crossed by Auvergnats traveling to work as woodcutters in the forests of the Loire and farther south, and by Limousins heading for the growing cities of Saint-Etienne and Lyon.[43] Farm workers came down from the densely populated mountains, especially the Monts du Forez, to work on harvests in the Plaine du Forez, then gradually worked their way back up the mountain slopes to their own farms. The industrial centers were also the destinations of temporary migrants: many rural out-migrants stayed in these cities for only a few years, earning enough to set up a farm of their own, returning to their native village when industrial fortunes turned down. Even if they made a career of mining or steelworking, eventually, many retired to the countryside when old age or ill health forced them to give up their industrial work.

The censuses also erected the residential household as a basic unit of analysis. In 1851 most country dwellers lived in households consisting of only a married couple and their unmarried children, but there were some areas in which household complexity was more prevalent (see Figures 3.9 and 3.10).[44] This was most noticeable in the western mountain cantons,

---

42 A.D.L. 49 M 176, 184, 188, 203, *Listes nominatives de recensement de 1872*, cantons of Montbrison, Charlieu, Roanne, Saint-Héand. This was the first census to ask this question.

43 Duplessy, *Annuaire*, 171–172; Corbin, *Archaïsme et modernité*, 180–182; Garrier, *Paysans du Beaujolais et du Lyonnais*, 98–99; Abel Chatelain, *Les Migrants temporaires en France de 1800 à 1914* (Villeneuve-d'Ascq: Université de Lille III, 1976), 627; and Abel Poitrineau, "Aspects de l'émigration temporaire et saisonière en Auvergne à la fin du XVIIIe et au début du XIXe siècle," *Revue d'Histoire Moderne et Contemporaine* 9 (1962), 16.

44 These figures employ two summary measures of the structure of the residential household – adults per household and marital units per household – invented by William Parrish and Moshe Schwartz, "Household Complexity in Nineteenth Century France," *American Sociological Review* 37 (1972), 154–173. It will be apparent that in the construction of their indices, Parrish and Schwartz emphasize the particular characteristics of the family unit that have, since the mid-nineteenth century, dominated the study of the family. For a critique of these measures, see Lutz K. Berkner, Jr., "Household Arithmetic: A Note," *Journal of Family History* 2 (1977), 159–163.

X - data unavailable

Figure 3.9   Cantonal medians of adults per household (APH) in Department of
the Loire, 1851.

where unmarried adults and, less frequently, married siblings or children
were often a part of the household. But throughout the department,
nuclear and complex households could be found next door to each other.

v

As products of French culture, these economic, demographic, and household descriptions contributed to the construction of the French discourse
about the countryside, and we can see similarities with the novels, histories, and paintings discussed in Chapter 2. They created a story about the
countryside and its people that incorporates many of the qualities of
"peasants": the countryside was diverse, each part was isolated from the
others, and its inhabitants lagged behind "France" in adopting "modern"
productive and reproductive behavior. But statistical inquiries into the
economy and population of the countryside also ignored characteristics

Figure 3.10   Cantonal medians of marital units per household (MUH) in Department of the Loire, 1851.

of it, such as migration and rural industry, that contradicted this image. Their particular contribution was to portray the countryside as a place both unchanging and to be changed, to place it in a possible history even while it was denied its own history. As the head of the French census under the July Monarchy, Alexandre Moreau de Jonnès, wrote, "Statistics does not have the power to act, but it has the power to reveal, and happily, in our day, this is practically the same thing."[45] Resistant to change, requiring French intervention, "peasants" nonetheless were significant because of what they could become.

---

45 Quoted in Porter, *Rise of Statistical Thinking,* 29. See also Bernard Cohn, "The Census, Social Structure and Objectification in South Asia" in *An Anthropologist Among the Historians and Other Essays* (New York: Oxford University Press, 1987), 224–254; and Daniel Scott Smith, "The Meanings of Family and Household: Change and Continuity in the Mirror of the American Census," *Population and Development Review* 18 (1992), 421–456.

My argument is that the categories of "peasant" and "French," or their more general stand-ins, "traditional" and "modern," are not the most useful in understanding rural history. Such categories have their own implicit histories, and the purpose here is to move outside of and overcome such aspects of rural histories. The interrelations of the economic and demographic patterns described in the various sources constructed by the French state must be viewed as a part of the negotiation of the meanings of the category "peasant." This process can be seen more clearly if we reconstruct several examples of rural communities. Such reconstructions can be relatively straightforward, rehearsing the different kinds and levels of economic and demographic behavior.[46] But they also allow us to see several sides of the negotiating process.

Verrières was an agricultural village of around a thousand people in the mid-nineteenth century. Located in the canton of Montbrison in the foothills of the western Monts du Forez, its economy was dominated by family farmers. Most heads of household listed themselves as *propriétaires-cultivateurs* in the 1851 census, but their farms were probably composed of both their own land and sharecropping *domaines*. According to the 1852 *Enquête agricole décennale*, a majority of farmers were able to piece together farms of ten to twenty hectares that produced cereals (especially rye) and livestock. While much of the cereal was probably for local consumption, livestock was a valuable cash product that provided income for payment of rents, taxes, and expansion of holdings.[47] Saint-Hilaire, in contrast, was a smaller commune of about seven hundred people in the mountainous canton of Charlieu in the northeastern corner of the department. Landholding was more divided here than in Verrières, and most farms were less than five hectares in size, too small to employ more than a few family members and not productive enough to provide for the needs of an entire family. Agriculture was complemented in Saint-Hilaire by silk and cotton weaving for merchants in Thizy and Lyon in the neighboring department of the Rhône.[48]

Saint-Hilaire and Verrières were places in which agricultural production was low in the first half of the nineteenth century: in Verrières this could be attributed to sharecropping, in Saint-Hilaire to the small size of farms. For this reason, as seen by agricultural reformers, they were typical of many places that were in need of reform if they were to join the French nation. The most important aspect of this analysis is its longitudi-

---

46 For specific information on other communes in the department as comparisons, see Lehning, *Peasants of Marlhes*, which describes a commune south of Saint-Etienne during this period; and the information presented on La Fouillouse north of Saint-Etienne in Lehning, "Nuptiality and Rural Industry." Both Marlhes and La Fouillouse were silk-weaving villages in the middle of the nineteenth century.

47 A.D.L. 55 M 10, *Enquête agricole décennale, 1852.*   48 Ibid.

nal approach, placing country dwellers in a history whose end point was the integration of the countryside into a market that linked it to "France," the fundamental story about the countryside that lay behind the various *statistiques* collected in the nineteenth century. But it is also possible to see these two villages as instances in which rural families operated on their own terms, not those of "tradition" or "modernity."

When household structure and reproductive behavior are considered, the two villages are not easily placed on a scale of modernity. The overwhelming majority of households in Saint-Hilaire were nuclear in structure.[49] For most Saint-Hilairiens, therefore, marriage meant the formation of a new household separate from both sets of parents. Complex households made up a very small proportion of households in Saint-Hilaire in 1851, with only 14 percent including kin outside of the conjugal family. Household complexity did not follow any clear kinship pattern, although there were narrow limits to the kin network; no household members were more distant from the conjugal pair than niece or nephew, and most were siblings.

The household system in Verrières presents a contrast to the overwhelmingly nuclear pattern in Saint-Hilaire, although this does not necessarily make it more "traditional." A majority of households were nuclear in structure (61.5 percent, including those with servants). But almost one-third of all households in 1851 were complex in some way. Many of these complex households included several conjugal pairs (42 of 203 households), and households headed by older parents with married children also present made up the majority of these.

Most households were nuclear when the head was young and in middle age, but as the head grew older, complex households increased in importance, especially those involving the coresidence of a married child with parents. In the 65+ age group, this kind of multiple household included 38.5 percent of all households. In Verrières, therefore, a clear pattern of multigenerational household complexity appears. Much less frequently than in Saint-Hilaire did marriage mean the establishment of a separate household, independent of parents. Instead, many men and women remained in a subordinate position even after their marriage.

One way in which French discourses about the countryside operated is to reduce complicated behaviors to a simple category such as "peasant," and in that way to place it in a subordinated relationship to French culture. This effectively eliminates the intentions and motivations of the individuals involved in these behaviors, aspects of the question that the

---

49 I am considering a cross-sectional source, the nominal census list, as if it reflects longitudinal experience. The lack of a true longitudinal source leaves no other choice, but in any event the slowness of changes in household behavior suggests that this should not create a serious problem.

category of "peasant" answered itself and that were never, in the nineteenth century, the subject of any inquiries. In the absence of such direct information, we, like our predecessors, find a strong tendency to create versions of the "peasant family" that provide interpretations. But interpreting the forms that appear in the sources should be more complicated than simply assuming a "peasant" family similar to the one assumed in the early nineteenth century.

This is especially the case because of the history that is implicit in the French discourse about the countryside, and indeed virtually all modern discourses about country dwellers. These stories type "peasants" as both timeless and outside of the story of "progress." Giving rural people a history almost always means placing them in a story about national development, and in the absence of an alternative means keeping them out of that story makes them timeless.[50] We must not only give country dwellers a history – to recognize that the countryside is a place of change – but also give that history a focus in the countryside, not in cities or the nation. We should, therefore, focus not on the placement of the country dwellers that we find in the inquiries – that is, how "developed" they are – but rather on the cross-sectional linkages across the economy and family that appear at a given moment in time. This different perspective will not necessarily extricate us from the imperatives of modern discourses about "peasants," but it will make country dwellers the actors in their history, rather than shadows drawn from developmental categories.

Viewed in this way, the household and demographic systems in Saint-Hilaire and Verrières appear to be closely linked to the family economy, aimed at matching the household with the labor requirements and capabilities of the economy. There were two different patterns of family economy in Saint-Hilaire at midcentury.[51] In one, agricultural families supplemented the agricultural labor (and earnings) of some members with the manufacturing labor (and earnings) of other members of the household. This can be seen as a reflection of the smallholding prevalent in the village, with most farms less than five hectares in size, below the minimum needed to provide for a family and not requiring the entire family as a labor force. Agriculture, therefore, does not appear to have been productive or profitable enough to provide an adequate basis for a family in Saint-Hilaire. There was excess labor as well as a need for additional income in each of these households, and rural industry provided a supplement to agricultural work and income. A second pattern is also apparent,

50 As, for example, in the widely used theory of peasant economy that was articulated in the 1920s by A. V. Chayanov, *The Theory of the Peasant Economy*, Daniel Thorner, B. Kerblay, and R. E. F. Smith, eds. (Homewood, Ill.: Irwin, 1966).
51 Patterns of family economy have been outlined in more detail in Lehning, "Nuptiality and Rural Industry," and idem, *Peasants of Marlhes*, ch. 9.

in which rural industry was the sole means of support. These households (20.9 percent of the total) did not have access to land, and the entire household, not just some of its members, was labor on which rural industry could draw.

Reproductive and household behavior meshed with these family economies. The nuclear households found in Saint-Hilaire suggest the results of the poor prospects for agriculture – graphically underscored by the complete absence of exclusively agricultural families – as well as the ability of rural industry to provide the economic basis for a household. But fertility was high, as was mortality and out-migration (see Table 3.1). The opportunities in rural industry, as well as the possibility of migration out of the commune, seized by many, meant that there was little pressure to reduce natural population growth beyond the limits imposed by nuptiality.

It is possible to interpret the situation in Verrières in the same perspective. The principal form of land tenure in the village, *métayage*, affected households in several ways. That the greater part of the land worked was not owned but held under a sharecropping lease meant that the household had no control over the ultimate disposition of the land. Thus, holdings were not divided with each inheritance, but remained grouped together into relatively large farms. These farms also needed large amounts of labor. While some families had recourse to domestic servants (17.7 percent of households), kin were more frequently used (30 percent of households). The complex families in Verrières therefore were labor-sharing groups that made it possible for a family to rent and work a *domaine*. The absence of alternative employment in the village, such as the rural industry available in Saint-Hilaire, no doubt strengthened the position of parents as they sought to keep a child working for them even after marriage. But the most important point about this household system was that it made it possible for the tenants in Verrières to work large sharecrop farms, providing the labor required to work sharecropped *domaines*.[52] Mortality was lower than in Saint-Hilaire, although out-migration was more frequent. The system of *métayage* in Verrières encouraged large, extended households and high fertility.

The point here is not that there was a neat fit between the rural economy and different aspects of family behavior in Verrières, Saint-Hilaire, or other villages. Such cross-sectional reductionism is no more valid than that of "tradition" and "modernity." We need to notice, rather, that this fit implies a different but intelligible logic for these families, organized in flexible groups adapted to their particular circumstances, not molded as

52 John Shaffer, *Family and Farm: Agrarian Change and Household Organization in the Loire Valley, 1500–1900* (Albany, N.Y.: SUNY Press, 1982), 51–52.

Table 3.1. *Summary of demographic
and family changes in Verrières
and Saint-Hilaire between 1851 and 1901.*

	Verrières	Saint-Hilaire
I_g 1851	.792	.959
I_g 1901	.499	.284
I_h 1851	.000	.000
I_h 1901	.014	.000
I_m 1851	.382	.416
I_m 1901	.498	.459
I_f 1851	.302	.399
I_f 1901	.339	.130
APH 1851	2.62	2.26
APH 1901	2.40	2.02
MUH 1851	1.19	0.98
MUH 1901	1.01	0.87
CDR 1851	14.5	25.4
CDR 1891	15.5	18.1
CDR 1901	19.8	19.7
MIGR 1841–51	−32.1	−21.2
MIGR 1886–91	−10.3	2.5*

*Positive rate indicates in-migration.
I_g = Marital Fertility
I_h = Illegitimate Fertility
I_m = Proportions Married
I_f = Overall Fertility
APH = Adults per Household
MUH = Marital Units per Household
CDR = Crude Death Rate
MIGR = Net Migration Rate

"peasant" or "traditional." Trying to fit them into those categories and the history they tell is to miss a significant part of the ways these families were living, and to imply, as did the French discourse about the economic and demographic aspects of the countryside, that it was only by changing that the countryside could become a part of the French nation.

VI

Statistical inquiries and censuses inexorably tried to make country dwellers part of the French nation. But if country dwellers at times acted as if they were French, it is also evident that they imagined themselves to be members of other communities as well. On 22 Germinal of the Year 12, the brigadier and a *gendarme* from Chazelles-sur-Lyon arrived in the commune of Saint-Galmier, just north of the Stephanois Valley. They there arrested one Benoit Lapra, a conscript of the class of the Year 8. On 19 Brumaire of the same year, the *brigade* of Pélussin, in the hamlet of Virseaux to maintain order during a fair, noticed another draft dodger and arrested him. Two days later, the brigadier of Saint-Chamond, in the commune of Saint-Coucilleaux to keep order during a festival, spotted a deserter and a draft dodger and placed them under arrest.[53] Such arrests were certainly not unusual in the French countryside during Napoleon's wars, as the state attempted to conscript young men to fill out the ranks, and young men attempted to avoid such service. What happened next was also not unusual. Having taken prisoners into custody, the *gendarmerie* was faced with the problem of getting them out of the village and before a magistrate for prosecution. In Saint-Galmier, there was "some movement" among the inhabitants, and the *gendarmes* requested a squad of national guardsmen from the mayor to protect them as they left the village. The squad did not appear until after ten o'clock in the evening, and the three armed men who did show up seemed suspicious. These fears were realized when, near the *place* of the village, Lapra attempted to flee: the brigadier found himself attacked from behind by the guardsmen, and the prisoner escaped. In Virseaux, the *gendarmes* were attacked by several armed individuals; once again, their prisoner was able to escape, and patrols with the *adjoint* of the commune failed to discover the perpetrators of the attack. In Saint-Coucilleux, a crowd threw stones, fired shots, and attacked the police.

These incidents reflect a pervasive characteristic of rural France in the nineteenth century, the existence of local village communities that, while not immediately apparent to the historian, helped to shape the daily lives of those who lived in and were a part of them. This village community had its origins under the ancien régime. As a collection of lands (the *terroir*), a religious unit (the parish), a fiscal unit (the *collecte*), and a governing unit (the assembly of inhabitants), the village was one of the central institutions in rural life before 1789.[54] In many parts of the country it also controlled aspects of agricultural practice, restricting the rights of individuals to cultivate fields as they wished, and enforcing traditional

---

53 A.N. BB[18] 37. *Inspection géneral de la gendarmerie nationale, Loire.* 30 Germinal An 12; 3 Frimaire An 12; 6 Frimaire An 12.

54 For descriptions of the village community under the ancien régime, see Pierre Goubert, *The Ancien Régime: French Society, 1600–1750* (New York: Harper & Row, 1973), 78–94; and George Duby, ed., *Histoire de la France rurale: tome 2, L'Age classique* (Paris: Editions du Seuil, 1975), 282–300; and Jean-Pierre Gutton, *La Sociabilité villageoise dans l'ancienne France* (Paris: Hachette, 1979).

communal rights over individual property. It also controlled individuals in areas such as marriage, reproduction, and moral behavior.

The community in the Lyonnais,[55] of which the Forez was a part, was most apparent in the different organizations that maintained its collective life: confraternities of the Holy Spirit; "kingdoms" (*royaumes, reinages*); and the organized male youth of the village, called "abbeys of youth," "*enfants de la ville,*" or "*garçons de paroisse.*" While these three groups both overlapped and competed with each other, they held together the village community, joining different generations, the rich and the poor, and the living and the dead. The last several centuries of the *ancien régime,* however, saw an assault by the Catholic Church on the power of several of these institutions of the village community. Ironically, however, the attempt to Christianize the kingdoms and stamp out the abbeys led to their replacement by youth groups completely beyond the control of the parish and curé. As Philip Hoffman has shown, conflicts between the curé and the community increased dramatically in the last decades of the ancien régime.[56] By 1789, Jean-Pierre Gutton notes, "the Tridentine parish was integrated in the rise of a community which was traditional no longer but which, under the control of the state, became an administrative unit." But in spite of these efforts, a lay community existed, especially in the youth groups, outside of this administrative and religious community.[57]

That this community continued into the first half of the nineteenth century and longer is apparent in the responses to conscription and police activity and in the marriage ceremony already described. But it also pervades petitions to the administration concerning communal boundaries. Jean Berger, former mayor of Noailly (canton of Saint-Haon-le-Châtel), may stand for many in his response, dictated from his sickbed in 1844, to a proposal to place his village of Cours in a new commune, Bénissonsdieu:

M. Berger was born in the commune of Noailly, he received the sacraments there. More than twenty years ago he served in its contingent under the flag of the Empire. He was mayor there; his father and mother died there, and he wishes to be buried near them. He contributed to the taxes that constructed a beautiful and large building for the presbytery and primary school, and to the heavy taxes

55 Jean-Pierre Gutton, "Confraternities, Curés and Communities in Rural Areas of the Diocese of Lyons under the Ancien Régime," in Kaspar von Greyerz, ed., *Religion and Society in Early Modern Europe, 1500–1800* (London: Allen & Unwin, 1984), 202; *Villages du Lyonnais sous la monarchie (XVIe–XVIIIe siècles)* (Lyon: Presses Universitaires de Lyon, 1978); Natalie Zemon Davis, "The Reasons of Misrule," in *Society and Culture in Early Modern France* (Stanford, Calif.: Stanford University Press, 1975), 97–123.

56 Philip Hoffman, *Church and Community in the Diocese of Lyon* (New Haven, Conn.: Yale University Press, 1984), 152–153.

57 Gutton, "Confraternities, Curés and Communities," 210.

imposed for the church. In a word, if Noailly possesses all the public services needed, [he] contributed to the expenses made for these and wishes to enjoy [the benefits of] the sacrifices he has made. By affection and by interest he ardently wishes that Noailly, as commune and as parish, continues in its present boundaries, and he hopes that the higher administration will not break it up.[58]

Berger located himself in Noailly "by affection and by interest," and similar solidarities appear in other bits of evidence. In 1839 the mayor of Estivareilles (canton of Saint-Bonnet-le-Château) alerted the prefect to the attempts of the residents of four hamlets in the neighboring commune of Apinac to become a part of his commune, to which they had "since time immemorial" been attached in spiritual matters, and a petition to the prefect from these hamlets argued that their dead had always been buried in the cemetary of Estivareilles, not Apinac.[59] In 1860 a proposal was made to combine hamlets from Saint-Héand, La Fouillouse, Saint-Priest, and Sorbiers into a commune depending on La Tour, "where their church was found." The division of civil and religious jurisdiction made it impossible for residents to assist at Mass and also vote on election days.[60] The same demand was made by residents of several hamlets in the commune of Lezigneux (canton of Montbrison), who wished to belong to the same temporal and spiritual jurisdiction, Lerigneux.[61]

The rural community was therefore an important part of the way in which country dwellers in the Loire constructed their world in the early nineteenth century. In ways that had little to do with the integration into the nation that French discourses imposed on the countryside, the community connected the range of activities that made up the daily lives of the rural population. Activities of reproduction, residence, and earning a living were fitted together within the rural community, and these activities drew larger meanings from the rural culture that existed there.

Perhaps the most important of the meanings conveyed by the rural community was its distinctness from French culture. Incidents of active resistance to external interference throughout France are best documented.[62] But farming, weaving, reproduction, and residence were daily ways in which this separate identity was constructed. It was also evident in the principal opportunity given the rural community to speak under the ancien régime. In the *cahiers de doléances* solicited by the monarchy

58 A.D.L. 46 M 13, *Procès-Verbal de dire par les habitants des Cours, commune de Noailly*, 23 juin 1844. Sahlins, *Boundaries*, 157, discusses the development of this territorial conception of the village community.

59 A.D.L. 46 M 13, *Maire de la commune d'Estivareilles à M. le préfet de la Loire*, 17 avril 1839; *Demande en réunion de quatre villages à la commune d'Estivareilles*.

60 A.D.L. 46 M 15, 30 janvier 1860, *Projet de commune de La Tour*.

61 A.D.L. 46 M 15, 22 avril 1841, *Demande à M. le préfet de la Loire*.

62 Charles Tilly, *The Contentious French* (Cambridge, Mass.: Belknap, 1986).

in 1789 in preparation for the meeting of the Estates General, this community told stories about its separateness from the rest of the country.
The parish of Bard (canton of Montbrison) requested that parish priests
be allowed to validate wills, "since notaries are so rare in the countryside
and especially in the mountains." Bully (canton of Saint-Germain-Laval)
lamented not only the absence of a fair, market, or commerce in the
parish, but also the difficulties involved in going to Roanne, "three
leagues distant and always by roads placed on the sides of hills and
in deep gorges, along different streams." Chalmazel (canton of Saint-
Georges-en-Couzan) was "placed in the western edge of this province on
the summit of the highest and most inaccessible mountain, covered with
snow for eight months each year." Chambéon not only had to face a
swamp that separated it from the Loire River, but the stagnant water gave
its inhabitants fevers, a difficulty at least matched by the plaint from
Saint-Just-sur-Loire (canton of Saint-Rambert) that avalanches threatened
its cultivators. Saint-Christo-en-Fontanès (canton of Saint-Héand) and
Sainte-Colombe (canton of Néronde) complained of their distance from
sovereign courts, and Saint-Denis-sur-Coise (canton of Saint-Galmier)
protested about the amount of time it took young men to travel to the
drawing for military service.[63] Even given the likely purpose of these
complaints, to reduce tax burdens and other inconveniences, there is
good reason to believe that they were true, but that is beside the point.
The *cahiers* created a particular image of the countryside, that contact
with the outside world was difficult for many rural communities in the
Loire. But telling the king about these difficulties also suggested that he
should leave the "isolated" countryside alone. Such arguments were a part
of the negotiating process: however difficult the passage was to the outside world, they went anyway.

VII

Birth, marriage, death, migration, residence, field work, and the weaving
of ribbons and cloth all stood for something else in rural culture. They
were the ways in which country dwellers represented themselves to others, and how these activities were carried out were complex portrayals of
the person, family, and village. Husbands and fathers, for example, were
responsible for the cultivation of their farms. But they were also bound
by the need to do this "as a good father of a family": destruction of the
land, squandering the heritage of one's children, may have provided for

63 Etienne Fournial and Jean-Pierre Gutton, *Cahiers de doléances de la province de Forez*
(Saint-Etienne: Centre d'etudes foréziennes, 1974), vol. 1: 64, 72, 84, 87; vol. 2 347,
313, 323, 320.

that family today, but implied irresponsibility toward the future. Actions expressed meanings in rural culture, and everyone played a variety of roles. These activities also provided the sites for the reproduction of this culture. Boys learned how to be men from their fathers and other men. Girls learned how to be women from their mothers and other women. This learning took place in virtually every activity: farming, weaving ribbons, attending weddings, baptisms, funerals, eating meals, and socializing with neighbors.

This chapter has intentionally emphasized the localized character of these activities. But even though these activities seem far from the centers of French civilization, it has proved impossible to describe them without reference to many aspects of "France." Even before 1789 events such as births, deaths, and marriages had to be registered with a representative of the French state, and as censuses began to be taken, living arrangements also had to be reported. The administration of the country is a well-known feature of the ancien régime, and meant that local events inevitably were written in a "French" framework. Agriculture and rural industry aroused interest beyond communal borders, and the police were occasional visitors to the local community. That community itself had, for centuries, been subjected to the interference of entities outside of itself, as the Church and the state tried to influence its organizations, purposes, and actions. The isolated countryside may be seen as a fiction that served multiple purposes. For French culture it helped place those who lived in the countryside, and their way of life, in a peripheral position in discourses about "France." For the country dwellers themselves, as they used it for example in the *cahiers* of 1789, it served as a way of arguing against the demands – for money, men, and produce – of "France." These fictions met each other in the cultural category "peasant."

Each of the activities described in this chapter, therefore, operated as metaphors in several different planes of meaning: rural, "peasant," and French. As metaphors subject to different meanings, they provided cultural spaces within which their significances could change. Tensions existed in these different meanings in the first half of the century, as is apparent in the emphasis on the individual that the state's *Enquêtes* assumed even in the face of a rural community that gave collective meaning to people's lives.[64] In the second half of the nineteenth century, different representations came to the countryside. These new representations, and their carriers, provided a powerful force in the negotiation of rural identities. On a number of sites, both old and new, country dwellers found their world open to question. Farming, weaving, having families, worshiping God, and socializing within the village acquired new reso-

64 Bourguet, *Déchiffrer la France*, 213.

nances; formal schooling and electoral politics changed the cultural terrain. The movements in and around these places are the ways in which the notion of "peasant" changed meaning in the second half of the nineteenth century, and with it the placement of country dwellers in the French nation.

4

Changes in the landscape

The positioning of country dwellers outside of history by the French construction of the countryside has made it difficult to construct fictional or historical images of country dwellers that give them an active role in stories of national development. Change in the countryside therefore has had to be fundamental and essential: turning "peasants" into "Frenchmen" involved reconstructing those who lived in the countryside. Even given the relatively slow and gradual character of the French movement toward an urban and industrial society in the second half of the nineteenth century, this period brought out the ambiguities of the French discourse about the countryside, as the different nature of "peasants" coexisted with the prospect of their incorporation into the French nation. But while this discourse, and histories that participate in it, speak of a transformation of country dwellers, it makes more sense to describe rural history as a process in which country dwellers changed their placement with regard to French culture. Rural culture coexisted with French culture, leading to a renegotiation of rural and French identities and new meanings for the term "peasant."

The physical setting in the countryside, especially away from Paris and the new industrial regions, remained much the same from the French Revolution until well into the twentieth century. Schools and *mairies* were built, and hedgerows and other obstacles might be torn down or constructed, but these only added to the legacy of centuries of rural civilization. Alice Taverne, a folklorist who gathered materials on rural life in the Loire after World War II, described settlements in terms similar to those used in the preceding chapter. On the Plaine du Forez, bourgs surrounded by isolated farms were the norm, while on the hillsides and in the mountains, farms were grouped in hamlets away from the bourg. But the overall patterning of settlement on the land did not change: she notes that, while these hamlets have their own life, "the bourg, with the church, the school, the *mairie* and a few stores, remains the communal center."[1]

Even with the relative continuity in the French countryside, however, there were some changes in types of habitation in the last part of the nineteenth century, and in this area we can begin to see hints of larger patterns of cultural contact. While the first three-quarters of the century had not been a period of much construction, the forty years before the Great War witnessed significant additions to the rural housing stock of the nation. In the Loire, especially in areas favored by economic growth, the size and complexity of farmhouses increased, with greater differentiation in uses and more privacy within the house itself.[2] New constructions also brought more comfort to rural families and reinforced the distinction between the farmhouse and the outside world. New buildings, either principal residences or annexes used for farm functions, were built at right angles to existing in-line buildings, turning the houses that were open to the passing road or pathway into structures more closed in on themselves. In the Roannais, the fourth side was typically kept open to the road, but in the Seuil de Neulize, the Plaine du Forez, and the eastern border, with the Lyonnais, the typical farmhouse had all four sides closed off.[3] Within these houses, the kitchen continued to carry the name *la maison*, but now there was a *salle* next to it, in which guests were received. The folklorists Robert and Madeleine Bouiller describe the new houses in the mountains as "larger, higher, and more cheerful."[4] Nonetheless, some new constructions did not fit this model: the Maison Muron, at Croix du Mort in Saint-Didier-sur-Rochefort, was built at the end of the nineteenth century by "people of very limited resources" and consisted of a single room with a sleeping area above; a small stable with the hayloft above was connected.[5]

The reconstruction of rural housing in the late nineteenth century is significant because the farmhouse was one of the most important metaphors by which country dwellers represented themselves to the world. The buildings were the focus of the farm, a distinct part of the patrimony of the family, the place within which most social interaction occurred, where the reproduction of the family and culture took place. The physical

---

1 Robert Specklin, "L'achèvement des paysages agraires," in *Histoire de la France rurale* (Paris: Seuil, 1977), vol. 3: 255–305; Alice Taverne, *Coutumes et superstitions foreziennes: l'habitat* (Ambierle: Editions du Musée Forezien, 1973), 26.
2 Eugen Weber, *Peasants into Frenchmen* (Stanford, Calif.: Stanford University Press, 1976), 155, refers to a "revolution in *habitat*." See also Robert and Madeleine Bouiller, *Les Constructions traditionelles dans le département de la Loire* (Ambierle: Musée Forezien, 1977), 15.
3 Ibid., 39–40.   4 Ibid.; Taverne, *Coutumes et superstitions*, 45.
5 André Bréasson, "Maisons paysannes d'un coin du forez," typescript in Archives de la Diana (janvier 1964).

evidence makes clear that changes were made in the rural housing stock. But this evidence gives a conflicted representation, showing the ambiguous relationship of country dwellers to patterns in French culture. As families in the Loire rebuilt the houses and farm buildings of working farms, they sought more room, comfort, and privacy even as the buildings served the needs of the farm. In doing so they appear to model the emphasis on comfort, privacy, and separation from the rest of the world that was a preeminent part of the family vision of urban, bourgeois France.[6] These new buildings thus paradoxically seem to aim at turning a structure whose functions had revolved around the needs of the farm into one in which concerns about privacy, comfort, and sociability predominated. Yet these houses could not in fact become bourgeois. Even as they acquired spaces that could be read as "bourgeois" and took forms that protected familial privacy, they still had to include the stables and barns needed for the farm, and they still housed elements that would be out of place in a bourgeois house, namely, livestock and grain.

Rural housing therefore suggests, in tantalizingly ambiguous fashion, that rather than French culture replacing rural culture there was instead a combination of the two in the same forms. While we lack the same kind of physical evidence for the rural community that exists for rural housing, the process by which a cultural site holds ambiguous meanings depending on one's perspective seems to have occurred there as well. Certainly, in an economic, political, and social sense the community did not define the village world as firmly as under the ancien régime. Farmers sold and bought goods in national and international markets; they traveled frequently across the boundaries of the commune and canton to bring their livestock and crops to harvest. While there, they stopped to drink and talk with men from outside their village in cafés. Sons and daughters of the village moved miles to find work, often in the large cities of the region – Roanne, Saint-Etienne, or Lyon – or in Paris, and they frequently found husbands and wives as well. Other migrants passed through the villages, heading for these urban centers or for work in the countryside as woodcutters or harvest workers, and after the middle of the nineteenth century, railroads made this travel easier.[7] Country dwellers worked as spinners and weavers for merchants in the cities, and nursed the infant

---

6 Peter Gay, *The Bourgeois Experience* (New York: Oxford University Press, 1984), vol. 1: 445.

7 The Loire was one of the first departments in France to have an extensive railway network. The line from Saint-Etienne to Lyon was opened in 1832; that from Andrezieux and Saint-Etienne in the south to Roanne in the north was opened in 1833, and improvements were made in both of these lines during the 1850s. See Louis-Jean Gras, *Histoire des premiers chemins de fer français et du premier tramway de France* (Saint-Etienne: Théolier, 1924).

children of urban artisans, shopkeepers, and workers. The state came into the village to collect taxes, enforce the laws, and draft sons. The village community as an enclosed economic, social, or political entity, if it ever existed, had certainly disappeared by the late nineteenth century.

Developments like this, which occurred across rural France, fit well into the French discourse about peasants becoming French. But there is other evidence that the community continued to play a significant role in the realm of mentality. As we saw in the previous chapter, country dwellers' lives revolved first around the family, and the persons and physical surroundings connected with it. Beyond that, however, was the local community. The family itself was a part of that community, acknowledging new families in the community and with an accountability to the community for familial actions such as childbearing and marriage. Each person had a place in that community, defined by age, gender, and marital status. Each person interacted frequently with the other members of that community. This occurred occasionally during daily activities, in spite of the barriers that geography and the family placed between the individual and the community, but most significantly at highly ceremonial occasions that marked great events in life and in the year, such as baptisms, marriages, funerals, markets, and the festival of the village's patron saint. This community was as real as the larger economic, political, social, and demographic structures that increasingly pulled country dwellers out of their local surroundings and forced them to deal with outsiders.

There are traces that this set of allegiances continued to exist in the second half of the nineteenth century, even as country dwellers were caught in the pressures engendered by the presence of a different language about social relationships.[8] The community surfaced at odd moments, but what is significant about these moments is the way in which they present the community as at odds with "French" forms of behavior. During the disputes of the 1880s over school laicization,[9] for example, the republican schoolteacher could not help but implicitly contrast the behavior of a model republican with the "absurd prejudices" of the population in La Valla, which continued to follow its curé.[10] And the parents in Saint-Julien-en-Jarez and Saint-Galmier were clearly not "free" since they persisted in sending their children to clerical schools. In Saint-Martin-

---

8 For the survival of the community in the neighboring southern Massif Central, see P. M. Jones, *Politics and Rural Society: The Southern Massif Central c. 1750–1880* (Cambridge University Press, 1985), 232, 245–249, 303, 308–309.

9 See this volume, ch. 6; Evelyn M. Acomb, *The French Laic Laws (1879–1889)* (New York: Columbia University Press, 1941); and Mona Ozouf, *L'Ecole, l'église et la République, 1871–1914* (Paris: Colin, 1963).

10 A.N. F¹⁷ 9181, *Laicisations des écoles publiques.*

L'Estrat, this was the doing of "mothers of families" over whom the curé exercised great power.[11] A principal characteristic of "peasants," then, was that they differed from the "French" of the early Third Republic by their enmeshment in restrictive social relations that made them act not as French men and women but as "peasants." The restrictions organized by the rural community distinguished its members from France even if they participated in markets or moved more often.

The work of the folklorist Paul Fortier-Beaulieu in the early twentieth century also makes clear the persistence of older community practices as well as their ambiguous cultural position. A series of maps of traditional customs of the village community indicate the extent to which a number of different practices had been preserved or had fallen into disuse by the 1930s. In categorizing these customs as "folklore" Fortier-Beaulieu and French culture of course indicated that they were not "French." Fortier-Beaulieu's maps of these customs then become descriptive of "peasant" and "French" parts of the department. The persistence of "traditional" folkloric customs in specific geographic areas emerges from these maps: the western Monts du Forez, and the southern Monts du Pilat. In these areas the custom of toll barricades, erected by the village youth to stop the wedding party outside of the bourg, was still in existence in the 1930s.[12] These are also the places in which the custom of the groom not appearing at the house of the bride persisted to that decade; in the center, the eastern Monts du Lyonnais, and in the Roannais, the groom was present by the time of Fortier-Beaulieu's survey.[13] Traditional courting practices (*fréquentation aux champs*) more successfully resisted greater freedom for young men and women, but the western mountains are clearly the favored region for these practices.[14] The evening community gatherings known as *veillées* also reproduce this geography.[15]

Both in allowing the construction of "peasant" and "French" cultures and in providing a cultural basis for geographic distinctions in the department, the study of the persistence of linguistic particularism coincided with the study of "traditional" community practices. In the southern and western mountains a Provençal patois resisted the incursions of northern French, just as the village community seems to have resisted the incursions of better communications and industrial development in those areas of the department.[16] Finding patois means, of course, deciding what is

---

11 A.N. F[17] 9182, *Laicisations des écoles publiques.*
12 Paul Fortier-Beaulieu, *Mariages et noces campagnards* (Paris: G. P. Maisonneuve, 1937), Carte No. 10.
13 Ibid., Carte No. 7.   14 Ibid., Carte No. 3.   15 Ibid., Carte No. 1.
16 Pierre Gardette, "Carte linguistique du Forez," *Bulletin de la Diana* (1943), 269–281. See also Gardette et al., *Atlas linguistique et ethnographique du Lyonnais* vol. III (Lyon: L'Institut de linguistique romane des facultés catholiques de Lyon, 1956).

different enough to be considered such, a process that in the Loire served to define the western mountains as the locus of the "true patois forezien." Louis-Pierre Gras, who in the 1860s conducted research into the languages of the department, argued that "if you wish to find the "true patois forezien," without too many alterations," it is necessary to go look in the mountains of Saint-Georges-en-Couzan and Chalmazelle, of Saint-Just-en-Chevalet and Crémeaux; for [in] the cities of the nobility, of the bourgeoisie, or of chicanery, such as Montbrison, official French has left profound traces."[17] One could hardly imagine a better expression of the way in which language could be read to distinguish "peasant" from "French" culture.

Both linguistic particularism and the village community were reinforced by the mountainous terrain and limited communication in these areas. These "persistences" allowed a typing of regions within the department in terms comprehensible in French culture, as either more or less incorporated into the French nation; in the second half of the nineteenth century these readings were underlined by interpretations of economic and social behavior as well.

II

All activities in the rural Loire during the late nineteenth century were subject to ambiguous interpretations similar to those given housing and the rural community. But this period saw a particularly strong series of readings of the countryside that revolved around economic and demographic behavior, and the remainder of this chapter will outline contact between French and rural cultures on these sites. In each of these we will see the same pattern as existed with housing and community: change there is, without any doubt. But the tendency noted in Chapter 3 to focus on the activities of the "average man" tended to obscure most differences coexisting in the countryside. Instead, descriptions of change reflected the insistence of French culture that only certain kinds were describable, those in which the end result was to make the countryside more "French." These descriptions solidified the geographic division of the department into regions that could be categorized in terms of how well they conformed to models of economic and demographic behavior laid out in French culture.

The economic aspects of this process of becoming "French" were articulated by a generation of French economic liberals writing during the

17 Louis-Pierre Gras, *Dictionnaire du patois forezien* (Lyon: A. Brun, 1863), 199. R. Balibar and D. Laporte, *Le Français national: politique et pratique de la langue nationale sous la Révolution* (Paris: Hachette, 1974); and R. D. Grillo, *Dominant Languages: Language and Hierarchy in Britain and France* (Cambridge University Press, 1989).

middle years of the century. Their liberalism emphasized individualism and the desirability of a free-market economy dominated by large producers. A leading theorist of that generation, Frédéric Bastiat, for example, argued that in selfishly pursuing his own advantage in a free market the producer contributed to lower prices for the consumer. By the second half of the nineteenth century, the most prominent voices in this discourse belonged to the economists associated with the journal *L'Economiste Français*, and especially to its founder, Paul Leroy-Beaulieu. The writings of Leroy-Beaulieu emphasize free labor, the encouragement of individual initiative and effort, and a competitive free market, although he did moderate the earlier antipathy to state intervention in economic matters. These ideas, with their insistence on the selfish individual and the free market, circulated among politicians and the upper bourgeoisie, finding expression for example in the 1879 Freycinet Plan for railroad development. The terms of market culture had also become unquestioned assumptions in industries such as textiles by the second half of the nineteenth century, making it difficult to find language to describe nonmarket aspects of the workplace.[18]

It is important not only that these elements of the French discourse about the economy emphasized individuals and the competition of the free market, but also that they conceived of economic activity in terms best suited to large enterprises run by entrepreneurs who sought to maximize their own profit. While finding a political value in small property holding, they tended to consign to the figurative dustbin those unable to compete with large enterprises. This is also apparent in one of the treatises on nineteenth-century agricultural development in the department of the Loire, written in 1895 by the Vicomte de Meaux, a former minister of the early Third Republic and a large landowner in the Plaine du Forez. The vicomte emphasized the importance of transportation improvements such as a bridge over the Loire and the railroad, and commended a number of large landowners for their initiative in carrying out improvements on their lands. But small rural producers who oriented their production toward family goals of subsistence found no place in his discussion.[19]

A Popular Front inquiry into agricultural conditions in the 1930s began

18 Charles Gide and Charles Rist, *Histoire des doctrines économiques* (Paris: Société du Recueil Sirey, 1922), 377–405; Dan Warshaw, *Paul Leroy-Beaulieu and Established Liberalism in France* (De Kalb: Northern Illinois University Press, 1991), esp. ch. 7; Sanford Elwitt, *The Making of the Third Republic* (Baton Rouge: Louisiana State University Press, 1975), 146–147; William Reddy, *The Rise of Market Culture* (Cambridge University Press, 1984), part 3.

19 Vicomte de Meaux, *Le Progrès agricole dans la Plaine du Forez depuis cinquante ans* (Montbrison: Imprimerie d'Eleuthère Brassart, 1895), esp. 9, 19–25, 40.

by dividing the Loire into three regions: "the mountains, the plateaus, and the plains, each of these regions corresponding to a great geological period."[20] The land remained a fundamental place in which observers defined rural society, although in the second half of the nineteenth century it increasingly was represented as a place of either significant change or resistance to change. No prefect or notable would use the term "agricultural revolution," but there is no doubt that agricultural improvement was the focus of activity and discourse in the second half of the nineteenth century. This created a division in the countryside between areas of development and areas of stagnation. Development was most striking on the traditionally poor Plaine du Forez, but was seen in virtually every part of the department; the only exceptions were the cantons in the Monts du Forez on the western boundary. But the forms of economic development in the countryside took on meanings that distinguished between developing and stagnant parts of the department.

The principal representation of this uneven development was in the periodic agricultural *Enquêtes* carried out by the prefectoral administration. As we have already noted, these inquiries focused on particular aspects of rural economic activity, such as agricultural production conceived in market-related terms. Their figures show an overall increase in the amount of grains produced in the department:[21] wheat increased from 232,921.25 hectolitres in 1852 to 708,726 hl in 1902; production of oats went from 235,329.30 hl in 1852 to 356,611.95 hl in 1902. The rye harvest, in contrast, fell slightly, from 617,310 hl in 1852 to 581,981.40 hl in 1902. The increase in wheat and decrease in rye, the two principal grains used in making bread for human consumption, is particularly significant: farmers were moving to a better quality grain, wheat, and decreasing their production of rye, the traditional grain in the local diet. The increase in oat production testifies to a rise in livestock production.

Only a very small part of these overall increases in wheat and oat production, however, was due to increased yields. The average wheat yield increased only from 11.3 to 12.3 hl/hectare; oats increased from 16.2 to 17.1 hl/h; rye also increased in yield, from 9.5 to 11.9 hl/h, in spite of the decreases in the total harvest for this crop. The real cause of the increased production of grains in the department was a tremendous increase in the amount of land being cultivated: the area planted in wheat, for example, increased from 20,612.5 hectares in 1852 to 57,620 hectares in 1902, while that planted in oats rose from 14,526.5 hectares to 20,854 in the same period. Only rye saw a decrease in area planted, from 64,980

20 Musée des arts et traditions populaires, *Enquête sur l'ancienne agriculture*, 13 avril 1937.
21 A.D.L. 55 M 10, 11, 12, Enquête agricole décennale, 1852; A.D.L. 55 M 77, Enquête agricole décennale, 1902.

hectares to 48,906. The records show a rise in the amount of land being cultivated of around 25 percent in the second half of the nineteenth century. There was also a jump in the area planted in potatoes. This crop, a favorite of agricultural reformers, increased from 13,890 hectares in 1852 to 37,594 in 1902. Its spread appears almost universal; only in the major industrial canton of Saint-Etienne and in Pélussin did planting of this crop decrease.

In that they asked about particular aspects of rural activity, the *Enquêtes agricoles* called for certain kinds of agricultural progress and provided the basis for distinguishing between regions on the basis of how they participated in this progress. The *Enquêtes* therefore are places in which rural and French approaches to agriculture met each other. This begins to become apparent in the ways in which different parts of the department extended the land under cultivation. Working with these records, the historian Robert Estier has drawn a contrast between the cantons to the northeast and those in the western Monts du Forez.[22] One method of changing agriculture was to clear and improve land, another was to change rotation systems so that less land remained fallow each year. In the canton of Saint-Just-en-Chevalet, in the western Monts du Forez, what improvements did occur in the second half of the century were the result not so much of declining fallow (it had been 46 percent of the farmland in 1852, and was still 37 percent by 1892), but rather of the extension of cultivation to wastelands. Agriculture in this canton was therefore extensive but of low productivity.[23] In contrast, in the cantons to the northeast of Roanne, fallowing had been lower even at midcentury, and it was dramatically reduced by the end of the century. In the canton of Belmont in the northeast, for example, fallow fell from one-quarter of the land in 1852 to a minuscule 4.3 percent by 1892.[24]

The contrast between Belmont and Saint-Just can be extended throughout the entire department. The prefectoral reports show that the cantons of the Plaine du Forez increased their acreage in wheat dramatically (see Tables 4.1a and 4.1b), but so did the cantons of the Stephanois region and the Monts du Lyonnais. Yields did not increase spectacularly in any part of the department and, if anything, the Plaine du Forez simply maintained its position of the first half of the century as a net exporter of cereals.[25] Only in the western Monts du Forez, in the cantons of Noiretable, Saint-Georges-en-Couzan, and Saint-Jean-Soleymieux, did wheat

22 Robert Estier, "Productions agricoles et industries rurales: l'exemple du roannais textile au XIXe siècle," in P. Bairoch and A-M. Pinz, *Des Economies traditionelles aux sociétés industrielles* (Geneva: Droz, 1985), 237–256.
23 Ibid., 249.   24 Ibid., 240.
25 Joseph Duplessy, *Annuaire du département de la Loire* (Montbrison: Cheminal, 1818), 270.

Table 4.1a. *Agricultural production in the Loire, 1852—1902, by canton*

	Wheat				Oats			
	Return		Area		Return		Area	
Canton	1852	1902	1852	1902	1852	1902	1852	1902
Bourg-Argental	13	—	15	67	18	13.7	810	788
Le Chambon	6	15	268.5	1,196	20	17	265.5	424
Pélussin	13	17.5	200	632	15	18.5	600	140.:
Rive-de-Gier	15.4	15	1,610	2,578	22	20.3	210	495
St-Chamond	14	15	847	1,355	12	21	441	283
St-Etienne	12	12	600	391	11	18	250	155
St-Genest	—	16	0	6	20	16.6	382	400
St-Héand	10	12.9	552	2,075	10	17.2	723	895
Böen	8.6	9.9	905	3,659	19.6	11.7	895	1,932
Feurs	10	5.5	2,191	7,799	18	18.4	1,948	1,264
Montbrison	12	10.9	2,464	3,279	22	17.5	1,000	1,648
Noirétable	—	10.8	0	50	12	14.6	300	383
St-Bonnet	—	11.5	0	113	12	15.1	1,320	1,193
St-Galmier	12	13	1,007	4,726	16	18.6	1,007	1,263
St-Georges	10	11.6	34	89	16	17.1	195	366
St-Jean	12	13.9	53	449	20	20.4	180	472
St-Rambert	—	10.2	—	3,225	—	19.4	—	1,464
Belmont	14	10	283	1,550	—	15	0	115
Charlieu	10.5	14	2,032	2,712	12	18	567	423
Néronde	10	14	392	1,697	18	20	235	942
La Pacaudière	12	11	1,078	3,705	17	14.2	591	606
Roanne	11.6	12	1,824	3,172	17.4	21.5	451	526
St-Haon	12	10	1,229	2,813	16	15	650	241
St-Just	—	12.2	—	433	—	11	—	673
St-Symphorien	15	12	1,554	4,575	16.2	20	1,079	1,948
St-Germain	6	9.5	299	2,709	12	14	25	1,034
Perreux	10	15	1,175	2,565	16	20	402	781
Totals	11.3	12.3	20,612.5	57,620	16.2	17.1	14,526.5	20,854

— = Data unavailable

not become the dominant crop. Running against the trend, these cantons actually increased their planting of rye.

In the terms of a discourse about the countryside that emphasized agricultural development, the ways in which the different regions of the department increased agricultural production carried profoundly different implications about agricultural change in these different areas. This

Table 4.1b. *Agricultural production in the Loire,*
1852—1902, by canton

	Rye				Potatoes	
	Return		Area		Area	
Canton	1852	1902	1852	1902	1852	1902
Bourg-Argental	10	11.3	2,500	2,210	500	1,587
Le Chambon	12.5	13	2,440	1,800	435	1,582
Pélussin	10	17.4	2,500	1,611	1,300	936
Rive-de-Gier	12.5	10.4	820	285	295	678
St-Chamond	11	14.5	1,730	352	522	728
St-Etienne	10	9	1,217	241	310	193
St-Genest	8.4	12.5	1,186	2,245	212	562
St-Héand	8	12.2	2,585	1,360	524	1,062
Böen	6.9	15.5	6,398	2,336	899	2,572
Feurs	9.5	10.7	4,691	2,703	1,507	2,445
Montbrison	12	11.2	5,208	3,619	1,200	2,154
Noirétable	8.2	8.7	1,794	2,367	150	862
St-Bonnet	6.4	10.4	3,005	3,722	1,004	1,649
St-Galmier	8	15.8	4,645	2,145	503	2,360
St-Georges	8	11.7	3,086	3,190	332	1,159
St-Jean	10	12.3	1,250	2,432	210	1,132
St-Rambert	—	9.5	—	4,035	—	2,896
Belmont	10	10	1,654	530	325	1,105
Charlieu	10	13	760	113	424	1,060
Néronde	12	14.3	2,194	1,300	235	1,557
La Pacaudière	9.1	10.1	2,026	561	285	1,349
Roanne	9.5	11	2,202	846	506	948
St-Haon	10	10	1,853	920	376	666
St-Just	—	7	—	3,369	—	1,774
St-Symphorien	11	12	5,123	2,066	1,114	2,377
St-Germain	4	10	2,354	2,148	472	1,551
Perreux	11	20	1,759	400	250	650
Totals	9.5	11.9	64,980	48,906	13,890	37,594

— = Data unavailable

discourse privileged the maximization of profit over subsistence as a mo-
tive for economic behavior. In these terms, the extension of land under
cultivation was a traditional means in European agriculture to increase the
agricultural product. Yet bringing worse land under cultivation meant
actually reducing yields per hectare and made it difficult to change the

cereals being planted. The canton of Saint-Just, for example, remained a canton of rye, while that of Belmont was leading the department in the move toward grains of higher quality.[26] Connected with this move on the part of Belmont, however, was a change in the crop rotation system: the two-field rotation of midcentury (cereal, fallow) was replaced by a four-field system (wheat, rye, forage, fallow). These new rotation systems reduced the amount of land lying fallow each year, allowing farmers to gain the production of the increased land planted. They were possible only because there was more livestock: the additional strain on the soil of more frequent planting and more demanding crops was offset by the fertilizer provided by livestock. Further, this improved fertilizing allowed the move to more demanding wheat, in fact increasing the yield of wheat even as land previously planted in rye was brought into wheat production.

The version of the countryside found in these *Enquêtes* therefore fits that countryside into an account about national economic development that distinguished between "French" and "peasant," and built on the long-standing identification of France with civilization and constructed "peasants" as timeless. In the central Plaine and the eastern mountains, farmers were adopting practices that brought their agriculture closer to the model of "developed" or "modern" agriculture implicit in the structuring of the *Enquêtes*. The amount of land planted each year increased as a result of clearances and improvements, but above all improved rotation. Rye was replaced by wheat as the principal cereal, while at the same time yields of this more demanding crop increased. The net result of both of these developments was an increase in the total amount of cereals, especially wheat, produced in the department by the second half of the nineteenth century. Yet these changes took place only in certain parts of the department, and the reports also created distinctions, based on conformity to these criteria for development, between different regions. The isolated western mountain cantons remained mired in a traditional agriculture, easily linked to the ignorant "peasants" of the French discourse about the countryside, while the rest of the department slowly improved its use of the land and the quality and quantity of food produced, transforming its attitudes and behaviors into ones similar to those of the "French" entrepreneurs favored by liberal economists.

The prefectoral reports and their description of a countryside divided into developing and stagnant regions located the rural Loire in a particular kind of discourse about its economy. It is by now a truism that peasant cultivators do not necessarily aim at maximizing production of high-quality cereals and livestock for a market, and thereby maximizing in-

26 Estier, "Productions agricoles," 249.

come.[27] But clothed in the language of science, the prefectoral emphasis on agricultural development enjoyed a strong position. To the dismay of agricultural reformers, however, some "peasants" refused to adopt the newer methods of rotation and fertilizing. This refusal is worth pondering, for the logic of nineteenth- and twentieth-century Western culture makes little sense of people who refuse economic development. Portraying these people as, at best, "peasants" isolated from the benefits of modern science serves only to reinforce the premises of the nineteenth-century discourse as it constructed "peasants." Rather, we need to understand this behavior as a practice in which these country dwellers represented their own identities.

The seemingly "backward" behavior of these western mountain families can be understood in its own terms as pursuing local goals rather than national aims, if we keep several factors in mind. While the area under cultivation in the Loire was increasing, as was the proportion planted in wheat, market agriculture was entering a period of crisis in France. Beginning in the 1870s and continuing until the last years of the century, prices of virtually all agricultural products fell. Grains were most dramatically struck by this depression: the decline from 1870–75 to the later low point was around 27 percent for cereals, almost 33 percent for wheat. It was also significant for other products. Potato prices fell by 35 percent; butter around 20–22 percent in the province of Normandy; adult cattle, 19 percent, calves, 10 percent. Wine prices fell even further: after a rise in price of 35–40 percent due to the impact of phylloxera in the early 1880s, the rest of the century saw a dramatic drop due to overproduction and increased imports, and prices fell by about 50 percent.[28]

Prices for the Loire suggest the same pattern. The mean price of wheat rose slightly from the 1831–40 decade to the 1841–50 decade, and continued to rise in the 1850s. It dropped (by 7 percent) in the next decade, but then recouped some of this loss in the 1870s. The mean price of a quintal of wheat was, in the 1870s, almost the same as in the 1840s (21 francs 41 centimes vs. 21 francs 38 centimes). But the 1880s were a period of sharp decline, as the mean price fell by 14 percent over the preceding decade, and the 1890s added another 6 percent drop onto this. The decline in the

27 A. V. Chayanov, *The Theory of the Peasant Economy*, Daniel Thorner, B. Kerblay, and R. E. F. Smith, eds. (Homewood, Ill.: Irwin, 1966); Olwen Hufton, *The Poor of Eighteenth-Century France, 1759–1789* (Oxford University Press [Clarendon Press], 1974); Jan DeVries, "Peasant Demand Patterns and Economic Development: Friesland, 1550–1740," in William N. Parker and Eric Jones, eds., *European Peasants and Their Markets* (Princeton, N.J.: Princeton University Press, 1975), 205–266; Paul Hohenberg, "Change in Rural France in the Period of Industrialization," *Journal of Economic History* 32 (1972), 219–240.

28 Gabriel Desert, "La Grande dépression de l'agriculture" in *Histoire de la France rurale* (Paris: Seuil, 1976), vol. 3: 395–397.

1880s became most apparent in 1884, with an 11 percent drop over the previous year, and bottomed out in the following year. In the 1890s, there was a slight recovery in the first few years of the decade, but prices in 1895 and 1896 were lower than they had been since 1831, and the following years only mildly improved the prospects for wheat producers in the department.[29]

Shifting to production oriented primarily toward the market in the period after 1880 could therefore bring benefits but could also be quite dangerous to the individual family farmer. In the official discourse about agricultural development, the emphasis on the monetary returns on production served to efface other ways of conceiving agriculture that were less tied to the market, such as autoconsumption or barter, yet took place at a time when monetary returns form agriculture were declining. A shift from lesser grains to wheat could mean that, even as prices of wheat declined, individuals' revenues from land planted in cereal increased, because wheat prices remained above those for other grains. This perception may help account for the shift in cereal production in those parts of the department typed as "developing." Further, as agriculture became more commercialized, and complementary agricultural goods such as meat and dairy products became more frequently a part of the produce of a farm, lost revenues from cereals could be recouped and even surpassed by those from other agricultural products. But such strategies required that individual farmers shift their efforts to products whose unit prices were declining. It should be no surprise that for some regions a strategy aimed at protecting the family farm from agricultural failure while producing not for the market but for home consumption made more sense.[30] This strategy defined some parts of the department as stagnant: their attempts to insulate themselves from the consequences of the falling prices for agricultural goods placed them in this category. Along with isolation and inadequate land tenure systems such as sharecropping, the western mountains also produced the wrong crop (rye), and increased production not by adopting new rotation arrangements but by clearing new fields.

29 This paragraph is based on data drawn from Louis-Jean Gras, *Histoire du commerce local et des industries qui s'y rattachent dans la région stéphanoise et forézienne* (Saint-Etienne: Théolier, 1910), 590, 605, 632, 644. Gras is not specific about the location of the market(s) from which he has drawn his prices, nor about the time of year to which the prices pertain. Nonetheless, his own connection with Saint-Etienne (he was the secretary of the Chambre de Commerce de Saint-Etienne) suggest that the data were drawn from that city. One quintal equals 220.46 pounds.

30 George W. Grantham, "Scale and Organization in French Farming, 1840–1880," in Parker and Jones, eds., *European Peasants and their Markets*, 293–326, emphasizes the ability of seemingly backward peasant family farms to be more profitable than capitalist farms in circumstances in which labor costs were significant, since family members could be used.

But in assuming the desirability of a market orientation for country dwellers, this discourse overlooked that employment and support of all members of the household could be the goal. These may have been disincentives to development as officials conceived the process, but were logical within the framework of country dwellers' conceptions of their fields.

The import of these discourses about development for our understanding of the rural society in the Loire in the late nineteenth century has less to do with which pattern was "correct" and which "false" than it does with the ways in which these notions about agricultural development created a particular version of the rural Loire. The fields of the Loire were sites that displayed different approaches to agricultural production. These competing notions of agricultural development served to mark different regions in the department as "developing" or "stagnant," and to create two different kinds of "peasants."

As we saw in the preceding chapter, the official discourse about rural economic development increasingly focused almost exclusively on agriculture.[31] This emphasis ignored a significant amount of the activity that actually went on in the countryside, for country dwellers were industrial workers as well as farmers. But even as the reporting format of the administration insisted on a division between an agricultural countryside and industrial cities, the older distribution of activities that countered this perception was itself being rearranged, for in the second half of the nineteenth century, rural by-employments tended to disappear. The Stephanois silk industry went into a long period of decline following the American Civil War in the 1860s. The war cut off the supply of cheap cotton used in *mélangés* (cotton was used for the weft of the ribbon); Paterson, New Jersey, replaced Saint-Etienne as the principal supplier of ribbons to the United States. Basle, in Switzerland, also made severe inroads against the Stephanois on the Continent, and the Cobden–Chevalier Treaty of 1860 opened up the French market to English ribbons produced in Coventry. These competitors moved more quickly toward factory production of cheap ribbons for the mass market than did the Stephanois manufacturers, and by the last quarter of the century the once-prosperous Stephanois silk trade was experiencing hard times. The labor force shrank, and small factories replaced the numerous rural families that had once depended on the trade.[32]

The movement to factory organization also reduced opportunities for

31 The 1862 *Enquête* did ask about rural industries, but this was an unusual question. See Bertrand Gille, *Les Sources statistiques le l'histoire de france* (Paris: Librairie Minard, 1964), 240, for a discussion of the midcentury inquiries.

32 See L.-J. Gras, *Histoire de la rubannerie* (Saint-Etienne: Théolier, 1906); for the rural effects of this decline, see James R. Lehning, *The Peasants of Marlhes* (Chapel Hill: University of North Carolina Press, 1980), 30–33.

cottage work elsewhere in the department. The Lyonnais silk trade followed this path in the last quarter of the century, reducing the demand of labor in the eastern mountains. And by the 1870s, the Roannais cotton industry had moved into factories located in the city of Roanne and its suburbs. Throughout the department, therefore, the opportunities for employment outside of agriculture shrank between 1850 and 1890.[33] This rearrangement of economic activities meant that increasingly the focus in the *Enquêtes agricoles* on agriculture as the defining activity of the countryside found some basis. Yet it served to obscure the process of deindustrialization itself as a part of the experiences of "peasants."

The effect of the structure of the official *Enquêtes* becomes apparent if we look again, even through the lens of those official reports, at the communes of Verrières and Saint-Hilaire. In both, there are traces of the model of rural economic development that formed the basis of the administration's representation. But in both we can also see that the transformation was incomplete, and can be construed in terms other than those of that model of development.

By the end of the nineteenth century, a significant change had occurred in the agrarian structure of Verrières, one in a direction favored by agricultural reformers. The *métayage* leases that were omnipresent in 1852 had disappeared, and most farms were cultivated by *propriétaires* with the help of their family or others. This change in land tenure was accompanied by some reduction in the size of farms: whereas in 1852 most farms were between ten and twenty hectares, only 17 percent were larger than ten hectares in 1892. Almost half (48 percent), however, were between five and ten hectares.[34] It is difficult not to see a relationship between the end of *métayage* and the fragmentation of farms: sharecropping spared the participating family from the necessity of dividing property among several heirs in each generation.[35] Proprietorship, however, exposed the farm to division and, over time, could lead to reduced farm size. In the place of sharecropping, therefore, Verrières had become a village of family farms that, while smaller in size than the *domaines* of midcentury, were still of substantial size for this part of France. But the shift from sharecropping to proprietorship did not necessarily open up Verrières to a growing agricultural economy; in a time of declining prices

33 See Charles Dechelette, *L'Industrie cotonière à Roanne* (Roanne: Imprimerie Souchier, 1910); E. Pariset, *Histoire de la fabrique lyonnaise* (Lyon: A. Rey, 1901); and Yves Lequin, *Les Ouvriers de la région lyonnaise (1848–1914)* (Lyon: Presses Universitaires de Lyon, 1977).
34 A.D.L. 55 M 44–46, *Enquête agricole décennale de 1892.*
35 John Shaffer, *Family and Farm: Agrarian Change and Household Organization in the Loire Valley, 1500–1900* (Albany, N.Y.: SUNY Press, 1982), ch. 8.

for cereals, it meant that the farming families who now bore the entire risk of the agricultural operation were placed in a difficult position.

Saint-Hilaire did not experience significant changes in the system of land tenure or size of farms between midcentury and the beginning of this century, and it was spared the complete deindustrialization that was the lot of many protoindustrial villages in late-nineteenth-century Europe. Nonetheless, the economic outlook for Saint-Hilaire was not bright by the end of the century. Returns on seed in wheat improved, although those for the other major crop, oats, did not. Fragmentation of landholding, however, continued to make it difficult for a family to employ many family members in agriculture: probably no more than two adults could profitably be used on the majority of farms, and the almost half of the farms that were under one hectare were little more than gardens. Indeed, by the 1901 census, most heads of household were listed as *fermiers* rather than *propriétaires*.[36] In these circumstances the wage sector of the economy was a vital part of the family economy, and there was an increase in the proportion of households working entirely in the textile sector. But the last part of the nineteenth century and the beginning of the twentieth was a period of stagnation for the Roannais cotton industry, and mechanization was proceeding rapidly, concentrating the industry in Roanne and its suburbs.[37] Wages are difficult to judge in such a dispersed industry, but it is hard to believe that textile work could support a family at the turn of the century better than, or even as well as, at midcentury. The textile industry remained in Saint-Hilaire at the turn of the century, and this was a positive factor in the family economies of the residents of the village. But mechanization and stagnation were the principal features of the industry, and these suggest that it was a tenuous way to make a living.

There is no doubt that the second half of the nineteenth century witnessed improvements in agricultural productivity as well as concentration of manufacturing in cities, and these processes occurred in many parts of France. My argument is not that the prefectoral reports created an image of change where it did not exist. Even within the terms of those reports, however, we must emphasize that the pace of rural change in the Loire was, as in many parts of France, painfully slow. Improvements in agricultural production were most apparent in the northeastern cantons, but even there the levels of improvement were below those elsewhere in the country. Protoindustry was moving out of the Loire countryside in the

36 A.D.L. 55 M 45, *Enquête agricole décennale de 1892;* 49 M 332, *Liste nominative de recensement de 1901.*
37 Lequin, *Les Ouvriers de la région lyonnaise,* vol. 1: 93–94; Dechelette, *L'Industrie cotonière,* 48.

course of the second half of the nineteenth century, and although it persisted in communes like Saint-Hilaire, it was of reduced importance.

What we must add to the description of economic change in the countryside that emerges from the prefectoral reports is the realization that these reports would capture only certain kinds of economic activity, and that they would tend to marginalize some activities even in reporting them. Just as agriculture became marginalized in the industrial cities of the department such as Saint-Etienne, so was manufacturing marginalized in those parts of the department that remained visibly "rural" and whose inhabitants remained visibly "peasant." Monetarized activities were highlighted, while those that did not find a place in the capitalist economy did appear in the reports. This bureaucratic marginalization of rural industry served to mask the potentially devastating process of rural deindustrialization. Both agricultural and protoindustrial work had, earlier, often been combined within the domestic economy of the household, and a significant part of that domestic economy did not aim at production for the market. As rural families represented themselves through their economic activities, therefore, they often engaged in either market-oriented or non-agricultural activities, but did not exclude the other. But such a combination of activities was virtually incomprehensible to the version of the countryside that informed French culture, especially as represented in the reports organized by the state. In this sense, the economic activities of the countryside, both agricultural and manufacturing, were further places in which "peasant" and "French" found different representations.

III

The population of the department of the Loire experienced significant changes in the ways in which families were formed during the nineteenth century. It is common to describe these behaviors in terms of such population characteristics as fertility, mortality, nuptiality, household structure, and migration, and in these terms the department's varied countryside moved from the demographic ancien régime characterized by high mortality, unrestricted fertility within marriage, and the limited nuptiality described in Chapter 3 to the pattern of low mortality, relatively widespread marriage, and limitation of fertility within marriage that characterizes most Western populations of the twentieth century. The frequent migration and nuclear household structure characteristic of these populations were already widespread in the Loire in the first half of the nineteenth century. But to a large extent it was in the period after midcentury that these changes came home to most rural families in the Loire. Because of this similarity between the family patterns of those living in the Loire countryside and the urban bourgeoisie, the family itself became a location for the contact between French and rural cultures. Yet here, as with economic development, we need to be aware of the ways in which the family and reproductive behavior of the country dwellers of the Loire was fitted into particular versions of population development, and how these versions impose their own logic of "peasant" behavior while eliminating others.[38]

A prominent part of public discourse in nineteenth-century France was devoted to questions surrounding issues of sexuality, family, and reproduction. Debates about the regulation or abolition of prostitution, the slow growth of the French population, and the organization of the family and household make clear both the extent of public concern about private matters and the particular way in which the dominant discourse of the period structured these questions. In an era given to both moralizing and science, the discussion revolved around questions of virtue and vice, and also invited scientific arguments. Prostitution was viewed as dangerous to the family and to public health; repopulationists were concerned that a population that was not growing had lost its vitality and fallen prey to the lure of individual accomplishment and mobility; commentators on the family argued that in increasingly nuclear households the French population was placing individual aims above the needs of kin and the French nation. There was not agreement within French culture even about the methods to be used to analyze these social developments, but the argument was usually carefully presented in scientific form, as medical experts such as Alfred Fournier studied the effects of prostitution as a medical problem, and social scientists such as Paul Leroy-Beaulieu, Arsène Dumont, and Frédéric Le Play utilized their versions of social-science methods to "document" the decline of the French population and family.[39]

38 This section will not directly address questions concerning the explanation of changes in family formation in the rural Loire. On this question, see James R. Lehning, "The Decline of Marital Fertility: Evidence from a French Department: La Loire, 1851– 1891," *Annales de démographie historique 1984*, 201–217; idem, "The timing and Prevalence of Women's Marriage in the French Department of the Loire, 1851–1891," *Journal of Family History* 13 (1988), 307–323; and idem, "Socioeconomic Change, Peasant Household Structure and Demographic Behavior in a French Department," *Journal of Family History* 17 (1992), 161–181.

39 See Michel Foucault, *The History of Sexuality*, trans. by Robert Hurley (New York: Random House, 1978); Thomas Laqueur, *Making Sex: Body and Gender from the Greeks to Freud* (Cambridge, Mass.: Harvard University Press, 1990), esp. ch. 6; Jacques Donzelot, *The Policing of Families*, trans. by Robert Hurley (New York: Pantheon, 1979). Karen Offen has considered the interrelationships of public discussions of depopulation, the French nation, and feminism in "Depopulation, Nationalism, and Feminism in Fin-de-Siècle France," *American Historical Review* 89 (1984), 648–676. On prostitution, see Jill Harsin, *Policing Prostitution in Nineteenth-Century Paris* (Princeton, N.J.: Princeton University Press, 1985); and Alain Corbin, *Les Filles de noce* (Paris: Flammarion, 1982), 315–379. On the population question, see Angus McLaren, *Sexu-*

The rural family was given a particular place in the French nation in this discourse. It was not a place of complete equality, and as in other instances the ambiguity in the construction of the "peasant" – as both savage and the repository of what was virtuous about France – colored this positioning. The rural family was to ignore and even counteract the pursuit of individual profit that was granted or claimed by other groups. This is most apparent in social criticism by Le Play and his followers, in which rural families were castigated for adopting forms that seemed to be aimed at maximizing individual happiness rather than subordinating individual wishes to family or national needs. More generally, and especially after the Franco-Prussian War of 1870, the populationist arguments that resounded through French culture insisted – even as the French bourgeoisie was itself limiting the size of its families – that rural families needed to maintain high fertility levels either to remain virtuous or so that France would be able to counter its larger neighbor. These arguments were brought into the countryside by the representatives of the Catholic church, who portrayed such reproductive behavior as a duty to God and a question of salvation, as well as by the lay schoolteachers who after 1880 played a growing role in rural education.

It was in this context of a powerful dominant discourse about families that the country dwellers of the Loire developed their own representations of families, and in particular of families in which fewer children and smaller residential units became predominant. As with economic development, however, these changes placed rural families in an ambiguous position, between rural and French family behavior. We need to consider not only the ways in which, by many measures, the family and demographic behavior of the Loire country dwellers went from a "demographic ancien régime" to a "modern" demographic system, but also what the significance is of phrasing the change in this way and in what ways this kind of description itself is a part of the discourses of rural and French cultures and the construction of the "peasant."

ality and Social Order: The Debate over the Fertility of Women and Workers in France, 1770–1920 (New York: Holmes & Meier, 1983), esp. Part 2; Joseph J. Spengler, *France Faces Depopulation* (New York: Greenwood, 1968), esp. chs. 6 and 7; Katherine Lynch, *Family, Class, and Ideology in Early Industrial France* (Madison: University of Wisconsin Press, 1988); Etienne van de Walle, "Motivations and Technology in the Decline of French Fertility," in Robert Wheaton and Tamara K. Hareven, eds., *Family and Sexuality in French History* (Philadelphia: University of Pennsylvania Press, 1980), 135–178; Yves Charbit and Andre Béjin, "La Pensée démographique," in Jacques Dupâquier, ed., *Histoire de la population française* (Paris: Presses Universitaires de France, 1988), vol. 3: 465–501. On Le Play, see Michael Brooke, *Le Play: Engineer and Social Scientist* (London: Longman Group, 1970). On mortality, see William Coleman, *Death Is a Social Disease: Public Health and Political Economy in Early Industrial France* (Madison: University of Wisconsin Press, 1982).

The movement of overall fertility levels in the department of the Loire follows a pattern relatively similar to that of France as a whole, at least in the nineteenth century. Etienne van de Walle's departmental calculations show a consistent decline from 1831 (the earliest year for which data is available) until 1851; the downward trend resumes in the 1860s and continues until 1930, although there is a minor upward movement in 1881.[40] A sample of rural villages (see Table 4.2) shows a similar decline: overall fertility (I_f) fell from a mean level of .369 in 1851 (about 10 percent higher than the estimate for the entire department) to .255 in 1891 (only slightly higher than the departmental estimate of .251).[41] The closeness by 1891 suggests that, by that date, reproductive behavior in the department was becoming more uniform.

A principal component in this decline in overall fertility was the widespread adoption of family-limitation practices within marriage and the consequent decline in marital fertility. The summary data show that marital fertility (I_g) declined initially in the 1830s, then leveled off until the beginning of a rapid decline in the late 1870s and 1880s that brought it to a very low level by the eve of the First World War.[42] Data on the sample of villages in 1891 clearly indicate that the forty-year period between 1851 and 1891 saw the onset of the fertility transition. For these thirty-three villages, the mean level of I_g fell from .767 in 1851 to .512 in 1891, a drop of one-third. The 1891 level suggests the strong probability that the majority of the department had shifted from uncontrolled to controlled

40 Ansley J. Coale and Roy Treadway, "A Summary of the Changing Distribution of Overall Fertility, Marital Fertility, and the Proportion Married in the Provinces of Europe," in Ansley J. Coale and Susan Cotts Watkins, eds., *The Decline of Fertility in Europe* (Princeton, N.J.: Princeton University Press, 1986), 100.

41 Van de Walle's figures are based on revised estimates of different characteristics of the population, such as number of births and women in each age group, which, along with the expected variance of a sample from the total population, probably accounts for much of the difference. It should be noted that his inclusion of urban areas in his calculations does not account for the differences, since urban areas had higher birth rates than rural areas in the Loire. The crude birth rates for major cities had a mean value of 37.5 per thousand in 1851 (included as cities are Le Chambon-Feugerolles, Firminy, Saint-Chamond, Saint-Etienne, Outre-Furens, Beaubrun, Montaud, Valbenoite and Roanne; data were unavailable in 1851 for Rive-de-Gier and Montbrison), whereas Van de Walle estimates an overall female birth rate of 31.6 for the 1846–50 period; the mean CBR for the sample used here was 33.5. Differences in age structures of the populations – the younger urban populations – probably account for much of this. See, for example, Michael P. Hanagan, "Proletarian Families and Social Protest: Production and Reproduction as Issues of Social Conflict in Nineteenth-Century France," in Steven Laurence Kaplan and Cynthia J. Koepp, eds., *Work in France: Representations, Meaning, Organization, and Practice* (Ithaca, N.Y.: Cornell University Press, 1986), especially Appendix 15.1, which attributes much of the differences in child/woman ratios between Le Chambon-Feugerolles and Rive-de-Gier in 1856 to age-structure differences.

42 Coale and Treadway, "Summary of the Changing Distribution."

Table 4.2. *Mean values of family formation variables for village sample in 1851 and 1891, by arrondissement*

Variable	St-Etienne Mean	Std. Dev.	Montbrison Mean	Std. Dev.	Roanne Mean	Std. Dev.	Entire Sample Mean	Std. Dev.
I_f 1851	.407	.082	.358	.086	.351	.099	.369	.090
I_g 1851	.782	.175	.779	.164	.741	.194	.767	.173
I_m 1851	.486	.067	.451	.088	.468	.054	.466	.072
I_h 1851	.018	.019	.022	.021	.010	.016	.017	.019
CDR 1851	25.5	6.8	22.8	6.9	22.3	6.8	23.4	6.5
APH 1851	2.20	.18	2.36	.31	2.08	.15	2.22	.25
MUH 1851	1.04	.04	1.09	.10	.98	.05	1.04	.008
I_f 1891	.247	.056	.298	.071	.210	.044	.255	.069
I_g 1891	.511	.151	.579	.135	.433	.077	.512	.135
I_m 1891	.487	.083	.510	.104	.473	.042	.491	.081
I_h 1891	.010	.008	.015	.008	.010	.009	.012	.008
CDR 1891	19.2	3.6	21.6	5.0	19.5	3.7	20.2	4.3
APH 1891	2.49	.21	2.46	.22	2.26	.09	2.40	.21
MUH 1891	.92	.06	.94	.07	.86	.06	.91	.07
D_{IF}	.160	.062	.060	.093	.140	.114	.114	.101
D_{IG}	.271	.081	.200	.155	.308	.196	.255	.155
D_{IM}	−.001	.090	−.059	.071	−.005	.060	−.025	.076
D_{IH}	−.007	.024	−.007	.021	.000	.019	−.004	.021
D_{CDR}	6.3	9.3	1.2	10.2	2.8	6.6	3.1	8.9
D_{APH}	−.29	.10	−.10	.14	−.18	.15	−.18	.15
D_{MUH}	.11	.06	.14	.07	.11	.04	.12	.06
Number of Cases	9		13		11		33	

I_f = Overall fertility
I_m = Proportions married
CDR = Crude death rate
MUH = Marital units per household
D_{IG} = Change in I_g, 1851 to 1891
D_{IH} = Change in I_h, 1851 to 1891
D_{APH} = Change in APH, 1851 to 1891
I_g = Marital fertility
I_h = Illegitimate fertility
APH = Adults per household
D_{IF} = Change in If, 1851 to 1891
D_{IM} = Change in Im, 1851 to 1891
D_{CDR} = Change in CDR, 1851 to 1891
D_{MUH} = Change in MUH, 1851 to 1891

fertility behavior within marriage. Moreover, the decline in marital fertility was apparently almost universal: in none of the thirty-three villages in the sample did marital fertility fail to decline. The drop in marital fertility was not, however, completed by 1891, and while many communes had already experienced dramatic decreases in the level of I_g, for others they had just begun. Thus, while there can be little doubt that the secular decline of marital fertility began in the Loire during the 1851–91 period, a corollary must be the diversity within the department, from commune to commune, of the timing and speed of the decline.

The nuptiality behavior of the population of the Loire also changed during the second half of the nineteenth century. There is a slight increase in proportions married (I_m) between 1831 and 1901, from .483 to .518.[43] The increase appears to have taken place in two phases: a first increase in the 1850s, and a second in the first decade of the twentieth century. Rising proportions married were not, therefore, a gradual process in the Loire, but rather appear from the summary data to have been located at specific points in time. The sample of villages also shows an increase in proportions married, of about the same magnitude as the summary figures, although the sample level of I_m is slightly higher than the departmental figure.

There was gradual improvement in mortality during the course of the nineteenth century. Estimates of female expectation of life at birth show an improvement of ten years in the century between 1801 and 1901, from 37.0 years to 47.4 years. Much of this improvement occurred after 1850, but even at the end of the century the Loire was still one of the most dangerous departments in the country.[44]

Hidden in these summary figures were significant local variations of family and reproductive behavior. This is apparent in the breakdown by arrondissement in Table 4.2.[45] In 1851 overall fertility in the southern arrondissement of Saint-Etienne was highest, driven by higher marital fertility and more frequent marriage than in the other two arrondissements, where I_f was approximately .05 lower than in the Stephanois region. By 1891, however, a substantial decline in marital fertility and the stability of nuptiality had reduced overall fertility in the South below that of the Montbrisonnais, where more frequent marriage limited the effects of controlled fertility within marriage. In the arrondissement of Roanne, in the North, overall fertility in 1891 was lower than anywhere else in the department, the effect of widespread family limitation.

The breakdown by arrondissement in Table 4.2 also helps locate geographically the changes in marital fertility and nuptiality. The figures for marital fertility in 1851 are relatively similar from one arrondissement to the next, although the Roannais shows the influence of the early decline

43 Ibid.
44 Van de Walle, *Female Population of France*, 191–195; see also Lehning, *Peasants of Marlhes*, 55–58.
45 Age and marital status distributions of the populations of each commune are available only for 1851, and it has therefore not been possible to calculate many demographic indices for later in the century for more than the sample used in this table.

of the northwestern cantons. The Montbrisonnais was most resistant to change between 1851 and 1891, while the decline had accelerated in the northern arrondissement. The arrondissement of Saint-Etienne had also seen a substantial decline, although this was limited to the parts of the arrondissement north of the industrial valley, which are heavily represented in the random sample of villages.[46] This southern third of the department, the arrondissement of Saint-Etienne, showed virtually no change in proportions married, nor did the northern third, the arrondissement of Roanne. Only in the center, the arrondissement of Montbrison, was there significant change. These communes had the lowest proportion married in 1851, and the highest proportion married in 1891.

The most substantial improvements in mortality occurred in the arrondissement of Saint-Etienne, especially in the industrial cantons of Le Chambon, Saint-Chamond, and Rive-de-Gier[47] (see Figure 4.1). There were also substantial improvements in mortality in the eastern mountains, with the cantons of Noiretable and Belmont leading the way, and to some extent on the Plaine du Forez, in the canton of Boën. In contrast, with the exception of a dramatic improvement in mortality in the canton of Saint-Just-en-Chevalet, mortality declined little in the western Monts du Forez; indeed, in several cantons in this part of the department the crude death rate rose between 1851 and 1891.

The geographic movement that was a major part of population behavior in the early nineteenth century continued in its second half. If there was a change in the migration flows in the department in that period, it was that the cantons that had been modest contributors to the streams moving from countryside to cities joined in the movement (see Figure 4.2). Many areas that had been important in 1851 continued to be so in the late 1880s, such as the cantons close to the Stephanois Valley, and those in the Northeast. There is some evidence that the industrial cities, especially Roanne in the North and Le Chambon and Saint-Chamond in the South, became more dependent on migrants to sustain their populations. But the Plaine du Forez saw increases in out-migration in the second half of the century, and the western Monts du Forez, which had minimal emigration at mid-

---

46 Compare, for example, the experience of the village of Marlhes, located in the Monts du Pilat south of Saint-Etienne. There is no evidence in that village of the control of fertility even within marriages contracted as late as the 1870s. See Lehning, *Peasants of Marlhes*, ch. 5. For urban fertility in this area, see Elinor Accampo, *Industrialization, Family Life, and Class Relations: Saint-Chamond, 1815–1914* (Berkeley and Los Angeles: University of California Press, 1989), especially ch. 4; and, on Rive-de-Gier and Le Chambon, Hanagan, "Proletarian Families and Social Protest."

47 Accampo, *Industrialization*, 124–133, argues that in the city of Saint-Chamond, mortality either worsened or remained stable in the second half of the century. This suggests that the improvement in the canton was the result primarily of changes in the rural communes of the canton.

X - data unavailable

Figure 4.1   Crude death rates by canton, 1891.

century, became heavy senders of population by the 1880s. In spite of the fact that these were areas of only modest decline in the birth rate in this period, many communes in the cantons of Noiretable and Saint-Just-en-Chevalet in the Monts du Forez experienced declines in population between 1851 and 1891.

The reproductive behavior of the rural population in the Loire in the second half of the nineteenth century therefore can be described as moving closer to the bourgeois model of low overall and marital fertility, more-frequent marriage, frequent migration, and less exposure to the dangers of high mortality that was becoming the norm in France and western Europe at this time. In describing the overall pattern this way, we also reinforce the geographic division of the department that appeared in the description of economic developments, since the most marked discrepancy from this model of demographic development is found once again in the western Monts du Forez. As a region not only of low agri-

Figure 4.2   Net migration rates by canton, 1886–1891.

cultural output and traditional agricultural practices but also of high overall fertility, high mortality, and uncontrolled fertility within marriage, the
western mountains seem confirmed in their place as "peasant."

The same stories might be told about the residential behavior of these
families. Residence was distinctly marked in nineteenth-century French
culture, as in particular the school of family sociology associated with
Frédéric Le Play connected forms of residence with particular virtues or
vices. Advocates of extended families such as Le Play insisted that there
was more to an extended household than just the presence of kin outside
of the conjugal pair. Extended households were the repositories of morality and values that led to a willingness to subordinate individual desires to
the needs of the family. Nuclear households, on the other hand, reflected
individualism. The transition from extended to nuclear household systems was linked to the progress of industrialization and urbanization,
processes that were themselves viewed in terms of moral degradation:

industry and the cities it spawned destroyed the basic values on which society was built. Their end result was the decay of authority within the family, fewer children, higher illegitimacy, and improvident "beggar marriages."[48]

This transition so feared by conservative critics of the nineteenth century appears to have been under way in much of the rural Loire. Somewhat countervailing tendencies in living arrangements occur between 1851 and 1891. The household moved toward a nuclear structure with a vengeance, as multiple-marriage households became less frequent in the population. At the same time, however, there was an increase in the number of adults in each household, which can occur only through increased coresidence of unmarried men or women, whether relatives, servants, or boarders, with married couples. At the same time, however, there is a tendency toward greater uniformity in both aspects of household structure in the department.

This tendency toward uniformity in household-structure characteristics can be seen in the breakdown by arrondissement in Table 4.2, as the means of both measures showed significant changes over the forty-year period. In all three arrondissements, adults per household increased, as the presence of unmarried adults in households became more common. This increase was perhaps more startling in the north, around Roanne, and the south, around Saint-Etienne, than in the Montbrisonnais, where APH was significantly higher in 1851. Similarly, marital units per household (MUH) declined in all three arrondissements, as households everywhere came closer to the nuclear-family ideal. Perhaps most striking is the level of MUH in the arrondissement of Montbrison, which in 1851 had been a region of complex households but by 1891 had moved very close to the pattern of nuclear households that was increasingly the case in the other two arrondissements and, indeed, in western Europe.[49]

Both in terms of reproductive behavior and household formation, therefore, significant parts of the rural population of the Loire adopted patterns of behavior that seemed to bring them closer to the ideals practiced by bourgeois French culture. Their families were small and often limited in membership to the conjugal pair and their (few) children. But

48 Frédéric Le Play, *L'Organisation du travail* (Tours: Mame, 1870); idem, *L'Organisation de la famille* (Paris: Tequi, 1871).
49 See Peter Laslett, *Family Life and Illicit Love in Earlier Generations* (Cambridge University Press, 1977); John Hajnal, "Two Kinds of Pre-Industrial Household Formation System," *Population and Development Review* 8 (1982), 449–494; William M. Parrish and Moshe Schwartz, "Household Complexity in 19th Century France," *American Sociological Review* 37 (1972), 154–173; William Goode, *World Revolution and Family Patterns* (New York: Free Press, 1963); and Talcott Parsons, "The Kinship System of the Contemporary United States," *American Anthropologist* 43 (1943), 22–38.

as in the case of housing, the identity between rural and bourgeois families should not be pressed too far, as the growing presence of unmarried adults in households shows. Servants were needed for farm work, and siblings often retained the right, thanks to partible-inheritance laws, to remain in the household. Increasingly missing were those individuals that more complex forms of household structure had cared for: retired parents. These patterns raised the specter that these families were guided by precisely those motives that so terrified conservatives like Frédéric Le Play: individualism, selfishness, and a lack of respect or concern for aged parents.

Susan Cotts Watkins has recently characterized as "demographic nationalism" a pattern of increasing conformity of demographic behavior within western European countries, and we might extend the concept to include "household nationalism" as well. Watkins's term is intended to include two different explanatory hypotheses: that demographic diversity declined either because factors such as market integration, state formation, and nation building made economic and social conditions more similar; or because these developments promoted a sense of belonging to a national community.[50] Implicit in both hypotheses is that similar behaviors were the result of similar factors, and that behaviors would change once conditions changed: to quote her paraphrase of Eugen Weber, the process was one of moving "from Peasants into Frenchwomen."

The inevitability of such a process, enhanced by its narrative cleanness, suggests that it does not focus elaborately on individual motivations. It views the changes in family formation that occurred in the late-nineteenth-century Loire as the result of the adoption of similar motives, and implies that nonconforming areas (such as the western mountains of the Loire) would eventually do the same as the result of a diffusion of motivations and behavior. Conceptualizing demographic and household change in this way serves to obscure as well as illuminate, and what it obscures most effectively are the ways in which some "peasants" did not become French men or women, but pursued their own logic in the formation of their families. As was the case with economic development, the discourse of which Watkins's argument is a part insists that the only way in which rural behavior might change is through ceasing to be "peasant" and becoming part of the French nation. Yet we need again to recognize that the family was a site of cultural negotiation between French and country dweller, and we must look for other possibilities than those suggested by the notion of demographic nationalism.

To do this it is useful to return to the villages of Saint-Hilaire and

50 Susan Cotts Watkins, *From Provinces Into Nations: Demographic Integration in Western Europe, 1870–1960* (Princeton, N.J.: Princeton University Press, 1991), esp. chs. 6 and 7.

Verrières and attempt to understand the changes in family formation that occurred there. In both communes a movement toward higher proportions married, control of fertility within marriage, and a nuclear-household system occurred in the second half of the century (see Table 3.1). I_m increased between 1851 and the end of the century, I_g decreased (in the case of Saint-Hilaire, dramatically), and adults per household and marital units per household decreased. However, whereas in Saint-Hilaire these changes led to a much lower level of overall fertility (I_f), this measure actually increased in Verrières. Mortality also showed some improvement in Saint-Hilaire, which in combination with the dramatic decline in reproduction meant that immigration was necessary to maintain the population size. In Verrières, in contrast, mortality remained at about the same level (albeit still lower than in Saint-Hilaire) and, with overall fertility even higher than it had been at midcentury, emigration remained an important part of the demographic mechanism. In general, while Saint-Hilaire appears in this span of two generations to have entered full tilt into a twentieth-century pattern of demographic and family behavior, Verrières, although somewhat closer to this behavior in 1851 than was Saint-Hilaire, moved more gradually in that direction during the fifty-year period.

These changes in family formation could be read as moves imitative of bourgeois French patterns of family behavior, but they also need to be understood in the context of the pressures social and economic changes placed on families in these two communes. The household system in Saint-Hilaire at the end of the century was overwhelmingly nuclear, as it had been at midcentury. A substantial number of households (69.8 percent) were nuclear, either with or without servants. About the same proportion of households as in 1851 were complex, and these households again showed no clear pattern but were scattered almost randomly over the different forms of complexity. One notable change, however, is that in 1901 there were substantially more households in spite of the smaller population of the village – almost 25 percent more than in 1851. A large part of this increase is in the number of households without any family; that is, those consisting of unrelated persons or, most often, of a single individual. These households were composed primarily of either the young or the old. If any fact were to underline the essentially nuclear character of the family system in Saint-Hilaire, it is this. The household of origin did not hold young adults as they grew up, nor did it provide an occupation or shelter for the elderly. Statistical data do not shed light on emotional aspects of family and household life, but that by 1901 most individuals in Saint-Hilaire left home when they could and did not depend on their adult children for care in old age suggests that the household as a collective-support institution was under severe strain.

The evolution of the household system in Verrières presents a contrast to the overwhelmingly nuclear pattern in Saint-Hilaire. While a majority of households were nuclear in structure at midcentury (61.5 percent, including those with servants), almost one-third of all households in 1851 were complex in some way. This household complexity remained an important part of the family system in Verrières in 1901. A smaller proportion of households were nuclear (55.1 percent vs. 61.5 percent) in 1901, and there was some increase in the proportion of households consisting of unrelated or single persons (15.2 percent vs 8.4 percent). But while this increase in nonfamily households was to some extent at the expense of complex households, almost one-fifth of the households in the village were vertically extended (19.3 percent).

The household systems of Saint-Hilaire and Verrières, and their changes between 1851 and 1901, were linked to social and economic structures. The household in Saint-Hilaire in 1901 had roots in the village economy. As in 1851 smallholding and the presence of weaving in particular encouraged independence from the family of origin: exclusively agricultural households did not need much labor outside of the conjugal pair and their children to work the family farm and, while as in 1851 some households supplemented the agricultural work of the household head with weaving, these were overwhelmingly nuclear in structure (forty-seven of fifty-four, only two of which had servants). The households with no related persons in them were often able to exist because of the opportunities provided by weaving: ten out of thirty-five were exclusively dependent on weaving for their livelihood, and even those dependent on agriculture were *cultivateurs* or *ménagères* rather than *propriétaires*. Indeed, it is apparent that, other than the curé, *instituteur*, and a few *rentiers*, those who lived in this kind of household were overwhelmingly drawn from the part of the social structure of the village dependent for their livelihoods on some kind of wage labor.

Change in the family and household system of Saint-Hilaire had, therefore, been modest between 1851 and 1901, but it certainly could be construed as a move in the direction of an increased emphasis both in practice and, possibly, in attitudes toward individualism at the expense of concerns with the well-being of the entire family, and especially its dependent members.[51] A similar reading could be placed on the widespread adoption of family limitation within marriage and the move toward more frequent marriage. But the proletarianization that was a consequence of the social and economic structures of Saint-Hilaire in the second half of the nineteenth century must be kept in mind as we interpret these changes in family formation. Given the relatively stagnant character of agriculture

51 As I interpreted it in an earlier analysis. See Lehning, "Socioeconomic Change," 173.

in Saint-Hilaire, the opportunities for employment outside of family farming seem particularly important in this village. Smallholding and the stagnation in the village of cotton manufacturing in the last decades of the nineteenth century placed heavy pressures on the family. Individualism may have been a part of the motivation for these changes, especially the increased prevalence of older individuals living in independent households and more frequent marriage, but the stagnation of agriculture and the loss of protoindustrial employments could lead families to choose to be smaller as well.

The development of the system of family formation in Verrières was also closely connected to the fortunes of the agricultural economy. The importance of complex households in Verrières in 1851 and 1901 suggests that household change occurred at a slower pace there than in the rest of the rural communes of the department, and the contrast with the overwhelmingly nuclear household system of Saint-Hilaire remains apparent even at the beginning of the twentieth century. But there was some change: the proportion of complex households declined, and the proportion of nonfamily households increased. Many of these nonfamily households were made up of older people: more persons aged over sixty-five lived by themselves than in complex households (eleven vs. ten). As in Saint-Hilaire, the number of households increased even though the population of the village declined.

It seems then that even in Verrières the complex family was losing its place. The labor needs of the smaller family farms there were still greater than on the minuscule farms of Saint-Hilaire, but these needs could be met from within the nuclear family, especially as the decline of *métayage* eliminated the contractual requirements for a larger labor force than had been typical of that form of tenure. As a consequence, by 1901, many people as they grew older either chose or were forced to live by themselves. Marriage and family limitation also became more frequent by the end of the century. But the levels of these aspects of family formation, as well as the rise in overall fertility, suggest that a significant number of families in the village continued to follow the practices of midcentury. Indeed, the continuation of a systematic form of extended household structure, tied to the labor needs of the agricultural system, meant that for those families that continued in this type of agricultural activity the imperatives were for extended households, restricted marriage, and high fertility within marriage. But for others, nuclear households, a greater possibility of marriage, and family limitation coincided with their needs.

Notions of demographic change in both the nineteenth and the twentieth centuries tend to place individuals and populations at one point in time into a larger history, either the story of moral decay told by Le Play or the one of demographic transition often used today. But we should guard against making such a quick leap. The families found in Saint-Hilaire and Verrières were very flexible, interacting with the opportunities and demands that the economic structure – reflected in the size of farms, the forms of land tenure, and the possibilities of industrial work – presented to members of the family. Family members were clearly individual actors in this process, and to that extent it is possible to ascribe any of these behaviors to the notions of individualism that marked French culture and its discourse about families. But even if there was some diffusion of "French" attitudes toward the family into the countryside, this does not mean that they became "French"; nor does it mean they were necessarily striving to fulfill the "French" conception of a "peasant." These families were firmly enmeshed in the system of social relations that surrounded the land and rural industry in the department. Their patterns of family formation, therefore, occasionally included anomalies in terms of expected patterns of change, such as the increase in overall fertility in Verrières. These anomalies are a reminder that the continuation of earlier patterns of behavior, and the adoption of patterns of behavior that resembled those of bourgeois France, were not necessarily the result of choices between "tradition" and "modernity," but part of an ongoing process of negotiation between two different perceptions of family behavior.

IV

Contact between rural culture and the culture of France during the second half of the nineteenth century led to significant changes in the organization of the cultural landscape in which the country dwellers of the Loire lived. Fields, families, and villages were not only aspects of the social, economic, and demographic organization of the rural community but also places in which the members of that community represented their identities and interacted with changing French readings of the countryside. The paucity of records makes it possible to see only traces of this contact in the ways in which such settings as the village and the house fit into this pattern of contact. But even there it is possible to see how the process of cultural contact involved misreadings and negotiations, as French observers operated within a discourse that summarized rural change as a process in which country dwellers would change their identities, adopting the behaviors and culture of "French civilization," while those country dwellers portrayed themselves in their own terms.

This process is more apparent in two principal sites of early nineteenth-century rural culture, the economy and the family. In each of these areas, rural culture encountered a well-articulated discourse in French culture that was expressed in the countryside by powerful agents and that sought conformity in the countryside to the French conception of a "peasant."

The economic discourse, articulated in the gathering of information, dividing agriculture from industry, and acknowledging only individual market-oriented activities, emphasized only those rural economic actions that contributed to either disparate individuals or the French nation. The family discourse cast reproduction and residence decisions in individual terms – often negatively, as was the case with Le Play's emphasis on the selfishness that lay behind nuclear families, early marriage, and restricted fertility – and also national terms, in the necessity of producing soldiers to fight unified Germany. Missing in both of these descriptions of "peasant" activities were the units around which rural culture organized its representations of peoples' lives, the village and the family. And while contemporary observers could not see the significance of these sites in the ways they described the countryside, an interpretation of rural behavior that emphasizes the continued significance of village and family is just as convincing as that provided by the spread of French culture. Indeed, this reading, by making sense not only of those who became market-oriented, set up their own households, and limited their fertility, but also those who did not, seems more coherent than one that categorizes these nonconformers as "backward."

Changes in the descriptions of economic and reproductive activities during the second half of the nineteenth century are as important as changes in those activities themselves, a point emphasized by "outlyers," those cases that did not conform to the expectations of French discourse, and that for that reason tended to be dismissed. In the Loire, patterns of economic and family behavior suggest that both those parts of the department that visibly conformed to French expectations, and those that did not, were pursuing their own aims, not imitating French culture. They were, however, operating within the boundaries set by French culture for "its peasants." Country dwellers could not escape the French discourse, and that placed them with regard to the rest of the nation. But the story is not always one of disagreement and resistance. At other cultural sites and in other instances of cultural contact, this same process of occasional conformity, occasional resistance, but always negotiation, was also at work.

5

Gender, places, people

I

The chapter organization of this book artificially separates different aspects of the cultures of France and the countryside, a separation that could lead to the false conclusion that, for example, the economic and reproductive discourses examined in previous chapters were not linked to the other sites of cultural contact that will be discussed in the remainder of this book. In no respect is this analytic separation more misleading than in the subject of this chapter, for gender – the social and cultural constructions of women and men – pervaded every aspect of the cultures of France and the countryside, providing and utilizing models that circulated through economic, familial, educational, religious, and political sites. It is impossible to find some aspect of French or rural culture that was not thoroughly imbued with notions about gender.[1] For this reason, it deserves specific attention.

The pervasiveness of gender in French culture is readily apparent in national intellectual, literary, and political discussions. *Masculinisme*, the presumption of male predominance over women, was a "totalitarianism of the commonplace" in nineteenth-century France, operating through the legal system, the Catholic church, the economy, the educational system, and subtle customs and practices.[2] Even as the political ideals of the Revolution of 1789 seemed to be achieved, women were placed apart. Jules Michelet expressed the common view that women had to be married to have an identity; Alexandre Dumas *fils* found a divine analogy to describe the power of men over women, drawing from the Bible the

1 See Joan Wallach Scott, "Gender: A Useful Category of Historical Analysis," *American Historical Review* 91 (1986), 1053–1075; and Gerda Lerner, *The Creation of Patriarchy* (New York: Oxford University Press, 1986), 238.
2 Patrick Kay Bidelman catalogs the ways in which this operated in *Pariahs Stand Up! The Founding of the Liberal Feminist Movement in France, 1858–1889* (Westport, Conn.: Greenwood, 1982), ch. 1.

lesson that woman is to man as man is to God; man was divinely conceived as movement, woman only as form.[3] In bourgeois families these attitudes were expressed in a focus on perpetuating the family, whose home became principally a site of reproduction.[4]

Such attitudes are representative of the ways in which patriarchal concepts defined male attributes as universals while women depended on men for identity and completeness.[5] It was a powerful discourse, and critics found themselves caught in several traps. A supporter of women's rights such as Victor Hugo could describe the situation of woman in France as "without political rights; she does not vote, she does not exist, she does not count," and argue that there should be female citizens just as males had become citizens. But for Hugo and many others the path to equality as citizens lay through the Republic. The establishment of the Republic became the principal priority, leading to the rejection of women's suffrage as a goal by many of the first generation of French feminists. Only a few feminists in the early Third Republic, led by Hubertine Auclert, sought the vote; most emphasized removing impediments to women's civil rights. But this strategy yielded few concrete gains. The leaders of the new republic failed to give the "woman question" much attention, and the nascent socialist movement of the last third of the nineteenth century never adopted feminist goals in spite of the efforts of a number of women.[6] Feminist critiques of the dominant discourse adopted its assumptions about women's unique role, leading to the increasing emphasis in the feminist movement on women as "mother-teachers." Léon Richer, the "founder of French feminism," spoke of how poor education undermined the mothering potential of women and argued that "the mother is the first educator of the child." The emancipation of women was needed to save the family and the Republic.[7] The idea of "separate spheres" became the principal way in which the feminist movement positioned women in French society, but this corroborated the marginal status of women in bourgeois French culture.

3 Ibid., 57, 79–80.

4 Bonnie G. Smith, *Ladies of the Leisure Class: The Bourgeoises of Northern France in the Nineteenth Century* (Princeton, N.J.: Princeton University Press, 1981), 56.

5 See Lerner, *Creation of Patriarchy*, ch. 11; Joan Wallach Scott, *Gender and the Politics of History* (New York: Columbia University Press, 1989), 83.

6 Joan B. Landes, *Women and the Public Sphere in the Age of the French Revolution* (Ithaca, N.Y.: Cornell University Press, 1988); Charles Sowerwine, *Sisters or Citizens? Women and Socialism in France since 1876* (Cambridge University Press, 1982), Part 1; and Marilyn J. Boxer, "Socialism Faces Feminism: The Failure of Synthesis in France, 1879–1914," in Boxer and Jean H. Quataert, eds., *Socialist Women* (New York: Elsevier, 1978), 75–111.

7 Claire Goldberg Moses, *French Feminism in the 19th Century* (Albany, N.Y.: SUNY Press, 1984), 201.

The essentialist assumptions about women that underlay this view did not lead to careful distinctions between women in different social situations, and the different versions of this discourse almost completely ignored rural women. Commentary from French culture about them came only indirectly and tended either to eliminate women from view, lumping together all "peasants," or to find among them the pastoral representation of virtuous family life, an alternative to the radical critiques of gender relations found in urban France. It was only in discussions of women's suffrage that "peasant" women, as distinct from bourgeois or working class women, received any attention. But these comments drew on French discourses about both women and country dwellers, and assumed the passivity and dependence of both. Richer, for example, wrote in 1877 that "out of nine million adult women, some few thousand would vote freely; the rest would receive their orders from the confessional."[8] The working conditions of rural women also did not excite much interest: farmers were exempted from legislation on labor, and women's domestic and reproductive responsibilities often outweighed interest in their productive roles.[9] With no active national role other than that of a danger to the Republic, and their productive role marginalized, women again faced the ambiguities of the French discourse about the countryside: to gain notice, they needed to become "French"; yet their significance for the nation lay in being passive "peasants."

Gendering, nevertheless, was a significant part of rural life, an important way in which country dwellers represented themselves. To some extent, these representations emerge from folklorists' accounts of rural ceremonies and sociability, or appear in the indirect lighting of census lists. But gender was a contradictory area in which clear distinctions between French and rural cultures seem to dissolve continually even as they are made. Rural culture distinguished between masculine and feminine space, representations of gender that could easily be seen in terms of the distinctions between these spheres made in French culture.[10] Many

8 Ibid., chs. 3 and 4; Susan Groag Bell and Karen M. Offen, eds., *Women, the Family, and Freedom: The Debate in Documents* (Stanford, Calif.: Stanford University Press, 1983), vol. 1: 511. Steven C. Hause and Anne R. Kenney note that feminism was an urban, essentially Parisian phenomenon, and have found no evidence of rural feminism; when provincial feminism was launched, it was confined to urban, middle-class women. *Women's Suffrage and Social Politics in the French Third Republic* (Princeton, N.J.: Princeton University Press, 1984), 43, 144.

9 Mary Lynn Stewart, *Women, Work, and the French State: Labour Protection and Social Patriarchy, 1879–1919* (Kingston: McGill-Queen's University Press, 1989), 24, 46, 197.

10 While gender distinctions in French culture were relatively strong, we should not assume that the boundaries were rigid or impermeable. In a number of instances, they could be crossed by women. See, for examples, Susan R. Grayzel, "Writers of *la Grande Guerre*: Gender and the Boundaries Between the Fronts," *Proceedings of the Western Society for*

traits of the *masculinisme* of French culture, such as the legal code and religion, penetrated into the countryside, describing a limited scope for female activities, even while daughters, wives, and mothers were significant contributors to the economic structure of the rural household.[11]

These contradictions existed in the cultural space enclosed by the term "peasant." As created by French discourse, this place constructed "peasant women" as different than, yet a reflection of, women in urban France. Country dwellers once again seemed a repository of desirable "French" values, helping observers define for themselves the way gender relations "ought to be" even as they obscured some of their characteristics in the countryside. But "peasant" notions of gender were also constructed through rural cultural practices, a part of the creation by rural women and men of their own identities. A central part of this was the particular symbolic and cultural position of women in the countryside. In the early modern period they controlled the intersection between the external world and the human body, transforming the raw into the cooked, nature into culture. This transformative power continued as an aspect of womanhood through the nineteenth century and into this century.[12] It was, however, a power exercised privately, in the home, and the distinction between public and private was also a powerful part of the way gender operated in the countryside.[13] Women's spaces were limited to domestic, localized areas. Men, on the other hand, enjoyed broader physical and cultural spaces: they moved across roads and fields, into markets and county seats.

These distinctions appear in descriptions of rural life, but less evident is their history. "Peasants" were timeless, without a history; the story of rural change meant ceasing to be "peasant" and becoming "French," an account that, we have already seen, implied a transformation of the coun-

French History, 21 (1994), 181–189; and Lynn L. Sharp, "Spiritist Women Mediums: Using the Beyond to Construct the Here-and-Now," ibid., 161–168.

11 Susan Carol Rogers, "Espace masculin, espace féminin: essai sur la différence," *Etudes Rurales* 74 (1979), 87–110; idem, *Shaping Modern Times in Rural France* (Princeton, N.J.: Princeton University Press, 1991); Yvonne Verdier, *Façons de dire, façons de faire: la laveuse, la couturière, la cuisinière* (Paris: Gallimard, 1979); Joan Wallach Scott and Louise A. Tilly, *Women, Work and Family* (New York: Holt, Rinehart, and Winston, 1978), esp. Part 1.

12 Robert Muchembled, *Popular Culture and Elite Culture in France, 1400–1750,* trans. by Lydia Cochrane (Baton Rouge: Louisiana State University Press, 1985), 66; Verdier, *Façons de dire, façons de faire.* See also Janet Thomas, "Women and Capitalism: Oppression or Emancipation?" *Comparative Studies in Society and History* 30 (1988), 534–549.

13 See Ana Maria Alonso, "Gender, Power, and Historical Memory: Discourses of *Serrano* Resistance," in Judith Butler and Joan Wallach Scott, eds., *Feminists Theorize the Political* (New York: Routledge, 1992), 404–425, for an analysis of the connections between gender, space, and public and private in a peasant society in Mexico.

try dweller through the acquisition of civilization. But it implied significant distinctions between men and women, and the French discourses
about women and the countryside proved powerful allies of rural gender
relations. Civilizing "peasant" men meant giving them the agency of
French citizens. As men, there was no contradiction involved in them
entering public spaces, and rural men by the end of the century had
entered several new arenas of cultural activity, not only attending primary
school but also participating in electoral politics. But rural women remained different. As women they seemed resistant to the transformation
into independent citizens that French citizenship implied. In spite of their
growing presence in primary schools, their role in the French nation was
closely tied, like that of their urban counterparts, to the home, as the
repositories and protectors of true French values. But the power women
held in rural culture raised issues, especially in the area of sexuality,
disquieting for a French culture that saw itself as the source of transformation and civilization. Gender, therefore, illuminates in an especially
straightforward manner the ambiguities of the French construction of
"peasants" and their history.

II

The significance of families in placing individuals in rural society meant
that both men and women "naturally" were parts of a family group, a
situation apparent in novels about rural life in which "peasants" were
members of families, and those who did not have families were suspicious. Men and women moved through a number of different roles in
their own and others' households as they grew up, and the normal life-
cycle progression in rural France was from the status of dependent child
to adolescent to married adult. But the gendering of the roles men and
women assumed throughout life was also a way of expressing inequality
and power relations in the countryside. The adult roles of father and
mother of a family were central to clusters of meanings that distinguished
between men and women, and preparation for these adult lives similarly
marked gender differences. These distinctions held men and women in
gendered positions that, as in French culture, were based on essential
characteristics of men and women, and placed those who acted differently
on the periphery.

In the Loire these different statuses usually but not always took place
within the framework of the predominant nuclear-family system. Within
the nuclear family, all individuals were important contributors to the
family's activities. As small children, both boys and girls spent much of
their time with their mothers at the farmhouse. As they grew up, work on
their parents' farm and domestic service on another farm were both nor-

mal parts of the life cycle. Census listings for rural villages typically show many domestics, both male and female, and these were a means of balancing the developmental cycle of households and their labor needs: servants were brought into households when members of the family could not provide sufficient labor to work the farm; they left when children became old enough to assist parents with the farm work.[14] Sometimes, no doubt, employment as a domestic was arranged between the parents and the farmer. There were also periodic fairs that brought farmers and domestics together. These were held in autumn and spring throughout the department, and were the occasion for not only job hunting but also socializing among the young men and women who attended them.[15]

As they grew older, men and women entered specifically gendered physical spaces. These physical – and then cultural – spaces implied certain kinds of activities that themselves carried gender implications, cementing the meaning in rural culture of the categories "man" and "woman." This gendering is most apparent in agriculture. Agricultural spaces away from the house appear to have been primarily male. The activities of men, who even as adolescents are usually listed in censuses as *cultivateurs*, were concerned with working the fields and maintaining the equipment necessary for agricultural work. Before they married, this work would be carried out under another male's supervision, either as a domestic servant or under the watchful eye and instruction of their father.

Women also carried out a wide range of activities on the farms of nineteenth-century France. These were of equal importance in the functioning of the farm, but they were above all and in contrast to male activities associated with the house.[16] This was underscored by the connection between women and the symbols of the distaff, the broom, and the cooking pot in the proverbs and folklore of rural France. Women's space also included the farmyard and the garden, as well as occasional work in the fields, and it seems likely that from a relatively early age daughters began to work in all of these areas.[17] This meant helping with cooking, getting water, gardening, and the care of the *animaux de bas*

14 James R. Lehning, *The Peasants of Marlhes* (Chapel Hill: University of North Carolina Press, 1980), 132–134. See also E. Todd, "Mobilité géographique et cycle de vie en Artois et en Toscane au XVIIIe siècle," *Annales E.S.C.* 30 (1975), 726–744; Ann Kussmaul, *Servants in Husbandry in Early Modern England* (Cambridge University Press, 1981), esp. 49–85; and Franklin F. Mendels, "La composition du ménage paysan en France au XIXe siècle: une analyse économique du mode de production domestique," *Annales E.S.C.* 33 (1978), 780–802.

15 Paul Fortier-Beaulieu, *Mariages et noces campagnards* (Paris: G. P. Maisonneuve, 1937), 44.

16 Cf. Rogers, "Espace masculin, espace féminin."

17 Martine Segalen, *Love and Power in the Peasant Family*, trans. by Sarah Matthews (University of Chicago Press, 1983), 35, 82–90.

cours, the chickens and other animals that filled the courtyard of the farmer's house. When older, a daughter might be assigned to other chores: certainly caring for younger siblings, and perhaps – especially on the western slopes and mountains – working as a shepherdess. There was also the chance that daughters would leave their own families' households and work for neighbors or relatives as domestic servants. Whether as a servant on someone else's farm, or assisting her parents on their own farm, young women in the countryside spent their time until their mid-twenties in a subordinate position doing heavy physical work.

The uneven positions of women and men in rural society are also apparent in the patterns of sociability and courtship that prevailed in the department. Accounts of these patterns portray a significant amount of supervision and control by adults over all youths, but there is no question that young women were more closely supervised. This close supervision seems to have kept young women closer to their families of origin and less linked to other unmarried women. Unmarried men are frequently portrayed as acting in groups, but accounts of young women either place them alone or with their families of origin, not other young women.

In much of rural France, *veillées* were a principal form of entertainment and sociability early in the century, especially during the winter, and this was the case in the Loire. While these evening gatherings brought young women and young men into contact with each other, the socializing was overseen by the entire population of the hamlet.[18] Other activities offered more opportunities for unsupervised actions, but it was primarily young men who enjoyed these. Occasional dances occurred during the year: in May, at the time of the feast of the village's patron saint, in the autumn and spring at the *foire aux domestiques*, and occasionally at cantonal fairs. Young men also joined with other young men in marriage celebrations and less reputable activities such as charivaris. These activities show them as able to wander unsupervised throughout the commune day and night.[19] Young women did not take an active part in these practices, except as objects of the activities of the young men. The night of the first of May, for example, it was the custom for the young men of a village to travel from hamlet to hamlet singing, playing musical instruments, or simply making noise by banging pots together, the kind of behavior that made up a traditional charivari.[20] But Paul Fortier-Beaulieu, the principal

18 See ch. 3 this volume and Edward Shorter, *The Making of the Modern Family* (New York: Basic, 1975), 124–127.
19 John Gillis, *For Better, For Worse: British Marriages, 1600 to the Present* (New York: Oxford University Press, 1985), 21.
20 On charivaris, see Fortier-Beaulieu, *Mariages et noces campagnards*, 314; Arnold Van Gennep, *Le Folklore de l'Auvergne et du Velay* (Paris: G. P. Maisonneuve, 1942), 61; Segalen, *Love and Power*, 41–49; E. P. Thompson, "Rough Music: le charivari anglais,"

folklorist of the department, specifically noted that these young men did not address themselves to young women and did not leave bouquets of flowers at the door of the girls' houses. These are small details, but they suggest that the village *jeunesse* might as a group harass young women. Individuals did not use this opportunity to court girlfriends, and young women did not join in the fun.[21] Similar group activities for young women may have existed, but they do not seem to have been as formalized or prominent.[22] Fairs and festivals – Carnival or the festival of the village's patron saint – also provided opportunities for socializing. But while these gatherings allowed common divisions of roles and territory to be abolished, they were still community affairs in which, even if parents were unable to supervise their daughters, other members of the community could do so.[23] Courting was almost always supervised by parents or other adults.

Folkloric descriptions of "peasant" customs such as charivari were among the ways in which French culture created its version of country dwellers. While they provide us with insights into some aspects of gender relations in the countryside, they are also part of a discourse that consistently viewed rural change as a process in which "peasants" became more integrated into the French nation and thereby lost their "peasant" qualities. Folklorists therefore saw rural change in courtship and sociability as revolving around a breakdown of isolated rural communities and the integration of country dwellers into larger social groups. At the same time, however, this story of change tended to act as a critique of urban patterns of sociability, in particular the problems apparent for bourgeois families in controlling their own children, especially their daughters, and the lack of control over working-class youth.[24] Similar concerns have pervaded many historians' descriptions of changes in rural family relations: these have focused on the spread of "romantic love" and companionate marriage, and have examined these processes in terms of the spread of capitalism and the diffusion of urban attitudes into the countryside.[25]

Annales E.S.C. 27 (1972), 285–312; and idem, "Rough Music and Charivari: Some Further Reflections" in Jacques Le Goff and Jean-Claude Schmitt, *Le Charivari* (Paris: Mouton, 1981), 273–283.

21 Fortier-Beaulieu, *Mariages et noces campagnards*, 68–69.

22 See, for example, the loosely organized group of young women described in René Bazin, *La Terre qui meurt* (Paris: Calmann-Lévy, 1987), 119–120.

23 Fortier-Beaulieu, *Mariages et noces campagnards*, 49, 57; Segalen, *Love and Power*, 147.

24 Bonnie Smith, *Ladies of the Leisure Class*, esp. ch. 7; Emile Zola, *Germinal* in *Oeuvres complètes* (Paris: Fasquelle, 1967), vol. 5: 23–421; Rachel Fuchs, *Poor and Pregnant in Paris* (New Brunswick, N.J.: Rutgers University Press, 1992), esp. chs. 2 and 3.

25 Shorter, *Making of the Modern Family*; François Lebrun, *La vie conjugale sous l'ancien régime* (Paris: Hachette, 1976). For different positions see Segalen, *Love and Power*; Scott and Tilly, *Women, Work and Family*; Gay L. Gullickson, *Spinners and Weavers of Auffay* (Cambridge University Press, 1986).

It is not therefore surprising that as the nineteenth century came to a close, evidence about changing patterns of courtship can be formed into a story about declining parental control. Folklorists like Fortier-Beaulieu both described "peasant" customs and documented their disappearance. Older forms of sociability such as the *veillée* disappeared in many parts of France; in the Loire, this was especially the case in the south, the north-eastern mountains, and the Plaine du Forez.[26] Local music societies began to give dances in the villages, providing youths with more opportunities for socializing. But gender differences appear in this story of the decline of "peasant" controls over youth activities, and in these differences concerns about sexual activity emerge. Martine Segalen has found these changes throughout France, and argues that because family honor tended to relate primarily to the unmarried daughter, close supervision remained the norm in many places.[27] The problem around which discussions of adolescent sociability formed therefore was that of controlling sexual activity. In the Loire, young women continued to remain closer to home than did young men, but the increased mobility of young men – both from neighboring villages and also from the urban centers of the department – brought young women into contact with a wider range of possible spouses or lovers.[28] Other new forms of socializing developed among young people as well. After the imposition of universal military service in 1889, the custom developed of each class of conscripts visiting their girl-friends [*conscrites*] and holding a dance. This certainly continued the older solidarity of the male *jeunesse* of the village, as the class of conscripts went around the village visiting their *conscrites*, with each conscript leaving a flower and a brioche with his girlfriend.[29] It also meant that opportunities for contact with those outside the immediate village increased, and much socializing, whether with outsiders or with young men from the village itself, now took place in circumstances in which parental and community supervision was perceived to be more difficult. But this greater freedom of movement was primarily experienced by young men: the continuing image of young men in a group with great mobility and independence contrasts sharply with that of individual young women in the parental home under closer supervision.

While rural parents no doubt were concerned about their children's sexual activity for a number of reasons, the differences between men and women that existed in the countryside were an instance in which the French discourse about the countryside could emerge. Rural sexuality in general, and adolescent sexuality in particular, was troublesome because it tied in so neatly with the French perception of "peasants" as irrational

26 Fortier-Beaulieu, *Mariages et noces campagnards*, 27–28.
27 Segalen, *Love and Power*, 21.
28 Fortier-Beaulieu, *Mariages et noces campagnards*, 29, 32, 33.   29 Ibid., 34, 43.

and instinctual, and because it reflected on problems closer to home. At a time when French culture was constructing careful limits to the sexual behavior of bourgeois women, and facing challenges to these limits from urban feminists and others, rural changes in courtship easily became part of the problem of "civilizing" country dwellers.[30] In this context, marriage not only marked the transition from dependent child to adult, but also ended the relatively dangerous period of adolescence. By containing illicit sexuality, marriage made it possible for "peasants," especially women, to reassume their position in French culture (and folklorists' accounts) as timeless repositories of virtue.

But the transition in status was different for men and women. Most first marriages for men occurred when they were in their late twenties. In the nuclear-family system, it meant independence for men as they moved out of their parents' homes and established their own residential families. This transition was often emphasized by the transfer of land between generations. This transfer may have occurred before the marriage, at the death of a father; often it was the subsequent inheritance that made possible the marriage of a son. It could also take place at the time of marriage through a donation between still-living parents and their son.[31] The acquisition of land meant not only an accentuation of the independence of a male, but also a turning of tables in his relationship to his mother. Even if he did not establish a separate household, he did acquire the trappings and many of the powers of adulthood as the farm passed to his control, and the woman on whom he had been dependent his entire life now became dependent on him. With marriage men took over the authority and responsibility of running either a rented or inherited farm, and their census listings show them as either *propriétaires-cultivateurs* or *fermiers-cultivateurs*. This was a position they would hold until old age, infirmity, or death removed them. The position of head of the household implied not only authority, independence, and responsibility; it also was normally associated with male adulthood, and it was physically associated with areas away from the farmhouse, in the more public space of outlying buildings and fields.

For most women marriage occurred in their middle twenties or a few years later, but it did not mean the kind of independence that married men enjoyed. The ceremony itself, in which the father "gave" his daughter to the groom, emphasized that the bride was not becoming indepen-

---

30 See, for example, Edward Shorter's description of rising complaints in the first half of the nineteenth century over declining popular morality, in *Making of the Modern Family,* 79–98.

31 On inheritance practices see Lehning, *Peasants of Marlhes,* ch. 8. See also the tensions generated by a donation of land to children in Emile Zola, *La Terre* in *Oeuvres complètes,* vol. 5: 761–1156.

dent, but was simply changing masters.[32] Early in the nineteenth century, this subservience was emphasized by the form of marriage contracts. The normal contract at this time established a modified dotal regime, in which the husband had the power to sell or mortgage the goods of his wife (although sometimes the wife reserved the power to borrow jointly with her husband against her property). After midcentury, the usual form was a community reduced to the acquisitions of the marriage.[33] In neither case, however, did French law give wives the power to act independently of their husbands even with regard to the property that they themselves brought to the marriage.

This rather pessimistic view of the transition for women from single to married status must, however, be somewhat tempered. While in complex family systems marriage meant that a woman competed for power and authority within the household with her mother-in-law, such families were not very widespread in the Loire. In the more common nuclear system, elevation from the status of daughter or servant to that of *ménagère* meant that, within the household, the wife was preeminent. In particular, as Martine Segalen has noted, control over numerous feminine tasks in the family and on the farm accentuated the sense of potential power that marked rural culture's view of women. The sphere of the *ménagère's* activities extended from the central place of the kitchen or common room, where the hearth was located, beyond the farmhouse to the farmyard and garden, and even farther to the stream or river where water was collected and laundry was done. Women also worked in the fields, and not only in exceptional times such as sowing and harvesting. But the role of mother also brought together numerous threads that centered on a particular kind of relationship between the woman and nature, a relationship that distinguished women from men through women's ability to transform nature.

This transformative power was clearly a part of rural views of women's sexuality. Such topics are often beyond the reach of the folklorist or the historian's vision, but they do become apparent at times, as in the numerous warnings one finds concerning menstruating women.[34] There was no attention by observers to sexual desire itself for either men or women in the countryside.[35] But there does seem to be a distinction made between men and women in their connection to the consequences of that desire,

32 Victor smith, "Un Mariage en Haut-forez en 1873," *Romania* 9 (1880), 547–60.
33 Lehning, *Peasants of Marlhes*, 125; Fortier-Beaulieu, *Mariages et noces campagnards*, 125–126.
34 Alice Taverne, *Coutumes et superstitions foréziennes: aspects de la vie quotidienne* (Ambierle: Musée forezien, 1973), 68.
35 As we might imagine, given legal restrictions on ways in which sexuality could be treated in fiction, there are few explicit descriptions. One of the few, Zola's *La Terre*, does not seem to systematically distinguish between men and women in the intensity of their sexual desire, although men are certainly more active in sexual relations than women.

reproduction. In the Loire as throughout France, chickens, the symbol of fertility, were symbolically related to women,[36] and it is certain that, whatever the relative knowledge and desire that bride and groom brought individually to the marriage bed, it was the wife who bore the consequences of sexual relations and who transformed sexual desire into the next generation. Obviously, she did so physically. But the activities of childbearing and child rearing also emphasized that this was perceived as an activity for women, not men. Birthing in the countryside was notable both for the absence of men, who were never present in the room where labor took place, and for the collection of women who were in attendance: mothers, neighborhood women, and the aptly titled *sage-femme* or midwife. New mothers remained in this female setting until they received the religious ceremony of purification after childbirth known as *décommèrage* (churching); only then could they visit family or friends.[37] As men continued after the birth of a child to journey away from the house to fields and more distant destinations each day, wives became mothers, nursing and rearing their children. In some parts of the department – the South around Saint-Etienne, the eastern mountains closest to Lyon – the birth of a child also often meant becoming a mercenary wet nurse, caring for an infant from the city.[38] Women, far more than men, were involved both physically and socially in the transformation of sexual desire into another human being.

Married women's metaphorical powers of transformation extended into areas other than reproduction. The elements of water, fire, and thread were normal symbols for women, and these represented her powers of transformation. Cooking was a significant aspect of the work of the *ménagère;* as Segalen notes: "It was in a very fundamental way associated with the woman, and not just any woman, not the servant, nor the daughter of the house. It was the responsibility of the mistress of the house; it was her privilege." The wife and mother was the mediator between nature and culture, the converter of raw food into cooked food. Knitting and spinning for domestic use – converting raw wool into thread and clothes – were also exclusively women's work. The mother not only knitted and spun to clothe her own family, but also helped teach her daughters to carry out these tasks, passing on the transformative powers of womanhood.[39]

---

36 Fortier-Beaulieu, *Mariages et noces campagnards*, 215.
37 J. Canard, *Folklore chrétien: coutumes d'origine religieuse, disparues ou en voie de disparition, en Forez et en Lyonnais* (Roanne: Imprimerie Sully, 1952), 33–36.
38 On mercenary wet-nursing, see George Sussman, *Selling Mothers' Milk: The Wet-Nursing Business in France, 1715–1914* (Urbana: University of Illinois Press, 1982), 103–105; and James R. Lehning, "Family Life and Wetnursing in a French Village," *Journal of Interdisciplinary History* 12 (1982), 645–656.
39 Segalen, *Love and Power*, 138, 141, 98, 88, 90–92.

The cultural role of *ménagère* was therefore marked by sharp differences from the central adult male role of *propriétaire-cultivateur,* especially in its emphasis not simply on production but on transformation. This difference – which meant that women and men were not interchangeable – implied a hierarchy in the household, but one with limits to male authority and dominance. The shift from subordinate daughter to *ménagère* did bring some autonomy to the woman even in rural cultural practice, expressed in the complementarity of the conjugal relationship, in which husband and wife joined together, working in different areas and activities, toward the common goal of the success of the family exploitation. And even in marriage rituals there are signs that run against the notion that wives were completely subordinate to their husbands. In the Loire, the customs of the *balai* and the *culotte* suggest that authority within the family was open to question: the newly married husband and wife, upon arrival at the farm after the wedding ceremony, competed to see who could reach a pair of men's pants tacked to the shutters of the house. The one who successfully reached them would be the authority; the one who lost took the broom.[40] This is, however, a complex and flexible ritual. The symbols used implied a certain ordering in the marriage relationship: it was, after all, a pair of pants, not a skirt, that the couple jumped for, and it was the loser, not the winner, who took the broom. These particular symbols suggest that the groom was *supposed* to best his bride in this competition: otherwise the normal order was overturned. Further, the bride and groom were aware of the ritual just as everyone else was; it may not affect their jumping ability, but the actual marriage relationship probably depended more on the relationship they had established while courting than on athletic skills.[41] This ritual suggests that whether that relationship was romantic, companionate, or complementary, the balance of power was weighted toward her husband, but the wife was not powerless.

While there may have been some change in status and control, however, continuity in women's lives before and after marriage is apparent in the work that they performed. For as long as she and her husband remained alive, the life of the agricultural *ménagère* involved the tasks of housekeeping, child rearing, and household management. Further, much of the social lives of married women remained separate from that of their husbands. Marriage did remove both men and women from the gender-exclusive social groups in which adolescents participated, and the focus of domestic activity in farmhouses in the single great room meant that, in the

40 Fortier-Beaulieu, *Mariages et noces campagnards,* 273–274; Natalie Zemon Davis, "Women on Top" in *Society and Culture in Early Modern France* (Stanford, Calif.: Stanford University Press, 1975), 124–151.
41 Segalen, *Love and Power,* 9, 26–27.

evenings at least, husband and wife were together.[42] Some socializing, such as that at Sunday Mass or wintertime *veillées*, brought husband and wife together along with their neighbors. But on normal days, women's sociability revolved around the river or stream where laundry was done, the spring where water was drawn, and the communal oven where bread was baked. It developed out of the domestic tasks of the *ménagère*, and it involved only other women.

In the parts of the department in which cottage industry was located, the agricultural work of women was supplemented by participation in these trades. This productive activity contradicted the focus on reproduction of the French discourse about women, but it also brought its own gendered hierarchization into the household and in that way reinforced the separate and subordinate position of the woman there. Clear skill distinctions existed between both town and countryside and men and women in the countryside. In the Lyonnais and the Stephanois silk industries, the most highly skilled tasks were carried out in the cities, not in the countryside.[43] The goods woven by a rural weaver were simple, lacking the elaborate patterns that made silk cloths or ribbons works of highly skilled artisans. Within the village, the least demanding tasks were the province of women. In the commune of La Fouillouse near Saint-Etienne, where families worked in that city's silk-ribbon-weaving industry, almost three-quarters of the *passementiers*, or ribbon weavers, were men; only 2 of the 175 *devideuses*, those who worked at the less-skilled preparatory task of cleaning the raw silk fiber before spinning, were men. In Saint-Hilaire, three-fifths of the *tisserands*, or weavers, were women, but only nine of the fifty-two *ouvriers en soie*, those who helped the *tisserand* by winding silk onto bobbins and doing other miscellaneous tasks, were males.

Because less-skilled tasks were placed in the countryside by the urban merchants who organized the textile trades, this protoindustry was overwhelmingly women's work. In La Fouillouse, women made up 76 percent of the labor force, and in Saint-Hilaire they were 66 percent of those indicating a protoindustrial occupation. Even in these villages, with their dependence on wage labor, adult men usually worked in agriculture, and those males who did work in silk weaving were, for the most part, young and single. Protoindustry was relatively low paying, and for most men, marriage meant moving into an agricultural occupation. Only those few men without the possibility of either inheriting or renting a farm made

---

42 Gillis, *For Better, For Worse*, 21; André Bréasson, "Maisons paysannes des environs de Saint-Didier-sur-Rochefort," *Bulletin de la Diana*, 39 (1965), 50–68.

43 See James R. Lehning, "Nuptiality and Rural Industry: Families and Labor in the French Countryside," *Journal of Family History* 8 (1983), 333–345, for fuller descriptions of these cases.

silk weaving their lifetime occupation. The labor of women, in contrast, was less firmly tied to farm work, and the low skill level needed in protoindustry made it possible for women to enter the trade in their youth, leave it when family and farm obligations became too time consuming, and return to it later in life when their child-rearing duties had diminished and there were older children available to take over some household tasks. These pressures can be clearly seen in patterns of participation in protoindustrial work. It was common among women in their late teens to late twenties, became less important in the thirties, and then, in the late forties or fifties, increased in importance once again.

This pattern seems to be a function of the availability of labor and the financial advantages of this work for the family economy. As a woman reached adult strength, she could begin to earn wages that were higher than any other kind of rural employment: at midcentury, for example, textile work paid an adult woman fifty to seventy-five centimes per day, compared with fifteen to thirty centimes per day paid children.[44] The only alternative to this employment was farm labor, and in these small-holding regions there was little possibility of employment either on the family farm or as a domestic on another farm. Work in domestic industry could therefore provide a significant contribution to the needs of a family at this time. After marriage, however, domestic demands reduced the availability of the mother's labor for protoindustry, lowering the rates of participation by wives in this kind of work. Only later, when children were old enough to allow the mother's return to wage earning, did wives return to the protoindustrial labor force.

While both French and rural cultures constructed gender overwhelmingly within the context of the family, even here it is apparent that the meaning of gender in the "peasant family" was contested. Rural women's transformative powers; their willingness, when able, to resort to wage labor; and their contribution in general to the family's productive capacity, all challenged the passivity expected by French culture. While the multiple readings of gender in the countryside did tend to converge, this was at the cost of inconsistencies and the marginalization of some aspects of gender relations.

III

Both rural and French culture placed women in a family, but as in the cities a significant number of women in the countryside were not members of family groups. This situation made it difficult to fit them into the usual ways of speaking about women, and placed them in a dangerous

44 A.N. C 956, 42 (Loire), *Enquête sur le travail agricole et industriel du 25 mai 1848.*

situation. As Robert Muchembled notes about early modern France, "Woe to the unmarried, to widows, orphans, or abandoned children – to any whom misfortune had deprived of a family! They lived apart, the objects of fear, indifference, or aggressiveness," a judgment that witchcraft accusations reinforce.[45] In rural society, it was the husband who socialized the woman and gave her a social and cultural existence.[46] Spinsters and widows were the women that demography and culture conspired to place in peril, in a kind of "twilight zone" that both marginalized them and made them difficult to interpret.[47] But they were not passive occupants of the position that their society and culture gave them; cultural practice in the countryside suggests that the boundaries between public and private, male and female, were permeable, if only in unusual circumstances.

The census descriptions of the situation of unmarried and widowed women in Verrières and Saint-Hilaire illustrate the ways in which women in these roles were placed in rural society, and how their experience provided a reflective surface for the French discourses about gender and the countryside.[48] Occupations of unmarried women in Verrières in 1851 indicate the overwhelming importance of agriculture, but their place in this sector was limited to some extent. Fully 45 percent of the spinsters in the village were engaged in agriculture, many of them (one-quarter of the total) as *propriétaires-cultivataires*. But in spite of the importance of sharecropping *domaines* in the village, spinsters rarely appeared as *métayers;* they may have been the heirs of small parcels, unable because of their sex and competition from complete families to rent the larger farms that were held as *métairies*. Other occupations also appear. A small number (13.8 percent) were listed as *indigente:* for them spinsterhood meant poverty. There were also four seamstresses. With this many in a commune of about a thousand their businesses must have been small, but their significance may lie elsewhere. In the twentieth-century village of Minot the seamstress played an important role in reproducing female culture, as

---

45 Muchembled, *Popular Culture and Elite Culture*, 35; E. William Monter, *Witchcraft in France and Switzerland: The Borderlands during the Reformation* (Ithaca, N.Y.: Cornell University Press, 1976), 141; H. C. Erik Midelfort, *Witch Hunting in Southwestern Germany, 1562–1684: The Social and Intellectual Foundations* (Stanford, Calif.: Stanford University Press, 1972), 195.

46 Segalen, *Love and Power*, 125.

47 See Olwen Hufton, "Women without Men: Widows and Spinsters in Britain and France in the Eighteenth Century," *Journal of Family History* 9 (1984), 355; and the very different fictional constructions of widows and spinsters in Zola, *La Terre*, and Bazin, *La Terre qui meurt.*

48 For a further analysis of the determinants of celibacy in the department, see James R. Lehning, "The Timing and Prevalence of Women's Marriage in the French Department of the Loire, 1851–1891," *Journal of Family History* 13 (1988), 307–327.

she not only provided the service of sewing for others in the village but also helped teach young women to sew and to develop their feminine identity. While outside the typical family group, the spinsters who worked as seamstresses were an important part of female society in the village.[49]

The most striking change in Verrières between 1851 and 1901 is the shift in spinsters' relationship to agriculture: occupations indicating property ownership disappeared. Those spinsters who remained in agriculture did so as *domestiques,* possibly a consequence of the decline of *métayage* and the consolidation of owner cultivation as the principal form of land tenure. In the absence of agricultural occupations, spinsters in Verrières in 1901 turned to service occupations, wage labor, and living on investments.

Agriculture was also an important activity for unmarried women in Saint-Hilaire, especially in 1851, although this was not solely as property-owners: more than one-fifth of them were proprietor-cultivators, but another 30 percent worked as either cultivators or domestics. The occupations of spinsters in Saint-Hilaire, however, also show the prominence of wage labor in the village's economic structure, especially the textile industry. Weaving and spinning employed two-fifths of the spinsters in the village. As in Verrières, agriculture lost some ground as an occupation for unmarried women in the second half of the century, and there may have been a shift in their role on the farm, as *ménagère* and *domestique* became the principal agricultural occupations. But wage labor continued to be an important source of support for the spinsters of Saint-Hilaire, and weavers made up the single most important occupational group in 1901. In contrast to the importance of service occupations in Verrières, unmarried women in Saint-Hilaire do not appear to have moved into this area, with only one *couturière* and two *institutrices.*

Occupational titles in censuses, especially those listed for women, can be misleading. But the ways unmarried women were listed in both of these villages suggest that the boundary between women's cultural position and that of men could be crossed, even if this was only in certain relatively rare situations. Given the close connection between agriculture and men, it is not surprising that wage labor and service occupations were prominent in the occupations of unmarried women. Yet that gendering of agriculture suggests that those women who were able to work in that sector had found an unusual place in rural culture.

Spinsters also lived in particular household situations. In Verrières, both in 1851 and in 1901, a large minority of spinsters were heads of households. About an equal proportion lived as lodgers.[50] In 1851, most

---

49 Verdier, *Façons de dire, façons de fair.*
50 This proportion was swollen in 1901 by the presence of a convent in the commune.

of the remaining spinsters lived in the households of either their parents or siblings, that is, in a subordinate position. Indeed, for more than half of these women in 1851, their household position implied a subordinate position, either the continuation of childhood status, in households headed by siblings, or (in three cases) in the household of a child of their sibling. By 1901 a significant number of unmarried women were still heads of their households, but the proportions listed as daughters and sisters of the head had dropped considerably. In contrast, the position of servant had become the most significant household role for unmarried women.

This shift away from the family of origin is also apparent in the types of households in which spinsters in Verrières lived. In 1851 only slightly more than 10 percent did not live in some kind of family household. A family unit therefore was the usual residential setting for an unmarried woman, and for many of them this family was an extended or multiple one. This situation changed dramatically by 1901: almost two-thirds of the spinsters in the village did not live in a kinship household. The family had apparently ceased to find a place for an unmarried daughter or sister, or these women were no longer willing to place themselves in the subordinate position that this necessitated. Whatever the reason, it is apparent that the position of spinsters changed significantly between 1851 and 1901 in Verrières, giving them, willingly or unwillingly, more independence from their families of origin. This independent position, however, was an ambiguous one for unmarried women. They acquired some of the cultural trappings of masculinity while separated from usual forms of familial organization. They were therefore transgressors against gender and familial roles, and for that reason suspicious to the rest of the community as their seventeenth- and eighteenth-century predecessors had been.

No such move toward independence from the family of origin occurred in Saint-Hilaire. A smaller proportion of single women were heads of household in that village than in Verrières; in contrast, a larger proportion were daughters or sisters of the householder, and while in 1901 there were no longer any sisters present, the proportion of daughters had increased dramatically, reaching more than three-fifths of the total. The households in which unmarried women in Saint-Hilaire lived also differed from those found in Verrières. In contrast to the rise of independent living in Verrières in the second half of the nineteenth century, the proportion of spinsters in Saint-Hilaire who did not live in family groups remained relatively constant. The number living in complex household forms was also less significant in Saint-Hilaire: nuclear household residence did increase in importance between 1851 and 1891, but in both years unmarried women lived most frequently in nuclear families in the subordinate role of daughter of the head. Spinsters in Saint-Hilaire did not make the same move away from their families of origin that spinsters in Verrières made at the same time.

The situation of unmarried women in these two villages suggests that the boundary between male and female space, while certainly relatively firm, was not impermeable. Spinsters were able to cross the boundary not only in their marital situation but also at times in their economic activities. They therefore acquired meanings that could arouse the suspicions of their neighbors.[51]

While similar to spinsters in that they were peripheral to the family group that provided many women with their cultural identity, widows had at one point in their adult lives made the break with their family of origin that marriage implied. What happened to them when that marriage ended therefore provides another view of the position of women in this rural society. While they often did not suffer the marginalization that was the lot of some spinsters, there were nonetheless a number of ways in which widows found themselves excluded by a rural culture that gave identity in terms of the family.

The occupations of widows in Verrières in both 1851 and 1901 placed them firmly in the agricultural sector, and in that sector as property owners. In both 1851 and 1901 virtually all widows owned and cultivated land. Throughout the period widows therefore enjoyed some economic independence. In both censuses the absence of many service occupations is notable: the business of families in Verrières was agriculture, and widows continued that business after the deaths of their husbands.[52] The same weakness of service occupations is apparent in Saint-Hilaire, although widows in that village did profit from the availability of wage labor in the textile industry. Nonetheless, agriculture was the most important single occupation of widows in Saint-Hilaire, as in Verrières. But the position of widows in Saint-Hilaire on agricultural exploitations was

---

51 Hufton, "Women without Men"; Judith Devlin, *The Superstitious Mind: French Peasants and the Supernatural in the Nineteenth Century* (New Haven, Conn.: Yale University Press, 1987), ch. 4.

52 We should take this conclusion with caution, for widowhood often meant geographic migration influenced not only by property ownership but by the location of the land owned. The widows listed in the Verrières census as property owners were those whose property was in the commune. While their husbands had been alive, they may have lived in the commune; they may also, however, have returned to Verrières after his death because that was where they owned land. Some widows, however, who lived in the commune while their husbands were alive owned no property of their own in the commune. If they remained in the commune they would appear as landless; they might also, however, leave after the deaths of their husbands because the land that French inheritance law assured them was located in their commune of birth, not in Verrières. See, for example, the high rates of out-migration among widows in Marlhes in the southern part of the department in Lehning, *Peasants of Marlhes*, 90–91.

not as strong as in Verrières, especially in 1851, when a large number were reduced to the position of day laborer. In 1901, however, the title *ménagère*, implying responsibility for running the household and caring for barnyard animals, had become the most important occupational title for widows. Many widows in Saint-Hilaire, therefore, seem to have been able to continue working on a farm after the death of their husbands. As elsewhere in France, they were probably helped in this by the gendered space of the commune, for the death of her husband meant that a widow had to find labor to work the fields, a problem that could be solved by hired hands or domestics, while her own work did not change.[53]

A significant change occurred between 1851 and 1901 in the household position of widows in Verrières. In 1851 widows in overwhelming numbers became the heads of the households that worked farms: four-fifths of widows were heads of households. In some cases these farms were worked by nuclear households, sometimes assisted by servants. But in many more cases the widow remained the head of a household that included other married persons, frequently the married son or daughter of the widow. Whether or not the death of the father made possible – or even required – the marriage of a child is not clear. What is apparent, however, is that a married child helped provide the labor necessary to work the farm without acceding to the position of head of household.

By 1901 this situation had changed. Widows in Verrières at that date no longer continued as head of their household when their husbands died. The most frequent outcome was again the marriage of a child, but the child acceded to the position of head of the household, creating a family in which the widow was the mother or mother-in-law of the head of household. While widows thus remained in the household, these were no longer *their* households but those of their children. Widows continued to be involved in agriculture and, as the occupational information indicates, many of them continued to own land. The *métayage* prevalent in Verrières at midcentury had made it possible for the widow, through her continued control of the land in the *domaine*, to be the head of the household after her husband's death. But the decline of sharecropping and inheritance laws that required that most of the father's land be inherited by his children rather than his widow meant that control of the farm, and with it the leadership of the household, passed to the next generation upon his death. Only if the farm included land of the widow, as well as or rather than that of her husband, or if he by testament gave her the use of a portion of his land, would she be able to maintain control of the farm and family.

Widows in Saint-Hilaire also were frequently heads of household in

53 Cf., Rogers, "Espace masculin, espace féminin."

1851, but were able to continue this with virtually no change to the end of the century: in both censuses, at least three-quarters of widows were heads of household. The households that they headed also differed from those in Verrières: a nuclear household, sometimes with servants, was the case for more than half of the widows in Saint-Hilaire (60 percent), in contrast to the low totals in Verrières (30.9 percent) for this kind of household structure. The remaining households included, in 1851, a significant number of widows living without a family group, although this had disappeared by 1901, and in both years there were a number of families containing widows and a married child.

We might attribute the frequency of widows in Saint-Hilaire as heads of their households to the existence of wage labor in the textile industry in that village, a source of income that may have allowed them to maintain their position. It is more probable, however, that the determining factors were the smaller size of farms, the consequently lower demand for labor on family farms in Saint-Hilaire, and the likelihood that a widow controlled the land either as owner or through a use right inherited from her husband; for even in Saint-Hilaire, widows had agricultural occupations more often than they worked in the textile industry.

The information from the censuses of Verrières and Saint-Hilaire argues against seeing a frozen, immutable position for rural spinsters and widows in this period. While *masculinisme* created many barriers for women, the legal system insured inheritance rights for them and allowed a husband to bestow a life use of a part of his land on his widow. It also assured unmarried daughters that they would inherit a portion of their parents' land. These conditions allowed some women to cross into what was primarily masculine space, as heads of household in charge of farms. There was therefore some room in which these women could create a position for themselves in rural society. Yet women were closely associated with the farmhouse and its spaces; more open, public spaces were marked as inherently male. This division was the case both in French culture and in rural cultural practice. The most likely way of gaining financial independence, domestic industry, was itself peripheral to the central activity of the countryside, agriculture. This meant that daughters could not inherit in the same ways as sons did, and widows could not really take their husbands' places. They could never be, in effect, men.

IV

French culture created significant distinctions between women and men, allocating public activities and the agency they required to men while placing women on the margins of the activities of the French nation and relegating them to bearing and rearing the next generation of French citizens within the home. Alongside these French perceptions, we must place rural constructions of gender, firmly rooted in every aspect of daily life, from the physical spaces in which people walked, to the tasks they performed, to the secrets they possessed, whether these were about working a field or having (or not having) a child. But genders in both cultures gained meaning from their differences from each other, and in this linkage was an inherent hierarchization. The activities that were reserved to men in both French and rural cultures were those that, being public, could lay claim to being the attributes of a full, active person, while women were portrayed as inherently limited and passive. In both cultures, some women could cross into male cultural space, but the roles that allowed this were clearly defined as unusual, tragic, or ambiguous.

Gender relations in the countryside were the outcome of the interaction and negotiation between rural cultural practices and the French discourses about women and country dwellers. Their contact in the second half of the nineteenth century did not bring into the countryside dramatically different conceptions of gender. Instead, this contact controlled the range of meanings of gender in the countryside and placed them in a national context. The limited meanings of male and female defined by French *masculinisme* reinforced the immobilism of gender relations in the countryside, and this is certainly an important consequence of that contact. But the second half of the nineteenth century was a period in which new cultural sites in the countryside were created, and existing ones given new meanings. For both men and women, this meant the incorporation of "peasants" into the French nation, although for both, this incorporation was partial and incomplete. The gender distinctions in both rural and French culture had profound consequences in this process. The claim to universalism that inhered in men's roles received reinforcement, as the Third Republic created spaces – the school and electoral politics – in which men could acquire civilization and assume their position in the nation. The construction of women as limited increasingly placed them in a peripheral position in this project of national construction, their national role consisting of essentially private activities viewed as essentially female. But this construction of rural women does not mean that they had no history in this period. Their history was one of marginalization, of placement as "peasant women" in a privatized sphere different from that found in their own culture, but also different from the one accorded their husbands as "peasant men." Gender, in short, made many differences.

6

The ambiguities of schooling

I

The contrast between a traditional society, one of whose principal qualities is a low level of schooling and literacy, and modern societies, characterized by mass schooling and high levels of literacy, is a staple of the way western societies speak about levels of development. In this view, the acquisition of literacy exposes people to new ideas, makes them more rational, and ultimately changes their behavior.[1] On a less fundamental level, educational attainment is seen as a basic part of the infrastructure of a modern society, needed for full participation in a complex industrial society.[2] Rarely questioned, education and literacy hold a central position in conceptions about transitions to "modernity."[3] This position revolves around constructions of nonliterates as different and nonrational, and of the educational process as a reconstitution of the individual. These notions are already familiar to us, as Abbé Grégoire, for example, drew on them in his analysis of the use of patois.[4] The extension of schooling, the rise of popular literacy, and the question of what should be taught and who should teach assumed major significance in the way French culture

1 Alex Inkeles and David Smith, *Becoming Modern* (Cambridge, Mass.: Harvard University Press, 1974), 15-24, lists characteristics of "modern" societies. François Furet and Jacques Ozouf, *Lire et écrire: l'alphabétisation des français de Calvin à Jules Ferry* (Paris: Minuit, 1977), Vol. 1: 358–359; Michel Vovelle, "Y a-t-il une révolution culturelle au XVIIIe siècle? A propos de l'éducation populaire en Provence," *Revue d'Histoire Moderne et Contemporaine*, 32 (1975), 89–141.
2 Mary Jean Bowman and C. Arnold Anderson, "Concerning the Role of Education in Development," in Clifford Geertz, ed., *Old Societies and New States: The Quest for Modernity in Asia and Africa* (New York: Free Press, 1963), 254. See also the essays in Leon Bataille, ed., *A Turning Point for Literacy* (New York: Pergamon, 1976).
3 David Levine, "Illiteracy and Family Life during the First Industrial Revolution," *Journal of Social History* 14 (1979), 40; and idem, "Education and Family Life in Early Industrial England," *Journal of Family History*, 4 (1979), 378.
4 See Ch. 2, this volume.

130

positioned itself in relation to the countryside during the nineteenth century. Education had long been informal in rural France, in the interaction between parents and other elders and children. This education focused on transferring skills concerning farming, crafts, and parenting, as well as the understanding of the world that French culture termed "folkloric." Formal schools, and schooling, were not new in the nineteenth-century countryside, but in the course of the century country dwellers were the recipients of an impressive effort to develop a national system of education intended to bring the benefits of not only education and literacy but also French culture to everyone in the countryside. This system, as it developed, was not neutral with regard to what it found in existence in the countryside, and the structure and intentions of schooling were shot through with an agenda tailored to the objects of the system. In particular, schooling begins to show the limits that were inherent in the category "peasant" as it was evolving in French culture. François Guizot, for example, while more prominent than the thousands of legislators, officials, and schoolteachers who influenced the education of French children between the Revolution and the Great War, may stand for many in his views on schooling. He saw popular education as an essentially moral experience, "cleansing, strengthening, and enlightening" the souls of the people so that they would be free to exercise "the influence that the laws of God give to man in life and in human society."[5] Guizot saw therefore an active role for schooling in the countryside, changing its residents in some way from their existence as unschooled country dwellers. But

---

5 François Guizot, *Mémoires pour servir à l'histoire de mon temps* (Paris: Michel Levy Frères, 1860), Vol. 3: 63; see also Harvey Graff, *The Legacies of Literacy: Continuities and Contradictions in Western Culture and Society* (Bloomington: Indiana University Press, 1987), esp. 12, 262; Eugen Weber, *Peasants Into Frenchmen* (Stanford, Calif.: Stanford University Press, 1976), ch. 18; R. D. Anderson, *Education in France, 1848–1870* (Oxford University Press [Clarendon Press], 1975); Maurice Crubellier, "D'Une culture populaire à une autre: l'école de la Troisième république," in Jacques Beauroy, Marc Bertrand, and Edward T. Gargan, eds., *Popular Traditions and Learned Culture in France* (Saratoga, Calif.: Anma Libri, 1985), 149–162; Raymond Grew and Patrick J. Harrigan, *School, State, and Society* (Ann Arbor: University of Michigan Press, 1991); Françoise Mayeur, *L'Education des filles en France au XIXe siècle* (Paris: Hachette, 1979); Laura S. Strumingher, *What Were Little Girls and Boys Made Of? Primary Education in Rural France, 1830–1880* (Albany, N.Y.: SUNY Press, 1983); Linda L. Clark, *Schooling the Daughters of Marianne: Textbooks and the Socialization of Girls in Modern French Primary Schools* (Albany, N.Y.: SUNY Press, 1984); and Phyllis Stock-Morton, *Moral Education for a Secular Society* (Albany, N.Y.: SUNY Press, 1988) provide useful insights into various aspects of French educational history. Robert Gildea, *Education in Provincial France, 1800–1914* (Oxford University Press [Clarendon Press], 1983); and Mary Jo Maynes, *Schooling for the People* (New York: Holmes & Meier, 1985) are two valuable regional studies.

Guizot felt the need for constraints that would remind rural students of their place in French society. Popular education should take place in a religious atmosphere, with religious impressions and habits penetrating every aspect of the educational process. For Guizot, as for so many participants in this discussion, popular education was not aimed at creating a completely free individual, but one who had been properly guided by education to appreciate his and her responsibilities to society. The relative prominence of religion in education was, of course, a considerable source of conflict within the French discourse, but throughout the nineteenth century, and even after the reforms of the Third Republic, education filled this guiding role: *la patrie* might replace the earlier religious objects of devotion, but schooling still served socially conservative ends. Along these lines, the Guizots, Fallouxes, Ferrys, and innumerable schoolteachers of nineteenth-century France created a modern educational system, one that by the end of the century was affecting virtually every French boy and girl.

The school became, therefore, one of the favored sites for the negotiations that went on between rural culture and French culture, a place that moved to the foreground in the creation of the "French" nation. Entering the classroom became a part of the process by which country dwellers were to be civilized and brought into the French nation. This notion, so strongly felt by the architects of rural schooling, has persisted, as the history of education in the countryside often seems to be modeled on putting new wine into old bottles. In this respect, histories of rural education have participated in the same discourse by which French culture positioned country dwellers in the nineteenth century. But formal schooling did not manage to efface rural culture, only to contain it. In this process the system of schooling was advantaged by the attributes of political, social, and cultural power available to it. However, it was disadvantaged by its narrow focus, a quality that made its most significant intention the contradictory one of educating individuals who would remain in the social and political position of "peasants."

II

The administrative focus from the early nineteenth century on was concerned with the provision of schools and attendance at them, and we can use this information, along with other information generated and preserved by the state, to create a version along those lines of the history of primary education in the Loire. This history in the Loire replicates that of France as a whole.[6] While some basic schooling had existed prior to the

6 See Maurice Gontard, *L'Enseignement primaire en France de la Révolution à la loi Guizot*

Revolution, a significant formal school system began to develop in the department only after the fall of the First Empire in 1815. Many schools were established during the Restoration, largely under the aegis of a Catholic Church that saw primary schooling as a means of preventing a recurrence of the horrors of the revolutionary period. In the early 1820s about one-third of communes had an *instituteur* providing some instruction, and by the time of the *Enquête Guizot* in 1833 this had risen to around one-half. A nascent school system had therefore been established, but it remained sparse. Of a sample of thirty-three villages in the department, nineteen did not have schools for boys in 1833.[7] The arrondissement of Roanne, roughly the northern third of the department, was particularly disadvantaged, but even in the central and southern parts the availability of primary schools was limited. An inquiry on women's religious communities and their activities from 1832 indicates that fourteen of these thirty-three communes, and approximately half of all communes in the department, had such communities engaged in education.[8] While some formal schooling existed, therefore, many children at this time were educated either informally, by their family or the parish priest, or through other institutions such as the army's regimental schools.

Over the next generation the network of schools developed to a remarkable extent. By 1846, only 16 percent of the communes in the department did not have a school, and by 1860, virtually every commune in the department had an *école des garçons*. In this period, therefore, primary schooling for boys became commonplace. Much the same occurred for girls, although it is difficult to document its state in the 1830s, since the *Enquête Guizot* did not concern itself with *écoles des filles*, and it was possible, if not frequent, for a single school in a commune to accept both boys and girls. But certainly by 1860 schools were available for girls as well as boys: at least 70 percent of communes had made some provision for girls' education within the commune, and many had separate *écoles des filles*.[9]

That schools existed did not necessarily mean that children attended them. From the administrative perspective, a number of factors worked

---

(1789–1833) (Paris: Belles lettres, n.d.); *Les Ecoles primaires de la France bourgeoise (1833–1875)* (Toulouse: Service de reprographie, Académie de Toulouse, 1976); Antoine Prost, *Histoire de l'enseignement en France, 1800–1967* (Paris: Colin, 1968).

7 A.N. F^{17} 10368, *Statistique générale de l'instruction primaire;* A.N. F^{17} 116, *Enquête sur l'instruction primaire, 1833.*

8 A.N. F^{19} 6307. *Etat général des communautés religieuses de femmes, situation au 1er décembre 1831,* dated 3 March 1832.

9 Information for 1846 from Annuaire du département de la Loire pour 1846 (Montbrison: Département de la Loire, 1846), 134–145; 184–193; 236–245; for 1860, see A.N. F^{17} 10413, *Etats de situation des écoles primaires publiques et libres et des écoles maternelles, 1860;* see also A.N. F^{20} 731, *Recensement des communautés religieuses, 1861.*

against attendance at school. Some of these were economic, as parents were forced to balance their perception of the benefits of schooling against its costs, both in expenditures for tuition and materials and the loss of the child's labor on the family farm. In many parts of the Loire, schooling came second. Annet Chalas, at Pouilly-les-Nonains (canton of Roanne), described students who arrived with only a poor reading primer and the diocesan catechism, and whose parents would not allow them to learn writing because they could not pay for the class materials. A more frequent complaint connected poor attendance with the work children were required to do around the family farm. Chalas had this problem, and Pierre Tamain, the *instituteur* at Valeille (canton of Feurs), complained in 1861 that "the greatest part of the children only attend school three or four months of the year, and these are the months when the bad weather keeps the animals in the barn." Jean-Claude-Marie-Poyet, *instituteur* at Nervieux (canton of Boën), had the same problem with children needed at home, and Jacques Chambodut, *instituteur* at Burdignes (canton of Bourg-Argental), voiced similar complaints, also blaming "the inertia of parents."[10] François Delorme, at Souternon (canton of Saint-Germain-Laval), noted in 1861 that not long before, "parents had the deplorable habit in the countryside of sending their children to school for three or four months each year, then withdrawing them; they continued this practice three or four years and that's the end of it."[11] The *Rapport général sur l'instruction primaire* for the arrondissement of Roanne in 1855 made the same complaint, linking indifference to education on the part of parents to their desire to use their children on their farms or place them as domestics.[12] Gender also played a role in school attendance. In 1859 the report on *écoles des filles* in the arrondissement of Montbrison noted that while girls were not needed as much as boys in agriculture, they were used as shepherds. It was also felt that girls needed education less than boys, and that "if it were not for the obligation of preparing them for First Communion, few girls would ever attend school."[13]

These were normal complaints throughout France, and the problem of convincing country dwellers that education had a value was itself an old one that continued into the 1860s. In 1836 the rector of the Academy of Lyon reported that "the greater part of the mayors are indifferent to

10 A.N.F [17] 10780, *Mémoire* of Annet Chalas, 31 janvier 1861; *Mémoire* of Pierre Tamain, 30 janvier 1861; *Mémoire* of Jean-Claude-Marie Poyet, 31 janvier 1861; *Mémoire* of Jacques Chambodut, 24 janvier 1861. See also A.N. F[17] 9347, *Arrondissement de Montbrison, inspection primaire: ecoles de garçons et écoles mixtes, 1860.*
11 A.N. F[17] 10780, *Mémoire* of Francois Delorme, 15 janvier 1861.
12 A.N. F[17] 9327.
13 A.N. F[17] 9344, *Rapport général sur la situation des écoles de filles*, 1859, arrondissement of Montbrison.

education, and therefore to the school."[14] A generation later, in Saint-Bonnet-des-Quarts (canton of La Pacaudière), the *instituteur*, Joseph Chrétien, described a conversation in his village: "One of them says, my father had no education, my grandfather the same, I have no more education [than them], but we are not ruined because of that, so my son had no need of education to carry on his business . . . The other says, look at that one, he is well-educated, and he has nothing, so what good is his education?"[15] In the arrondissement of Roanne in 1855, the inspector claimed that "there is in general . . . a certain indifference on the part of heads of family for education," although he quickly excepted religious education from this statement because parents thought it was necessary for their child's First Communion. The differences in approach between country families and representatives of the state can be gathered from the reason this inspector gave for their indifference: "Not having themselves received an education, since schools were not, fifteen or twenty years ago, what they are today, they [parents] do not understand either the happy influence or the necessity [of education]."[16]

The continued importance of these factors is visible in the 1861 memoir of Benoit Bernay, *instituteur* at the *chef-lieu* of the canton of Saint-Jean-Soleymieux: he cites the family's economic circumstances, the needs of the family economy for the child's labor, the cost of schooling itself, and parents' perception of the benefits of schooling.[17] Other reports show that indigent students were particularly disadvantaged. The education given to them, especially in schools for girls, was frequently minimal compared with that provided paying students.[18]

We can recognize in these comments elements of the French construction of country dwellers as passive and unenlightened. It seems remarkable, given the catalog of reasons that rural children would not attend, that there were any improvements in primary education. But school attendance was rising all the same, a development that the *inspecteur primaire* of the arrondissement of Saint-Etienne in 1861 attributed to the success "beyond all hope" of new systems of subscription, as well as the "*bon esprit*" of the rural populations, who seemed to be more and more

14 A.N. F[17] 9369, *Rapport sur l'instruction primaire*, Académie de Lyon, 31 décembre 1836.

15 A.N. F[17] 10780, *Mémoire* of Joseph Chrétien, 23 janvier 1861.

16 A.N. F[17] 9327, *Rapport général sur l'instruction primaire*, arrondissement of Roanne, 1855.

17 A.N. F[17] 10780, *Mémoire* of Benoit Bernay, 22 janvier 1861.

18 See, for example, the statements in A.N. F[17] 9338, *Rapport sur la situation des écoles primaires de filles pendant l'année scolaire, 1857–58*, arrondissement of Roanne; and A.N. F[17] 9344, *Rapport général sur la situation des écoles de filles, 1859*, arrondissement of Montbrison.

concerned with the education of their children.[19] Some indication of this can be seen in the figures for male students attending school in the sample villages in 1833 and 1860 (see Table 6.1): almost all schools showed an increase in attendance during that period. Even more striking is the increase in the proportion of eligible students attending school: the 744 students listed in 1833 probably represent only around 25 percent of those of school age. This figure reflects not only nonattendance but also attendance for only a few years. By 1860, 85 percent of eligible males (seven to thirteen years of age) were attending school: most were not only attending, but probably attending for five or six years. There are no data for girls in the 1830s, but by 1860, 83 percent of those age seven to thirteen were attending school. In the middle decades of the nineteenth century, therefore, schooling for an extended period of time became usual for most children.

Historians have generally attributed this increase in schooling to the wider availability of schools as the state assumed greater responsibility for the provision of education, and to a growing acceptance by parents of schooling for their children. There is, indeed, evidence from the Loire that supports these views: certainly the impetus given by the Loi Guizot to creation of primary schools for boys made wider education possible, and at least one inspector, in 1855, wrote that families were more appreciative of "the benefits of education."[20] This was the perspective from the point of view of French culture, which was not likely to question the value of acquiring French civilization. A closer examination of the 1860 attendance figures, however, permits more specific conclusions about why this occurred (see Table 6.2). There is no indication that school attendance for males was the result of efforts by certain social or economic groups to obtain an education for their sons. Wealth or type of landholding did not mean greater access to education; nor did the relationship of the village and its economy to the growing urban centers of Roanne and Saint-Etienne. Such factors may have played a role earlier in the century, but by 1860 all families appear to have decided that education was necessary for their sons.

The situation was different for daughters, with more selectivity in whose daughters went to school. The farther a village was from one of the major cities, Roanne and Saint-Etienne, the less likely it was that girls would be sent to school, suggesting that education was seen as a necessity in the new world created by urban and economic development. This was a slow process: *instituteurs* in such communes as Saint-Jean-Soleymieux

19 A.N. F[17] 9347, *Rapport, inspection primaire, écoles de garçons et écoles mixtes, arrondissement de Saint-Etienne*, 31 janvier 1861.
20 A.D.L. T 1537, *Rapport sur l'instruction primaire, commune de Marlhes*, 1842.

Table 6.1. *School attendance percentages
in sample villages in 1833 and 1860*

	1833 Male attendance	1860 Male attendance	1860 Female attendance
Thélis-la-Combe	—	66	74
Châteauneuf	—	0	100
Dargoire	—	79	50
St-Genis-Terrenoire	23	93	96
Doizieux	33	92	97
La Fouillouse	41	88	94
St-Christo	32	95	89
St-Priest	—	77	100
Villars	96	80	100
Cezay	78	85	72
Montverdun	—	86	66
Feurs	61	97	94
Jas	—	79	59
Valeille	111	88	88
Moingt	—	89	92
Savigneux	—	86	91
St-Jean-la-Vêtre	—	74	86
Estivareilles	46	72	73
Usson	30	100	70
St-Bonnet-le-Cour	31	69	80
Sail-sous-Couzan	—	93	73
Montarcher	—	82	87
La Gresle	—	72	83
Maizilly	136	89	50
St-Denis-de-Caban	—	89	84
Vougy	—	95	100
Ste-Colombe	—	87	87
St-Cyr-de-Valorges	—	80	77
Notre-Dame-de-Bois	—	81	84
Combre	102	91	92
Commelle-Vernay	—	90	95
Fourneaux	—	84	93
St-Symphorien-en-Laye	10	96	100

Note: Attendance figures greater than 100 percent in 1833 may result from children from outside the commune or outside the 7–13 age group attending the
school.
— = Data unavailable

Peasant and French

Table 6.2. *Multiple regression analysis of the determinants of school attendance (betas)*

Independent variable	Males in 1860	Females in 1860
Foncière/Capita	−0.218	−0.032
Proprietor %	−0.203	−0.397***
Textile %	−0.013	0.147
Railroad distance	0.207	−0.214
City distance	−0.114	−0.584***
South language	−0.106	0.399
Constant	96.6225	110.9982
Multiple R	0.3052	0.6659
R Square	0.0931	0.4434

*** = Significant at .001 level.
Foncière/Capita = Per capita assessment for land tax
Proprietor % = Percentage of population listed as proprietors
Textile % = Percentage of population listed as textile workers
Railroad distance = Distance from nearest railroad
City distance = Distance from nearest major city
South language = Located in southern language area (1=yes; 0=no)

(canton of Saint-Jean-Soleymieux) and Saint-Bonnet-les-Quarts (canton of La Pacaudière) complained that some parents, especially the poorer ones, still had difficulty seeing the value of education.[21] But increasingly those parents most likely to be exposed to urban influences were also most likely to send their daughters to school, providing them with an essential resource for urban life. It is among these parents that the "benefits of education" were most appreciated.

It was also less likely that girls would attend school in the areas of smallholding, where farms rarely exceeded five hectares, that encircled Roanne in the north and Saint-Etienne in the south, and that ran through the mountains along the eastern and western borders of the department. Attendance was higher, in contrast, in the areas of middling peasant farms

21 Roger Thabault, *Education and Change in a Village Community: Mazières-en-Gatine, 1848–1914*, trans. by Peter Tregear (New York: Schocken, 1971); cf., Maynes, *Schooling for the People*, 130; A.N. F¹⁷ 10780, *Mémoire* of Joseph Chrétien, 23 janvier 1861; *Mémoire* of Benoit Bernay, 22 janvier 1861.

of five to twenty hectares in the center of the department. It was not, however, greater wealth that allowed families with larger farms to send their daughters to school. Small farms near cities were increasingly emphasizing husbandry,[22] which usually employed female labor for herding and processing dairy products, while larger farms remained cereal producers, utilizing primarily male labor. Thus smallholders could employ their daughters year-round, while families with middling farms were less dependent on this family source of farm labor.

School-attendance patterns in 1860 therefore suggest that schooling was almost universally accepted for boys, but for girls still hinged on the integration of the village into an urban system – which made apparent the positive benefits of schooling – and on the different structures of the household economy between small- and middleholders. These conclusions, when taken with the available evidence from school inspectors' reports, suggest that while for religious reasons most families wished to send their children to school at least until their First Communion, other circumstances intervened in the final judgment. For all boys, by 1860, some schooling was apparently recognized as necessary; for girls, however, schooling was contingent on the extent of their parents' realization that their futures depended on the growing cities and the role of educational skills in that milieu, as well as on the possibility of sparing their labor at home. Rather than simple opposition to or acceptance of schooling, therefore, parents differentiated between children by gender as they made educational decisions.

It is also possible to reconstruct a history of a result of schooling, literacy, by measuring the proportions able to sign an act of marriage.[23] The development of literacy in the Loire during the nineteenth century reflects the patterns of schooling in the department and was typical of the slow pattern visible in the southeastern corner of the massif Central.[24] It improved gradually between the late eighteenth century and the 1880s, by which time virtually all men and women could sign their names (see Table 6.3). As was the case throughout France, male literacy was higher and spread faster than that of women: even by midcentury almost 70 percent of men could sign their names, while in the same period only slightly

22 James R. Lehning, *The Peasants of Marlhes* (Chapel Hill: University of North Carolina Press, 1980), 43–44.

23 This is of course a limited and limiting way of measuring a phenomenon as complex as literacy. In the French case, it is suggestive of some knowledge of not only writing but also reading, and therefore of a minimal level of skill at what might be termed "literacy." See Furet and Ozouf, *Lire et écrire*, Vol. 1: 20, 26. For this reason, and with this disclaimer, I will use the term.

24 Ministère de l'instruction publique, *Etat récapitulatif et comparatif indiquant, par département, le nombre des conjoints qui ont signé l'acte de leur mariage aux XVIIe, XVIIIe et XIXe siècles.*

Table 6.3. *Male and female literacy levels in the Loire, 1780–1892*

	1780s	1816–25	1846–55	1883–92
Males Signing Act (%)	32.3	47.1	68.2	96.3
Females Signing Act (%)	18.9	18.7	38.9	92.5

more than one-third of women could do so. These figures echo the pattern described above of acceptance of schooling for most males around midcentury, but selective school attendance for women. Areas isolated by geography, language, or both – those, as we have already seen, that were being defined as stagnant or backward in administrative recordkeeping[25] – were those in which literacy was least developed among young women at midcentury. While schooling and literacy cannot be equated – many no doubt learned to read and write outside of the school system even at midcentury – school attendance figures and the spread of literacy point in the same direction: by midcentury some schooling and some level of literacy were common for men, but remained selective for women.

By the 1880s literacy had become widespread – close to universal, in fact – among both men and women in the rural Loire. This level of literacy was reached before the educational reforms of the Third Republic, passed between 1879 and 1886,[26] had much opportunity to make an impact on the school system of the countryside. The development of primary schooling and literacy in the middle decades of the nineteenth century in the Loire, then, was not the work of the Third Republic and the Ferry Laws, but rather the result of an accelerating process begun under the ancien régime, pushed forward by the Loi Guizot of 1833, and especially achieved under the Second Empire. In this area, at least, the indications are that most parts of the department, including those in the western Monts du Forez, had by the early Third Republic escaped the description of backwardness that emerges from the administrative records. The most rapid improvements in female literacy between the Second and Third Republics, for example, came in villages in the region of Provençal patois. The result was to create a new social institution, the primary school, that assumed an important position in the process of growing up in the countryside; and to introduce a new set of skills, reading and writing, and make them an attribute of being an adult. The

25 See Ch. 4, this volume.
26 On these reforms, see Evelyn Acomb, *The French Laic Laws (1879–1889)* (New York: Columbia University Press, 1941); and Mona Ozouf, *L'Ecole, l'église et la République, 1871–1914* (Paris: Colin, 1963).

slow development of schooling in the Loire is testimony to the insistence by families that this new institution would function at least to some extent on their terms, not those set by the schoolteachers and inspectors who anguished over the unwillingness of parents to make education a universally high priority within the family. Nonetheless, by the end of the Second Empire, most men and many women had spent a number of years during childhood – perhaps as many as six or seven – sitting in a classroom, just as those teachers and inspectors desired.

III

The emphasis on the provision of schooling and attendance in official records and histories tends to obscure the cultural work of the school. This new institution carried in it several paradoxes. Its creators were not in agreement about what the product of education in the countryside should be. The most obvious distinction is between Catholics and secularizing republicans, but the broad range of views between these extremes testifies that French culture itself contained contradictory positions. These differences implied different meanings of the term "peasant," but all intended that education would create that cultural category, whose members would fulfill their responsibilities to the French nation but be different (and know their difference) from the carriers of culture at the national level. In both separating country dwellers from their earlier roles as "peasants," and limiting their access to the alternative role of "French," the system of mass education generated contradictions that opened spaces for "peasant" participation in the process by which schooling came to be a natural part of growing up in the countryside.[27] The nineteenth century saw the placement in a prominent position of an institution in which French culture was rewriting the meaning of the category "peasant," but that project was rife with contradictions.

The ambiguity of that process is apparent in a memoir written in 1861 by M. Perrin, the *instituteur* of Marcoux in the canton of Boën. Perrin clearly was unusual for his time, a schoolteacher who was a throwback (perhaps even a survivor; we do not know his career history) to those schoolteachers who had been purged in the aftermath of the Revolution of 1848 and the Loi de Parieu of 1850.[28] His essay can be taken as an early

27 For other perspectives on this, see Laura Struminger, "Square Pegs into Round Holes: Rural Parents, Children and Primary Schools; France, 1830–1880," in Beauroy, Bertrand, and Gargan, eds., *Popular Traditions and Learned Culture*, 133–147; Crubellier, "D'Une culture populaire à une autre"; and Ben Ekloff, "Peasant Sloth Reconsidered: Strategies of Education and Learning in Rural Russia before the Revolution," *Journal of Social History* 16 (1981), 355–385.
28 A.N. F¹⁷ 10780, *Mémoire* of Perrin, 1 février, 1861.

definition of what a "peasant" would become as schooling became more widespread. In it, he showed an understanding of the role of education in preparing country dwellers for the world that was slowly coming their way. "Today," Perrin wrote, "the inhabitant of the countryside needs to be educated; by means of the railroad, from the city to the countryside is only a step; the peasant throws himself into all sorts of speculations that require from him some instruction: understanding his language, writing it, speaking it; this is the goal toward which he should strive." But conditions of schooling severely restricted his ability to reach these goals. In an indication of the division in the attitude of French culture toward popular education, Perrin complained vociferously about both the interference of the curé in the work of the *instituteur,* and the priest's disinterest in any subject but the catechism: "This *haut personnage* does not at all work to propagate primary education among his flock, he would rather see them wallow in a stupid ignorance than see them educated." Perrin attributed this to the curé's jealousy toward the *instituteur,* and the former's fear that the children would grow up to be *magistrats du village.* Happily, in Perrin's eyes, many parents did not listen to the curé, and were even willing to pay to educate their children. Further, he saw a future in which the arrogance of the curé would come back to haunt him. "By the arrogance with which *Messieurs les curés* have for a long time treated the rural populations," he wrote, "they have attracted hatred; . . . even the most isolated peasants dislike them and no longer recognize them as the ministers of Christ, but as men who wish to govern everything, as little despots."

If Perrin was a throwback in terms of his political views, he suggests how the local elites of the French countryside could become divided among themselves. He was writing in 1861, soon after French participation in the War of Italian Unification had offended French Catholics. It is apparent that the curé and the *instituteur* had locked horns on this issue, for Perrin sarcastically notes that the parish priest repays the emperor's support of the Church in France by accusing Napoleon of being the author of all the events in Italy, and claiming that Napoleon is the "principal motor of the war against the pope."

But while Perrin might rail about the arrogance, influence, and meddling of the parish priest, his complaint was not that the catechism should not be taught – he in fact stated that "a schoolmaster ought to devote himself especially to having it learned" – but that his students needed other subjects as well. If the curé had his parishioners' true interests at heart, Perrin thought, he would be concerned that students not only knew the catechism but also that they could write well and know the mathematics "that was useful for them" to calculate the productivity of a farm and the gain or loss on merchandise. This was a practical education both for the country dweller, who became a better "peasant," and for France, which kept its category of "peasants." The aim of Perrin was not to give his students an ability to act outside of a hierarchy. Rather, he intended to replace the authority of the curé with that of a schoolteacher, who would provide his students with what they needed, but only what they needed.[29]

Perrin obliquely faced the dilemma of French culture as it sought to educate without eliminating "peasants." This dilemma meant that even as the French state gathered evidence that showed more schools in the countryside and more country dwellers attending those schools, the most significant aspect of the history of rural education lay not in the establishment of a system of mass education and the growing acceptance of that system in the countryside, but in the limits that the conditions of primary schooling imposed on the educational experience. These limits came from the contradiction between the French conception of the school and the physical setting of formal education, the role of language in the school, the social context of the literacy that the school brought, and the kinds of knowledge that this new technology made accessible to those who lived in the countryside.

Physical conditions for much of the century might be taken as a visual metaphor for the ambiguous cultural position of the school. The *inspecteur primaire* described in 1842 what was probably a typical rural school, in the village of Villars (canton of Saint-Héand) not far from Saint-Etienne, in terms that accentuate darkness rather than enlightenment:

It is difficult to call this a school. . . . It is a room about five or six meters square which one reaches by a narrow, rickety, and dirty stairway; the door is barely attached to its hinges; the floor is bad; the walls are black and ramshackle; the light comes in through a single window in harmony with the building; everywhere a dense cloud of smoke, or of pressing darkness, everywhere a disgusting uncleanliness, of worm-eaten benches and tables, which totter, the whole place badly maintained and showing in the most hidden places the sign of negligence.[30]

In Dargoire (canton of Rive-de-Gier) at about the same time (1840), the inspector commented that the furniture of the school was in a pitiable state, the stove was completely out of service, and the *instituteur* had only an open alcove for accommodations.[31]

In 1861 *instituteurs* were still complaining about the conditions of schooling in their essays written for the same contest, sponsored by the

---

29 See Ekloff, "Peasant Sloth Reconsidered," 373, for an argument that this was what Russian peasants wished from their schools.
30 A.D.L. T 1537, *Rapport de l'inspecteur primaire*, 2 juin 1842. Commune of Villars.
31 A.D.L. T 1537, *Rapport de 1840*, commune of Dargoire.

Ministry of Education, that had given M. Perrin a forum.[32] The essay of Etienne Roux, at Saint-Marcel d'Urphé (canton of Saint-Just-en-Chevalet), suggests that conditions had not improved much since 1842. "The greater part," he noted, "of buildings used for primary education, in the rural communes, are not designed for these uses: here, they are inadequate; there, badly ventilated; elsewhere, unhealthful."[33] Jean-Claude-Marie Poyet, at Nervieux (canton of Boën), ironically noted "happy the *instituteur* who does not lack a clock, some tables or benches, and who is not forced, above all during winter, to gather the children in a small, sordid, and in consequence badly ventilated apartment."[34] François Delorme, in Souternon (canton of Saint-Germain-Laval), said that the schoolroom was usually badly ventilated, too small, and missing indispensable equipment.[35] His opinion was seconded by Annet Chalas at Pouilly-les-Nonains (canton of Roanne).[36] Evidently it was still difficult to call these structures schools. What these comments suggest is the importance of a particular version of the school as a place with certain features: it was ideally clean, well-furnished, and airy, with a clock and other equipment.

It was also a place in which French was spoken, and the conformity of schooling to the "French" model was also limited for some by the existence of a local patois. Brittany is the part of France in which this has been best remembered, but in the tradition of Abbé Grégoire the definition of language as "patois" acted everywhere as a way of marking it as belonging to "peasant" rather than "French" culture. Administrators and some historians made much of this as an educational problem.[37] The problem should not be minimized. But educational difficulties concerning patois came as much from the civilizing mission of schools as from communication problems in classrooms. Teachers in Brittany themselves usually spoke Breton, and the extent to which the patois of the Loire, for example, was distinctive is open to some question. It also apparently deteriorated in the course of the nineteenth century. In the arrondissement of Roanne, where the dialect existed, in attenuated form, only in

32 See Guy Thuillier, "Une Source à éxploiter: les mémoires des instituteurs en 1861," *Revue d'Histoire Economique et Sociale* 55 (1977), 263–270, for a description of these sources.

33 A.N. F[17] 10780, *Mémoire* of Etienne Roux, 20 janvier 1861.

34 A.N. F[17] 10780, *Mémoire* of Jean-Claude-Marie Poyet, 31 janvier 1861.

35 A.N. F[17] 10780, *Mémoire* of François Delorme, 15 janvier 1861.

36 A.N. F[17] 10780, *Mémoire* of Annet Chalas, 31 janvier 1861.

37 Pierre Jakez Hélias, *Le Cheval d'Orgueil* (Paris: Plon, 1975), ch. 4; Maryon McDonald, *We Are Not French! Language, Culture and Identity in Brittany* (New York: Routledge, 1989), 35–50; P. M. Jones, *Politics and Rural Society: The Southern Massif Central c. 1750–1880* (Cambridge University Press, 1985), 120–122; Weber, *Peasants into Frenchmen*, 310–314.

those parts of the arrondissement close to the Plaine du Forez, the report on primary education in 1855 noted that there was no idiom, strictly speaking, and that the local language really consisted only of a "disfiguring" of French by changing pronunciation and word endings. "It is impossible," the inspector said, "not to recognize that the usage of French had made much progress in the last fifteen years," and he attributed this progress to the influence of the primary school.[38] A similar comment was made about the patois of the arrondissement of Montbrison, farther south. The school inspector considered the local language "close enough" to French; further, "it is understood and used by everyone."[39] But at about the same time, the *instituteur* of Saint-Jean-Soleymieux (canton of Saint-Jean-Soleymieux), complained that "when a student comes to class for the first time . . . it is often impossible for the *maître* to make himself understood, above all if the child lives in a hamlet far from the bourg."[40] In the arrondissement of Saint-Etienne, however, the inspector felt that "patois and French are so similar that, in the most distant villages, travelers are able to make themselves understood and to receive responses if not in a correct language, at least in intelligible fashion." But this inspector also brought out a further point: children were embarrassed to speak French to their parents, and forcing them to do so offended their self-respect. The contradictory aims of schooling – inculcating respect for authority, especially parental authority, yet also imposing a culture foreign to those parents, gave correct French an ambiguous position.[41]

There is no doubt that local dialects influenced the impact of schooling in the rural Loire. This was most obviously the case in the Southwest, where geography and language isolated country dwellers. By the late 1850s language was losing its impact, but it was still an instrument of control in the schoolroom. In the arrondissement of Saint-Etienne, for example, the inspector in 1861 claimed that "patois is strictly forbidden."[42] But it also had wider ramifications outside the school. Local dialects served as a focus of local identity, an identity that could be deeply

38 A.N. F^{17} 9327, *Rapport général sur l'instruction primaire*, arrondissement of Roanne, 1855.

39 A.N. F^{17} 9327, *Rapport général sur l'instruction primaire*, arrondissement of Montbrison, 27 avril 1856.

40 A.N. F^{17} 10780, *Mémoire* of Benoit Bernay, 22 janvier 1861.

41 A.N. F^{17} 9327, *Rapport sur la situation de l'instruction primaire en 1855*, arrondissement of Saint-Etienne. See also Ch. 3 in this volume and the discussion by Pierre Jakez Hélias of the use of Breton in Plodemet in the period between the wars: on the one hand, parents backed up teachers' punishments for speaking Breton, since French was a barrier that had to be climbed over to gain riches; on the other, Breton became a useful language in which to make fun of French speakers. *Le Cheval d'orgueil*, 235–237, 574.

42 A.N. F^{17} 9347, *Rapport de l'inspection primaire, écoles de garçons et écoles mixtes*, arrondissement of Saint-Etienne, 31 janvier 1861.

seated in structures such as that of the authority of parents over their children. The question is complex: dialects did not always separate "peasants" from the culture of their bourgeois countrymen; schools did not always manage to destroy such elements of local culture. What is clear is that the administrative definition of French and patois confounded learning academic subjects with broader cultural issues.

It is also not at all certain that being literate separated individuals from the nonliterate part of the village community. If anything, it seems most likely that literacy enriched the experience of both literates and nonliterates. Even in the more dispersed countryside there were activities in common that would allow such contact between literates and nonliterates. For most of the century the *veillées* that brought together rural residents in the wintertime could provide the opportunity for reading aloud by a literate person to his nonliterate neighbors. As we have already seen, these evening gatherings were, by the end of the nineteenth century, limited to the more isolated western parts of the department. But it is likely that the family group itself was a place for contact between literates and nonliterates.[43] While a substantial proportion of the rural population for much of the nineteenth century was unable to sign at marriage, there were many fewer families in which neither spouse was literate. If literacy was creating two separate cultures, most families would fall into the categories of "both signing" and "neither signing" shown in Table 6.4. This is somewhat true before the Revolution, when literacy was limited to a small elite. As literacy became more widespread, however, it became pervasive in the family context. Marriage therefore acted as a bridge between the literate and nonliterate populations in the Loire, providing all but a small minority with some access, direct or indirect, to the written culture that literacy made available. The social institution that organized much of the lives of individuals, the family, also provided them with access to literate culture. We should note, however, that this access was structured in several ways. While there is no indication that being literate necessarily gave prestige and power in the relationship between husband and wife, overwhelmingly it was the husband who was able to sign in the marriages in which only one spouse could sign. This placed husbands in a position to mediate between the world that literacy opened to the family and the other members of that family, especially their wives. Literacy therefore mirrored and reinforced the gendering of space in the village community. But there was a countervailing tendency, as this access took place within the context of a competing culture that both literate and nonliterate family members shared. A literate husband might read aloud

---

43 See the argument by David Vincent, *Literacy and Popular Culture: England, 1750–1914* (Cambridge University Press, 1989), 17.

Table 6.4. *Proportion of marrying couples in literacy categories*

	Both sign	Husband only signs	Wife only signs	Neither signs
1780–1785	8%	18%	1%	73%
1816–1825	19%	30%	3%	48%
1841–1850	33%	34%	7%	27%

Note: By the 1884–93 period, 96% of husbands and 92% of wives signed.

to the family, but his nonliterate spouse might also tell a story from the oral tradition.

This cultural ambiguity of literacy is underscored by the content of schooling and the new forms of knowledge that it made accessible to the countryside. In many places the educational system that taught reading and writing in the countryside during the nineteenth century was firmly in the hands of the Catholic Church, and until this link was broken by the Ferry Laws (after virtually universal literacy had been reached) the content of primary education was dominated by concern for reinforcing Catholicism. Once educated, country dwellers appear to have read materials that drew heavily on their existing oral culture.

The period following the fall of the First Empire was one of religious as well as political restoration in France, as the favorable policies of the government allowed the Church to reassert its role in French society.[44] The Archdiocese of Lyon was an important participant in this religious revival, and its most visible sign was a flurry of foundations of religious teaching orders.[45] Among orders for men, the Petits Frères de Marie, founded in the early years of the Restoration, was one of the most important of these establishments.[46] Among foundations of women's orders organized with a superior general in the nineteenth century, the Archdiocese of Lyon was a major part of the "larger Southeast" that accounted for a significant proportion of these foundations. The two principal orders were the Sisters of

44 Gontard, *Les Ecoles primaires,* 28; Pierre Zind, *Les Nouvelles congrégations de frères enseignants en France de 1800 à 1830* (Saint-Génis-Laval: Chez l'auteur, 1969), 108.

45 Pierre Zind refers to "a fever of foundations of teaching brothers in the Diocese of Lyon." Ibid., 209.

46 The Petits Frères de Marie did not receive canonical recognition until 1824, but they had been in existence since 1816. See ibid., 121–122. The order did not receive civil authorization until 20 June 1851, since the government had virtually ceased granting such authorizations in 1830. See Gontard, *Les Ecoles primaires,* 135.

Saint Joseph, first established in Le Puy in 1650, which moved to Saint-Etienne in 1808 and eventually established its mother house in Lyon; and the Sisters of Saint Charles, a late-seventeenth-century foundation also based in Lyon.[47]

The aims of these orders were more religious than educational and exemplified the strategy of the Church. The founder of the Petits Frères de Marie, Marcellin Champagnat, said as much in a letter to the members of the order. "We have undertaken," he wrote, "to teach them profane subjects only to have the opportunity to teach them the catechism every day and in that way to engrave more deeply in their spirit and heart the way of salvation." Above all, this meant teaching the catechism, the truths of the Catholic faith, which under the Restoration was the subject of three recitations a day.[48]

While this connection between religion and education was attenuated in some parts of the country after the Bourbon monarchy fell in 1830, it continued in the Loire. In 1833 many schools for boys remained in the hands of religious orders such as the Petits Frères, with the expenses of the teacher's salary borne by the parish vestry rather than the Municipal Council. Priests were jealous of their control over the school, and clerical aims in fact encouraged the development of the educational system at this time. In 1832 in Roanne, a priest attacked in his sermon a new mutualist *école communale*, asking, "Who is the stranger in charge [of this school]?" The rector of the Academy of Lyon wrote in 1836 that curés attached a great deal of importance to education, offering advice to the *instituteur*. If this was not accepted, however, the parish priest tried to establish an *école libre*, which he could control and which often meant the ruin of the communal school. As late as 1881, the curé in Saint-Martin-L'Estrat was threatening parents that their children would not receive First Communion if they did not attend the *école congréganiste*.[49]

Religious influence in the schools was directly related to social hierarchies, as the social elites threatened by the spread of revolutionary sentiments sought to cement their own social positions by supporting a congreganist school. In Feurs in 1881, the *école libre* was generously supported by the Marquise de Vivens, and "many parents were obliged to send their children there, or see their livelihoods disappear."[50] In the commune of Pouilly-les-Feurs in the same canton, the principal land-

47 Claude Langlois, *Le catholicisme au féminin: les congrégations françaises à supérieure général au XIXe siècle* (Paris: Cerf, 1984), 219, 75, 724, 722, 502.

48 Pierre Zind, *Les Nouvelles congrégations*, 384.

49 Gontard, *L'Enseignement primaire*, 448; A.N. F17 9369, *Rapport sur l'instruction primaire*, Academy of Lyon, 31 décembre 1836; A.N. F17 9181, *Laicisation des écoles publiques*.

50 A.N. F17 9181, *Laicisation des écoles publiques*.

owners forced their workers, farmers, and sharecroppers to send their children to the *école congréganiste* that they had founded. This influence, the "fanaticism" of the population, and his long service in this parish gave the curé a strong influence in the commune, which he used to make sure that children attended the *école libre*, not the *école communale*. In Saint-Génest-Malifaux, the *école libre* was supported by the "barons, masters of the countryside, by an army of *dames*, whose mission is to intimidate the families favorable to our [republican] cause, and by a Municipal Council which systematically opposes the secular school."[51]

This religious control of education had a distinctly gendered character. Virtually every commune in the department had an *école des filles* staffed by nuns in 1861. Such religious affiliations were also frequent in the *écoles des garçons* in the arrondissement of Saint-Etienne, but in the rest of the department most communes did not have men's religious orders teaching.[52]

The subjects taught continued to provide the teacher with opportunities to "engrave the way of salvation." While in communes such as Dargoire (canton of Rive-de-Gier) in 1840 some grammar, geography, and French history were taught, and reading, writing, spelling, grammar, arithmetic, and geography joined sacred history and the catechism in the curriculum throughout the department, these always took a religious cast. The inspector of the department in 1841, Coutard, reported that "the books used are exclusively religious."[53] In the following years, clerical control of education was reinforced by appointment of members of religious orders as public schoolteachers and the establishment of *écoles privées des filles* by orders of teaching nuns such as the Sisters of Saint Joseph and the Sisters of Saint Charles. The Bible and catechism, supplemented by grammar texts and manuals on personal conduct, were the principal books used in class in the 1840s.[54]

This use of religious materials appears to have continued in much of the department until the passage and implementation of the Ferry Laws late in the nineteenth century. An inspector commented in 1848 that in the *écoles des filles* of the arrondissement of Saint-Etienne, "Except for religious instruction and reading, the other subjects are neglected too much."[55] The same complaints surfaced in 1855 about both *écoles des*

51 Ibid.
52 A.N. F[20] 731, *Recensement des communautés religieuses, 1861.*
53 A.D.L. T 1537, *Rapport sur l'instruction primaire, 1840;* A.N. F[17] 116, *Enquête sur l'instruction primaire, 1833;* A.N. F[17] 9308, *Rapport géneral sur l'état de l'instruction primaire dans le département de la Loire en 1841.*
54 A.D.L. T 1537, *Rapport sur l'instruction primaire, 1842; 1843–44.*
55 A.N. F[17] 9312, *Rapport spécial sur la situation de l'instruction primaire dans le département de la Loire,* 18 septembre 1848, 5.

garçons and *écoles des filles*, where reading was taught as a part of religious instruction, through monotonous, often unintelligible reading of the catechism; writing, grammar, and arithmetic received only cursory attention even in the better schools.[56] In the Roannais in the 1850s the catechism was taught for at least an hour every day in the wintertime, when students came most frequently, and the schoolteacher, to avoid complaints from the curé, "devoted the greatest part of the time to teaching it." As late as 1880 an inspector commented that while the teaching of reading was good in the school in Marlhes, in the mountains of the southern part of the department, it was unfortunate that it was taught by the reading of the Bible. Such devotion did not mean enthusiasm, and inspectors frequently complained about the monotone in which the catechism was taught by the *instituteur*. The inspector in Montbrison in 1858, for example, noted that reading was less an intellectual exercise than a physical operation.[57]

The religious content of primary education reflected the concerns of parents for much of the nineteenth century, until laicization began to change the curriculum and brought many communities in conflict with the state over education. In 1848, the inspector claimed that "in our department, preference is generally given to *instituteurs* who belong to religious congregations." The result was clerical dominance of the teaching personnel. In 1852, in the arrondissement of Montbrison, there were only sixteen lay schoolteachers in girls' schools. The inspector in Montbrison in 1856 attributed this to the influence of the clergy, although they did seem to be more willing than before 1848 to accept a lay schoolteacher.[58]

As we have seen, an important factor in encouraging schooling was the necessity for the child to learn the catechism before receiving First Communion. This religious purpose led to conflicts over the aims of schooling. The same priest who denounced the new *école communale* in Roanne in 1832 also threatened to examine the students from this school scru-

---

56 A.N. F[17] 9314, *Rapport sur la situation des écoles primaires de garçons*, 1 février 1855; *Rapport sur la situation des écoles primaires de filles et des salles d'asile* (arrondissement de Saint-Etienne), 1 février 1855.

57 A.N. F[17] 9338, *Rapport sur la situation des écoles primaires de garçons pendant l'année scolaire 1856–57*, arrondissement of Roanne; A.N. F[17] 9314, *Rapport sur la situation des écoles primaires de garçons*, arrondissement of Saint-Etienne, 1855; A.N. F[17] 9338, *Rapport sur la situation de l'instruction primaire dans les écoles de garçons en 1858*, arrondissement of Montbrison, 1858; A.D.L. T 1545, *Rapport de l'inspecteur primaire, commune de Marlhes*, 7 décembre 1880.

58 A.N. F[17] 9313, *Exposé de la situation de l'instruction primaire accompagné d'un tableau statistique*, 1848–49; A.N. F[17] 9314, *Rapport sur la situation des écoles primaires de filles dans l'arrondissement de Montbrison pendant l'année scolaire 1852–1853*; A.N. F[17] 9327, *Rapport sur l'instruction primaire*, arrondissement of Montbrison, 1856.

pulously when they presented themselves for their First Communion, "for they will need it!"[59] In the *écoles des filles* of the 1840s, this was the principal aim: "They (Sisters of Saint Joseph and of Saint Charles) apply themselves in a special way to preparing the children for their First Communion."[60] Even in the *écoles des garçons* this religious aim dominated: "Attendance at school is considered by parents only as a nullity that children must do to be allowed to make their First Communion."[61] The situation was the same in the Roannais in 1856: "Once the First Communion is made, more than two-thirds of the students desert the school and never return." The inspector for the arrondissement of Saint-Etienne during the Second Empire permitted himself a little optimism on the results of two decades of educational improvement, arguing that "families appreciate the benefits of education."[62] Doubtless this appreciation did increase as time wore on, but it is less certain that, as he suggested, "superstition is losing its empire."[63] The religious interests of parents and clergy meant that "after [the First Communion] is accomplished the children no longer reappear at school." Education remained transitory and limited, and the results were students for whom, "save an incomplete knowledge of the catechism, there soon remains absolutely nothing of this instruction."[64]

Even beyond the concerns of the clergy, whether the curé who sat on the communal school board or the religious brother or sister who frequently was appointed *instituteur* or *institutrice publique*, most *instituteurs* had only limited aims in the classroom. In 1861, Denis Joseph Chapuis, in the commune of Gumières (canton of Saint-Jean-Soleymieux), wrote that students in rural communities had no need of an "education in depth," because "it would be injurious for those destined exclusively for agriculture because, if they take too much interest in science, they would neglect the cultivation of their fields, which is, nevertheless, the base of all industry; and they would wish to participate in politics." All they need to know was how to read, say their prayers, and read their catechism.[65]

59 Gontard, *L'Enseignement primaire*, 448.
60 A.N. F^{17} 9308, *Rapport général sur l'état de l'instruction primaire dans le département de la Loire en 1841*, 15.
61 A.N. F^{17} 9311, *Rapport sur l'instruction primaire, 13 janvier 1847*, 2; A.N. F^{17} 9338, *Rapport sur la situation des écoles primaires des garçons pendant l'année scolaire 1856–57*, arrondissement of Roanne. See also A.N. F^{17} 9318, *Rapport sur la situation des écoles de filles et des salles d'asile en 1855, arrondissement de Saint-Etienne*.
62 A.N. F^{17} 9318, *Rapport sur la situation des écoles de garçons en 1855, arrondissement de Saint-Etienne*.
63 A.N. F^{17} 9327, *Rapport sur la situation de l'instruction primaire en 1855, arrondissement de Saint-Etienne*.
64 A.N. F^{17} 9311, *Rapport sur l'instruction primaire, 13 janvier 1847*, 2.
65 A.N. F^{17} 10780, *Mémoire* of Denis Joseph Chapuis, 10 janvier 1861.

Antoine Lafont, *instituteur* at Andrézieux (canton of Saint-Rambert), would have made François Guizot happy with his comment, "The *maître d'école* is there to teach the inhabitants of the countryside morality, agriculture, and respect for the laws." He also felt that, while there was a statue of Christ in every school, a bust of Napoleon III should also be there.[66] Even those with more ambitious goals for their students were careful (perhaps because they knew their audience in the Ministry of Education) to underline socially and intellectually conservative aims. Etienne Roux, in Saint-Marcel d'Urphé (canton of Saint-Just-en-Chevalet), aimed at producing "instructed, active, intelligent, laborious men who loved the life of the fields; but, above all, it is necessary that he [the schoolteacher] knows that the school is the sanctuary from which should leave the pious child, the honest man, the good citizen." The emphasis on citizenship is not found in the goals of men such as Marcellin Champagnat, but Roux hardly wanted to produce students who would wish to leave the countryside.[67]

This educational practice seems intended to produce a new version of "peasant" placed in the nation, but not in the same place as those operating educational institutions. Schooling for girls similarly sought to bring them into French culture, but in a different way. A particular aspect of education for girls was the emphasis on using schooling to prepare them for their future roles as housekeepers. The emphasis on religious education was important for future mothers, the guardians of the family's morality. More pragmatically, housekeeping skills were a part of the curriculum. The inspector in the arrondissement of Montbrison in 1852–53 was pleased by the fact that many of the schools in the arrondissement were now teaching girls to sew, a skill that "no young person should be ignorant of, especially a mother of a family." Several years later, in 1858, the inspector in the same arrondissement noted that sewing and knitting were the object of particular attention in the girls' schools of his area.[68]

The emphasis on sewing in primary education for girls is interesting only partly for the obvious point that such schooling drew on a view that the principal reason girls needed to be educated was for their future role as *ménagère*, and in that way prepared for a very limited place in the French nation. More than that, however, using schools to teach sewing is a particularly striking instance of the way in which these schools ignored the customs and culture of those who were to be schooled. As we have

66 A.N. F¹⁷ 10780, *Mémoire* of Antoine LaFont, 25 janvier 1861.
67 A.N. F¹⁷ 10780, *Mémoire* of Etienne Roux, 20 janvier 1861.
68 A.N. F¹⁷ 9314, *Rapport sur la situation des écoles primaires de filles dans l'arrondisse-ment de Montbrison pendant l'année scolaire 1852–1853*; A.N. F¹⁷ 9338, *Rapport sur la situation de l'instruction primaire dans les écoles de filles en 1858*, arrondissement of Montbrison; and Clark, *Schooling the Daughters of Marianne*, 26–59.

already seen, village culture distinguished between tasks and places in terms of gender, and one of the most important aspects of the feminine side of this division lay in the layers of meaning that surrounded the role of *ménagère*. It was in this role that rural women found not only power and authority within the household, but also the ties to village culture that defined their identities. And it seems likely that in nineteenth-century France, as in the village of Minot in more recent times, learning to sew was an important part of learning to be a woman; mothers and *couturières* were important figures in both processes.[69] The primary-school inspectors were no doubt proud of their achievement in seeking to improve homemaking in the countryside. It is possible that their emphasis on teaching these skills was viewed as a confirmation by French culture of an important aspect of rural culture. Their efforts, however, ignored and then severed a web of social and cultural relations, moving the training away from the rural spaces in which it had occurred and placing it in the hands of an outsider. It seems likely that in doing so they ensured that education would be seen as foreign to rural women and their daughters.

The content of formal primary education in the Loire was not, therefore, aimed at exposing students to new ideas and ways of thinking such as rationality and secularism. Developed not by a secularizing state, as was the anticlerical school system of the late nineteenth century, but as a part of a "religious restoration" after the tumultuous events of the Revolution, schooling was the instrument of a society dedicated to conserving its traditional character. In fact, there was a strong dose of social theory that came with learning to read and write in these schools. Yet this theory itself contained paradoxes. The *Catéchisme* of the Archdiocese of Lyon, which was probably the most frequently used book in rural schools in the Loire until the 1880s, provided students with a set of maxims that emphasized their duty to obey their parents. But it also demanded obedience to the parish priest, their social betters, and the government. The discussion of the Fourth Commandment obligation to obey one's mother and father emphasized subordination. "Father and mother" included grandfathers and grandmothers, mothers and fathers-in-law, tutors and curators, godparents, and "all those who have authority over us, such as pastors, kings, magistrates, schoolteachers." Reproduction was also emphasized, and those who married should do so with the intention of having children and raising them as Christians. Lest any students should decide that these duties could be ignored, punishment was made clear: the sin of those

69 See Ch. 5, this volume; Struminagher, "Square Pegs," 136; Susan Carol Rogers, "Espace masculin, espace féminin: essai sur la différence," *Etudes Rurales* 74 (1979), 87–110; and Yvonne Verdier, *Façons de dire, façons de faire: la laveuse, la couturière, la cuisinière* (Paris: Gallimard, 1979).

resisting the authority of the Church and its pastors was that of "temerity, blindness, disobedience; the sin of heretics and schismatics throughout the centuries, which leads to . . . eternal damnation." Membership in the local community was also emphasized. Those who spent the *fête patronale* in dissolution and disorder would attract the anger and condemnation of God, not only on themselves but also on their parish.[70]

This theory was all well and good when there was no disagreement between these various familial, social, and political authorities. Was that always going to be the case? Certainly the authors of the *Catéchisme* thought it should be. But even under the Restoration, it would be an optimistic reading of French politics to suggest that the state obeyed the Church, and the situation worsened as the century wore on. Would parents obey the curé? We have already seen that this depended very much on the needs of the family, and the demands that the curé was making on families. If the priest insisted that children be sent to the *école libre*, many families would do so; but, then again, some families did not send their children to school at all. Those children who went to school might speak French, rather than patois, in class, but they would not insult their parents by speaking it at home.

Even outside of the primary-school system, the possession of literacy does not appear to have exposed country dwellers to materials that separated readers from their rural surroundings. The books present in rural families were probably purchased from traveling peddlers whose winter tours took them through the Loire.[71] While the events of recent history began to appear in the books sold by these peddlers, they continued as under the ancien régime to draw on existing popular culture and reflect "the old fund of rural wisdom."[72] Beyond the *livres de colportage*, reading matter was limited. The *romans à quatre sous* and the *journaux-romans* that began to appear in the second half of the nineteenth century were limited in their distribution to urban workers and to more prosperous country dwellers.[73] Outside the school, therefore, country dwellers in the Loire probably read little, and what they did read tended to repeat the lessons of popular culture, not undercut it with "rationality and secularism."

IV

At least in chronological terms there is reason to think that literacy and formal schooling were significant contributors to the changes in the lives

70 *Catéchisme imprimé par l'ordre de S. E. Monseigneur le Cardinal Fesch, archévêque de Lyon, primat des Gaules; pour être seul enseigné dans son diocèse* (Lyon: Chez Lambert-Gentot, 1823), 80, 128, 32, 173.

71 Jean-Jacques Darmon, *Le Colportage de libraire en France sous le Second empire: grands colporteurs et culture populaire* (Paris: Plon, 1972), 47.

72 Ibid., 171.   73 Ibid., 190–200.

of the country dwellers in the Loire, just as the scholarly literature would have us believe. But this relies on a narrow reading of the history of what went on in the schoolhouses that spread across the countryside, a reading that believes, and continues to reinforce, the views of the French culture that brought these new forms of knowledge there. Schooling and literacy were part of a reassertion of religious dominance over the lives and minds of the "peasant" that began with the Concordat, predominated under the Restoration (especially with the foundations of religious teaching orders), continued through the July Monarchy, and was confirmed in the Loi Falloux and the policies of the Second Empire. It was therefore a part of the program of civilizing "savage peasants" by giving them French and a modest number of skills along with their religion.

But if schooling did not have in the Loire the corrosive content that is attributed to it as a matter of course, it also seems that it did not have the conservative and integrating effect that nineteenth-century educators, politicians, and religious leaders wished. The "traditional" culture that those men and women sought to inculcate in students was not rural culture. The absent voices in this chapter have been those of the individuals who sat in the miserable classrooms of the rural Loire during the nineteenth century, and we discover their reactions to schooling only in the odd anecdote. It seems likely that this reaction did not take the form of a transformation of their view of the world. There is little reason to think that they became convinced that the world was rational rather than irrational. Perhaps the most positive lesson of schooling was in the realm of social relations, where it presented a view of society in which individual initiative, innovation, and independence were not honored. Obedience and acceptance of the inevitable, whether it be crop failure, the whims of one's social betters, or the births and deaths of children, were presented in positive terms.

The primary school of nineteenth-century France as an institution sought to limit and contain the impact of the new cultural technology of literacy by imposing a particular version of education on its "peasant" subjects, a version that would prepare them for, but only for, their position in relation to "French" culture. It sought, therefore, to carry out the delicate operation of transforming the ignorant, reactionary peasants of the ancien régime into the educated but docile "peasants" of modern France. But there is enough in the sources to suggest that, even with the social and political forces arrayed on its side, the school was in a difficult cultural position. Many of its lessons would be irrelevant back at the farmhouse. If one never intended to go to Germany, one did not need to know where it was. More of them simply did not work. Did knowing how to count guarantee that one would not be swindled selling a pig, or did one still need to learn the art of haggling from one's father? And some of them, in the setting of the family, required the violation of not only other lessons of the school, but fundamental tenets of how life was to be lived. How, at the age of eight, speak to one's parents in a language they could not comprehend?

These were individuals' problems as they advanced through the institution. The cumulative effect of these problems, however, was to highlight the contradictions inherent in an attempt to educate "peasants." In becoming a principal site of contact between French and rural constructions of the countryside, the school itself destroyed the airtight boundaries between those categories as they had been constituted. This result was not quickly perceived by those who brought schooling to the countryside; but other contacts, on other sites, also encountered it. The school was not the only place in which French culture found itself seeking to contain its "peasants." As contact took place in churches and polling places, the same difficulties would surface.

7

Inside the parish church

I

In December 1814, the *gendarmerie* of the Loire reported that thieves had broken into the parish church in Buissières (canton of Néronde) and stolen about seventy francs. But, the report noted, "the silver Chalice was in a drawer that was opened, but [the Chalice] was not taken." A month later the subprefect of Saint-Etienne wrote to the prefect about a robbery in the church of Saint-Romain-en-Jarret. Thirty francs had been stolen, but "they opened the door of the sacristy, forced open several armoires, but took nothing; it seems that money was the only aim of their crime." These thefts seem to be confirmation that, as another police report in the Year 13 (1803) suggested, "those who make a trade of theft and brigandage seem to have placed their hopes on the riches of the Church."[1]

The entry of thieves into the churches of the Loire is a strikingly appropriate representation of the position in the countryside of that building and the religion it housed, for the Church as a cultural site was certainly invaded in the century after 1789. If the school was a newly prominent site of contact between French and rural cultures, the parish church was one of the oldest places in which representatives of French culture instructed country dwellers in the forms of social, political, and cultural discourse, and they in their turn negotiated with their social betters over these issues.[2]

1 A.D.L. 21 M 7, pc. 8, 1 décembre 1814; pc. 41, 20 janvier 1815; 10 M 6, pc. 37, Premier Trimestre An 13.
2 Natalie Zemon Davis, *Society and Culture in Early Modern France* (Stanford, Calif.: Stanford University Press, 1975); Jean Delumeau, *Catholicism between Luther and Voltaire: A New View of the Counter-Reformation*, trans. by Jeremy Moiser (Philadelphia: Westminster, 1977), 168: A. N. Galpern, *The Religions of the People in Sixteenth-Century Champagne* (Cambridge, Mass.: Harvard University Press, 1976), 20; Philip Hoffman, *Church and Community in the Diocese of Lyon* (New Haven, Conn.: Yale University Press, 1984); Keith Luria, *Territories of Grace: Cultural Change in the Seventeenth-*

Its significant positions both within French culture and in the country-side gave the French Catholic Church the means and authority to describe a version of the "peasant." This construction was a part of the French discourse about the countryside, focused specifically on the issues of what was sacred – chalices but not money boxes – and what was neces-sary for eternal salvation. It portrayed "peasants" as different, especially from urban workers; people who were acted upon – in this instance, who "were saved" – rather than as active participants in shaping their own lives; and as outside of history. In this respect it did not differ from the other ways in which that French version of the countryside was pre-sented. But French culture in the nineteenth century was scarcely unified in its own construction of the sacred, and controversies continually arose that, as they played out at the national level, are standard parts of the story of French history. These controversies also had ramifications in the countryside. Many representatives of French culture felt that the Catholic version of the countryside should remain in place, but others contested this way of positioning "peasants" and sought to redefine their place in the nation by making them a part of the "secular religion" of the Repub-lic. This conflict within French culture, which existed from the very beginning of the century, gained strength as time passed and as the Re-public triumphed after 1870.

For country dwellers, the Catholic church was another place in which they negotiated their identity with French culture. In this respect, the distinctions made by Claude Langlois between religious practices that were imposed, proposed, tolerated, or forbidden are relevant, for they suggest a whole range of forms of popular piety that, while usually falling within the limits of what was considered acceptable by the Church, often actively pressed against those bounds.[3] This religious contest was a long-standing feature of rural life, and the nineteenth century witnessed some significant shifts in emphasis within the church itself. Some country dwellers – those in Brittany are the best-known instance – remained closely tied to a fervent religiosity. But for many the importance of the church receded on the rural landscape. This happened in different ways in the course of the century. In the aftermath of the revolutionary and Napoleonic upheavals, disputes within the parish church showed that many country dwellers refused to accept the limits that the institution sought to place on them. Especially in the second half of the century, even

Century Diocese of Grenoble (Berkeley and Los Angeles: University of California Press, 1991); Edward T. Gargan, "The Priestly Culture in Modern France," *Catholic Historical Review* 57 (1971), 1–20.

3 Claude Langlois, *Un Diocèse breton au début du XIXe siècle: le diocèse de Vannes au XIXe siècle, 1800–1830* (Paris: Klincksieck, 1974), 603.

as the Catholic Church found its position in French culture under attack at the national level, it was also experiencing far-reaching troubles at the local level. In many places, country dwellers remained within a broadly conceived Catholicism but insisted on active participation in the definition of the sacred. For others the importance of religion declined in their lives, a kind of secularization.[4]

Because churches were often well organized and powerful institutions, the sources for the study of religious behavior tend to have been created by them. This makes most obvious to the historian the outward aspects of religion as it was defined by those close to the institution: adhesion to the Church at least in an exterior way, acknowledgment of the authority of its ministers, and acceptance of the social and political hierarchies in which religion was located.[5] The sources generated by the Catholic Church therefore allow us to piece together a partial history of religion, one that focuses largely on the question of adherence to the guidance of the Church. While in this story some parts of France had strayed from religion even in the eighteenth century, and the Revolution dealt a further blow to Catholicism with its concerted programs of de-Christianization, much of the country remained loyal. The countryside holds a prominent place in this story as the location of true devotion even as some members of the French elite and the growing worker populations of the cities left the fold. Its story is therefore about the extent to which country dwellers conformed to the Church's version of "peasant."

The Loire fits easily into this history of religion in France. There were some disputes, but a relative homogeneity of religious practice and belief marked the early nineteenth century, and even at midcentury most areas were of relatively strong faith. But in the second half of the nineteenth century this homogeneity began to crumble, and although most of the Loire remained faithful to the Church, religion ceased to be as strong an influence on country dwellers as it had been previously. This version of the Loire countryside also describes a familiar geography: in spite of long-term movement away from the Church in much of the department, the mountainous west and southwest remained strongly religious. But if we expand the bounds of this history and try to judge the extent to which a "spontaneous confidence in the protective capacities of religion in case

4 John McManners, *Church and State in France, 1870–1914* (New York: Harper & Row, 1972).
5 The French school of religious sociology has focused its work on these questions. See Gabriel Le Bras, *Etudes de sociologie religieuse* (Paris: Presses Universitaires de France, 1955–56); Fernand Boulard and Jean Remy, *Pratique religieuse urbaine et régions culturelles* (Paris: Ouvrières, 1968); and Christianne Marcilhacy, *Le Diocèse d'Orléans sous l'épiscopat de Mgr. Dupanloup, 1849–1878* (Paris: Plon, 1962).

of calamity" was a part of the popular culture of the Loire, it becomes more complicated.[6] For most Foreziens, religion was more than adherence to the requirements of the Catholic Church. In the ceremonies surrounding major events in life and other actions that reveal to us popular piety, it is clear not only that there was more to religion than practice, but also that these forms of piety pressed hard against the limits set by the Catholic Church, its agents – the parish priests – and the other representatives of French culture in the countryside.

II

The boundary between religion and politics was never very clear in nineteenth-century France, and this is obvious in the way rural religion was described by outside observers. The three series of reports of pastoral visits to parishes in the Loire that survive in the archives of the Archdiocese of Lyon bear the marks of the concerns of the Church and suggest that the salvation of souls carried with it strong temporal concerns.[7] Under the Restoration, "morals" and "politics" were frequently confused: in Verrières (canton of Montbrison) the archbishop's notation indicated that there were no great disorders, and in Aveizieux (canton of Saint-Galmier), while morality was good, the people were "difficult to govern." By the end of the century, the problems were different but still political: in the parish of Saint-Etienne in Roanne, for example, the impious were infected by socialism. These reports, especially those from the 1820s and 1890s, therefore provide not only a first impression of the state of religion in the department and its changes in the course of the century, but also an indicator of the way religion participated in the French discourse about the countryside.

These reports constituted "peasants" as passive recipients of salvation, much like the figures in Millet's *Angelus,* and the *Visites pastorales* of 1826–28 indicate that much of the population of the Loire fulfilled their religious duties to the satisfaction of the clergy, even if they were not overly pious. Only in a handful of parishes were problems perceived. Most serious were those parishes where most of the population seemed to

6 The phrase comes from Gérard Cholvy, *Religion et société au XIXe siècle: le Diocèse de Montpellier* (Université de Lille III, 1973), vol. 2: 1536–48. See also Peter Berger, *The Sacred Canopy* (Garden City, N.Y.: Doubleday, 1967); and Thomas Luckmann, *The Invisible Religion* (New York: Macmillan, 1967); Pierre Chaunu, "Une histoire religieuse serielle," *Revue d'Histoire Moderne et Contemporaine* 12 (1965), 5–34; Michel Vovelle, *Piété baroque et déchristianisation en Provence au XVIIIe siècle* (Paris: Plon, 1973); Yves-Marie Hilaire, *Une Chrétienté au XIXe siècle? La Vie religieuse des populations du diocèse d'Arras (1840–1914)* (Villeneuve d'Asq: Université de Lille III, 1977).

7 Archives de l'Archdiocèse de Lyon (hereafter A.A.L.). *Visites pastorales,* 1826–28; 1844–49; 1879–96.

be slipping away from the Church. In La Fouillouse (canton of Saint-Héand), near Saint-Etienne, "morals, without being extremely bad, still leave something to be desired"; and in Saint-Romain-d'Urphé (canton of Saint-Just-en-Chevalet) in the Roannais, the situation was only "ordinary." In Fourneux (canton of Saint-Symphorien-en-Laye), in the Roannais, the mediocrity of religious belief at least had an apparent reason: the lack of zeal on the part of the curé. In other parishes the reports refer to a specific group lacking in religiosity. In Maclas (canton of Pélussin), "one part is good, another bad." At Saint-Etienne-la-Molland (canton of Boën), "there is some chaff among the wheat." More specifically, in some parishes it was the lower classes that were of most concern: in Saint-Génis-Terrenoire (canton of Rive-de-Gier), near Saint-Etienne, the morality of the lower class was not good, and in Saint-Martin-d'Estreux (canton of Feurs) there was "a great deal of ignorance" among the *"bas peuple,"* while the bourgeoisie behaved well. In the large town of Usson (canton of Saint-Bonnet-le-Chateau), the bourg had poor morality but the surrounding countryside was relatively pious. These problem villages were, it must be emphasized, perceived as islands in a department where religious practice was relatively good.

The *Visites pastorales* of the 1840s[8] give a repetition of reports of good religious behavior, and like the earlier reports they emphasize the close identity between general quiescence and religiosity. By the 1880s, however, the Catholic Church faced what it considered to be major problems with the religious behavior of the population in the Loire. These were most evident in the urban industrial centers, and became a way of establishing "peasants" as a positive alternative to urban workers.[9] In the parish of Saint-André in Saint-Etienne, the largest, most heavily industrialized city in the department, the report in 1888 was that "the population of the parish is exclusively worker and is under the direction of patrons who are scarcely Christian; it tends more and more toward religious indifference . . . however, it remains Catholic in the important events of life." The major problem was Sunday work, and one finds here a typical division in religious practice between men and women: 750 women but only 250 men performed their Easter duty. The situation was little better in Roanne, the principal industrial center of the northern part of the department. In the parish of Saint-Etienne in that city, while there were "those very bad, those indifferent, and those of excellent religiosity," nine-tenths of the parish was infected by socialism and impiety. Only 300 men and 1,500 to 1,800 women in this parish of 8,000 to 9,000 performed their Easter duty.

8 A.A.L., *Visites pastorales*, 1844–49. These records are not as useful as the other two sets due to a lack of information and comments.
9 A.A.L., *Visites pastorales*, 1879–96.

The contrast between the cities and the rural parts of the department that had been made at midcentury continued in these late-nineteenth-century reports, in spite of growing concern in a number of rural parishes. Many reports in the 1880s and 1890s, like those earlier in the century, indicated that piety was "good" in the countryside. Fraisse, a rural parish in the canton of Le Chambon-Feugerolles, was typical: "the population is Catholic and, generally speaking, practicing." But what sets these *Visites pastorales* of the late nineteenth century apart from those earlier in the century is the mounting concern for a portion of the population that seemed to be drifting away from the Church. Even in this concern, however, the perception was that true "peasants," especially "peasant women," remained loyal to the Church and compliant with authority, as both the feminization of religion and the connection between industry and impiety are apparent. Men were frequently mentioned as less devout than their wives. This could run from the sharp division evident in the urban parishes of Saint-Etienne and Roanne to problems even in small rural parishes still strongly religious. In Vougy (canton of Charlieu), for example, in general the population was very religious, and virtually all of the women practiced their faith, most men did so as well, but there were about sixty male abstentions in this parish of twelve hundred people. In Maizilly (canton of Charlieu), the same situation existed: the parish was religious, the women unanimously, the men with a few exceptions. And in Notre-Dame-de-Vernay (canton of Perreux), men and women fulfilled their Easter duty, but there were thirteen or fourteen abstentions by men. No matter what the religious fervor of a parish, men were less likely to be religious than women.

A second group singled out for concern were those affected by the growing industrialization of the department: workers and immigrants. We have already seen, in Saint-Etienne and Roanne, the difficulties the Church experienced with workers in large industrial centers. But these problems existed in smaller towns as well. In the parish of Saint-Martin-en-Crailleu in Saint-Chamond, the "rural half of the population [is] religious; the half [consisting of] workers [is] indifferent." Both Sunday work and other diversions were problems: in Saint-Génis-Terrenoire (canton of Rive-de-Gier), Sunday work in the mines was an issue, while in Sainte-Croix in Rive-de-Gier, "going to the cabaret on Sunday was a concern." A hint of the problems with industrialization is evident in the report from Villars (canton of Saint-Héand): "No hostility (to religion), but indifference among the foreigners who form a large part of the population." As the industrial areas became less homogeneous, the religious practice of the earlier period could not be sustained.

As religiosity declined in some areas, there was a growing defensiveness on the part of the Church even about areas that still appeared to be practicing. This was reflected in a large number of parishes with notations like "leaves a bit to be desired" (Sevelinges, canton of Belmont). Dargoire (canton of Rive-de-Gier) was "Christian, but little practicing," although most assisted at daily offices. This comment suggests the larger meanings that the clergy attached to the faith: it was not enough just to assist at daily offices. Urbize (canton of La Pacaudière) was "good enough" but "a little apathetic," and in Commelle (canton of Perreux) the problem was that the faith was "not vibrant." At Saint-Bonnet-les-Quarts (canton of La Pacaudière), people were religious, but not enlightened.

By the eve of the late-century controversies surrounding education, the status of religious congregations, and the legal position of the Church itself, the Catholic Church in the Loire was facing concerns very different from those of the Restoration or even the late July Monarchy. The Church in the Third Republic worried about losing its flock: men, especially workers and immigrants, were leaving the churches to women in disconcertingly large numbers, even if they maintained a form of religious practice at marriage, the birth of children, and death. The trickle of the 1840s threatened to become a flood, with a people "hostile to all religious authority"[10] a distinct possibility. The specter of secularization threatened even in this relatively Christian department.

If the *Visites pastorales* suggest a pattern over time of the devotion to religion, a rough idea of its geography can be gained from the 1848 *Enquête cantonale sur le travail agricole et industrie*.[11] This inquiry included a question on moral and religious education in each canton.[12] The report indicates the ways in which "peasant" morality was conceived by the cantonal committee and the *juge de paix* who prepared it, and it describes a geography of the department (see Figure 7.1). Four areas of religious practice stand out on this map. There is a belt of strong devotion along the western and southern border of the department, consisting mostly of the Pilat Mountains in the south and the Monts du Forez, with some extension into the western side of the Plaine du Forez in the center. Breaking this belt of strong religious belief, and dominating the southern part of the department, was a second region in which religion was either unsatisfactory or neglected. This area focused on the industrial valley around Saint-Etienne, and consisted of the cantons that had been the site of extensive urban and industrial growth in the decades prior to 1848. A

10 A.A.L., *Visites pastorales*, Paroisse de Saint-Romain-en Jarez, 26 août 1889.
11 A.N. C 956. See also the use of this *enquête* in Michel Lagrée, *Mentalités, religion et histoire en Haute-Bretagne au XIXe siècle: le diocèse de Rennes, 1815–1848* (Paris: Klincksieck, 1977), 47–52.
12 The reports for two cantons (Charlieu and Saint-Just-en-Chevalet) are missing; for a third, Pélussin, the report does not indicate enough about the religious situation in the canton.

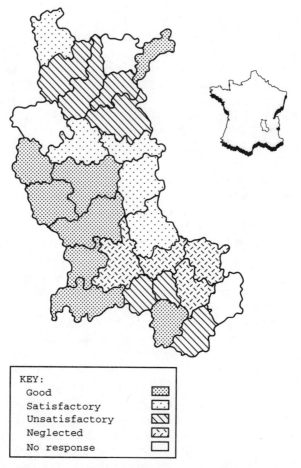

KEY:
Good	
Satisfactory	
Unsatisfactory	
Neglected	
No response	

Figure 7.1   Religion according to the 1848 *Enquête sur le travail agricole et industriel.*

third area, also of unsatisfactory practice, was in the cantons around Roanne in the north. These cantons contributed labor to the cotton industry of Roanne, and their lax practice suggests a linkage between industrialization and de-Christianization. From the perspective of the notables who contributed their views to the *Enquête*, both were dangerous to order. The fourth distinct area of religious attitudes in the department is found in the center and east, consisting of the eastern side of the Plaine du Forez and the Monts du Lyonnais, on the border with the department of the Rhône. The religious attitudes of this area, while not as strong or as intransigent as those to the west, were at least satisfactory. It therefore represents a somewhat moderated extension across the center of the department of the religiosity of the Monts du Forez.

The responses to the 1848 *Enquête* therefore reveal religious division in the department even at midcentury. From the perspective of the notables who drew up the responses to the *Enquête*, extremes stood out: the presence of an intransigent Catholicism in the rural, mountainous west and south, and the existence of growing pockets of de-Christianization in and around the growing industrial centers, Roanne and Saint-Etienne. Also troubling to those notables, however, was the moderate behavior of the rest of the department: practicing, but not fanatically Catholic, and therefore uncertain in their devotion.

Seasonal patterns of marriage, showing the extent of observance of the Catholic Church's ban on marriage during the religious seasons of Lent (March) and Advent (December) in a sample of rural villages in the department, shed further light on religious practice.[13] The data on seasonality of marriages are not without weaknesses, but these can be surmounted.[14] These indicators agree with the opinions of nineteenth-century notables and clergy: in the rural villages of the Loire, religious practice was relatively strong in the first half of the nineteenth century, but fell off

13 On the use of seasonality for this purpose, see the article by Jacques Houdaille, "Un Indicateur de pratique religieuse: la célébration saisonnière des mariages avant, pendant et après la révolution française (1740–1829)," *Population*, 33 (1978), 367–380.
14 As these data are examined, several points must be kept in mind. The unit of analysis is the commune, which in the sample varies in population from 205 to 4,180. Any summary statistic, such as a measure of seasonality of marriage, reflects the average behavior in the commune, not the behavior of any particular member of the commune. The smallness of the units may minimize the difficulties of using such ecological data, but it does not eliminate them entirely.

The data used for seasonality are the marriage registers in each commune, kept in A.D.L. Series 3 E. From raw totals of marriages in each month, standardized indices expressing the proportion of the year's marriages occurring in each month have been calculated. The actual measure used is the change in this proportional index between February and March, on the one hand, and November and December on the other. This figure is used in order to take into account different overall patterns of seasonality from village to village, isolating as much as possible the influence of the religious factor. In spite of this, the problem remains that other factors besides religion could affect seasonality: demand for labor or seasonal patterns of migration, for example, could depress the number of marriages in a religious season. The best guarantee against this is the use of data for both Lent and Advent, since it is less likely that both seasons would be affected by the same factors.

Finally, while the civil registers probably recorded most marriages, the periods of time for which these data have been drawn are relatively short. Fleury and Henry suggest that the seasonality of marriages be based on data from at least a full century. (See Michel Fleury and Louis Henry, *Nouveau manuel de dépouillement et d'exploitation de l'état civil ancien* [Paris: Editions de l'Institut nationale d'études démographiques, 1976], 103.) To do so in this case would vitiate the purpose, to discover variations over time in religious practice. There is therefore the possibility that small numbers have emphasized random variations in seasonality. Some confidence that this is not the case may be gained from the lack of significant differences between smaller (less than a thousand people) and larger (more than a thousand people) villages in the sample.

to a considerable extent after midcentury. Using as a measure the difference between the seasonal index of marriages for Lent or Advent, on the one hand, and the preceding month on the other, the reduced observance of the religious ban on marriage during Lent and Advent becomes apparent. Both seasonal measures remain at approximately the same very high level between the Restoration and midcentury, but decline by around 50 percent during the next forty years.

There is therefore considerable evidence that the religiosity of the country dwellers in the Loire was declining in the second half of the nineteenth century, from the decline in observance of Lenten and Advent restrictions on marriages to the concerns expressed in both the *Visites pastorales* of the late nineteenth century and the midcentury *Enquête*. These are certainly indicators of a changing position of religion in the lives of some country dwellers, and they are also a suggestion of a growing willingness on the part of country dwellers to assume a more active role with regard to received authorities. But we need to understand the full meaning of these trends. These new characteristics of religiosity – and most country dwellers did remain religious in some way – also served as a profound challenge to the ahistorical placement of "peasants" in French culture, and as a part of the ongoing negotiation of the meaning of that category. A change in the level of devotion on the part of country dwellers threatened to remove them from the timeless vacuum in which French culture typically placed them, and involve them in a process that, among urban workers, had produced all-too-apparent results in the revolts and disorders that sporadically marked French cities.

III

The comments by bishops and notables about religion make clear that they held a specific vision of the kind of popular piety that was acceptable, one that subordinated popular piety to the rules of the Catholic Church and popular behavior to priests and notables. If "peasants" were to be considered religious, they needed to conform to that vision. Such conformity may have been, in any era, simply a dream. But the eighteenth century and revolutionary period left a heritage of religious division in many parts of France between popular religious beliefs and the Church's forms of belief and expression that heightened tensions in village after village.[15] In some instances de-Christianization had preceded the tumult of the 1790s, while in others controversies between the de-

15 John McManners, *The French Revolution and the Church* (New York: Harper & Row, 1969); Jacques Gadille, *Histoire des diocèses de France: Lyon* (Paris: Beauchesne, 1983), 190–207.

Christianizing state and the local population during that decade left a legacy of bitterness. Even if the nineteenth century witnessed considerable effort on the part of religious and civil authorities to impose a religious "settlement" on the countryside, they did so in the aftermath of a revolutionary era in which the ancien régime pervasiveness of religion in "peasant" life had been seriously disrupted.

This was certainly the case in the Loire, although there was no single pattern of experience during the Revolution. Some parts of the department had become embroiled in disputes connected to the various oaths required by the revolutionary government, and as the repression of Catholicism became tighter under the Terror, a "hidden church" came into existence.[16] Religious disagreements persisted well into the first decade of the nineteenth century, even as the French state made its peace with the Papacy and sorted out local controversies: there were a number of incidents marking the installation of new parish curés in the Year 11 (1802–03).[17] But the following years saw apparent calm return. In the Year 13 (1804–05), the police reported that in the arrondissement of Saint-Etienne, "the ministers of the altars fulfill their duties with edification, the disagreements and quarrels . . . religious divisions and persecutions begin to embarrass the most obstinate; a perfect accord seems to reign among the pastors, and the docile sheep, following their example, seem now to belong only to the same flock."[18]

This police statement may have been optimistic, and it certainly drew heavily on the French notion of placid, docile "peasants." But it is apparent that in spite of the revolutionary disruptions, religion was pervasive in daily life, and religious sentiment remained strong in much of the countryside. Church bells rang out across the countryside to celebrate events, to warn of dangers, and to mark the time of the day with the Angelus. The feast of the patron saint of each village was the principal annual festival, and religious feasts such as Christmas and Easter helped mark the

---

16 A.D.L. L 974 (*Clergé: prestation de serments par des prêtres, 1790–1791*) includes numerous reports of both oaths and retractions of oaths. No reliable study of the oaths exists for the Loire, but see: E. Brossard, *Histoire du départment de la Loire pendant la Révolution française (1789–1795)* (Saint-Etienne: La Loire républicaine, 1905), Vol. 1: 376–378; R. Palluat de Bessat, "La Résistance à la constitution civile du clergé dans le district de Montbrison, 1791–1792," *Amitiés Foréziennes et Vellaves* (1926), 305–310, 398–410, 492–503; and Colin Lucas, *The Structure of the Terror* (New York: Oxford University Press, 1973); Timothy Tackett, *Religion, Revolution, and Regional Culture in Eighteenth-Century France: The Ecclesiastical Oath of 1791* (Princeton, N.J.: Princeton University Press, 1986). On the underground church, see Charles Ledré, *Le Culte caché sous la Révolution: les missions de l'abbé Linsolas* (Paris: Bonne Presse, 1949).

17 A.D.L. V 4, *Troubles survenus à l'occasion de l'installation d'ecclésiastiques.*

18 A.D.L. 10 M 6, pc. 17, Premier Trimestre An 13, *Compte Rendu de la situation de l'arrondissement de Saint-Etienne.*

passage of the year.[19] But this piety was not always expressed in ways that conformed to the wishes of the Church or notables, and it is clear that the lengthy negotiation process between Catholicism and popular religion continued. Magic was commonplace in the rural Loire, with animals such as wolves and cats particularly empowered. Even more striking is the way in which, in many places, the agents of the Catholic church and its ceremonies were enclosed in a magical context. Country dwellers believed that the Devil was present in numerous manifestations, especially domestic animals colored black. The Devil's representatives, sorcerers, were relatively common in the countryside in the middle of the nineteenth century, and every important village had at least one. But priests were also granted magical powers – they were believed to be able to stop frosts and fires – that certainly exceeded those claimed for them in Catholic doctrine.[20]

The enveloping of Catholicism in a context of nondoctrinal beliefs is also apparent in the major events marking transitions in the lives of individuals. The Church devoted great efforts during the seventeenth and eighteenth centuries to controlling these celebrations, and it is therefore no great surprise that a religious rite marked most major events. But beyond the requirements of the Church, popular culture insisted on the importance of the religious element in life transitions. Philippe Ariès has argued that as rural folklife was reconstructed after the disruptions of the revolutionary era, it became more Christian, a process by which traditional village society adapted to the modern family by means of the church ceremony.[21] The "familization" of piety had as its complement a resurgence of popular religiosity.[22] This continued, however, the uneasy combination of Catholic doctrine and rural belief. Baptism, for example, was an important part of birth, and not just because the Catholic Church insisted that children should be baptized. This was a popular concern: in case of danger of death, the midwife baptized the infant; if death occurred before baptism, the child was buried not in the cemetery with the rest of

---

19 J. Canard, *Folklore chrétien: coutumes d'origine religieuse, disparues ou en voie de disparition, en Forez et en Lyonnais* (Roanne: Imprimerie Sully, 1952), 71, 91.

20 Thomas A. Kselman, *Death and the Afterlife in Modern France* (Princeton, N.J.: Princeton University Press, 1993), esp. ch. 2; Judith Devlin, *The Superstitious Mind* (New Haven, Conn.: Yale University Press, 1987), ch. 1; Alice Taverne, *Coutumes et superstitions foréziennes: médecine populaire, sorcellerie; diable et lutins* (Ambierle: Musée forezien, 1971), 32–34, 44, 51.

21 Philippe Ariès, "Culture orale et culture écrite," in Bernard Plongeron and Robert Pannet, eds., *Le Christianisme populaire: les dossiers de l'histoire* (Paris: Centurion, 1976), 237.

22 Gérard Cholvy, "Réalités de la religion populaire dans la France contemporaine. XIXe-début XXe siècles," in Bernard Plongeron, ed., *La Religion populaire: approches historiques* (Paris: Beauchesne, 1976), 154–155.

the village community but at a crossroads, an indication of the importance of baptism for membership in a community firmly marked by Christianity. Baptism also created a special bond between the child and his or her godparents. These might have been blood relatives, but the custom that the godparents provide gifts for the children of the village after the ceremony in the church marked the special nature of the relationship.[23] Godparents were responsible in the eyes of the community and the Church for the religious upbringing of the child. Through gift giving on behalf of the child, they also established the first contact between the newborn infant and the community in which he or she would live.[24] Distinguishing the Catholic elements in these customs is useless; this was a seamless blend of religious doctrine and family and community concerns.

First Communion ceremonies show this same pattern. The importance of this event seems to have increased throughout rural France in the nineteenth century.[25] In the Loire the rite required by the Church marked a stage of life, and was another instance that recognized in popular custom the special relationship between the child and his or her "religious" kin, the godparents. First Communion clearly marked the transition from childhood to adolescence, and in many places – to the dismay of educators, as we have seen – meant the end of schooling. Beginning to receive communion meant that the child had advanced one step further into the religious community. As a part of the ceremony the child was given a Mass book and an ornamented candle. These gifts came from the godparents, who once again linked the child and the village community.[26] As with baptism, popular custom insisted that there was more to a religious rite than the fulfillment of a requirement of the institutional Church.

Religious activities also marked the next major event in life, marriage. We have already seen that the Church's requirements about marriage were generally observed in the rural Loire at least until midcentury. But there was more to the popular approach to marriage and courtship than simply adherence to canonical requirements. Young women who wished to marry went on pilgrimages. Bonfires were burned in honor of couples married less than a year, but only those married in the Church. The marriage ceremony itself, in the detailed description from the 1860s provided by the folklorist Victor Smith, suggests that the religious ceremony in the church took precedence over the civil ceremony. But at the same time the

23 Louis Gachon, *L'Auvergne et le Velay* (Paris: G. P. Maisonneuve, 1975), 175. Arnold
   Van Gennep, *Le Folklore de l'Auvergne et du Velay* (Paris: G. P. Maisonneuve, 1942), 21,
   76.
24 Canard, *Folklore chrétien*, 20; Langlois, *Un Diocèse bréton*, 514.
25 Ariès, "Culture orale," 236.   26 Gachon, *L'Auvergne et le Velay*, 176–177.

actual marriage ceremony was only a part of a complex collection of rituals consecrating the marriage of two members of the community, and the rites of the Church were only a part of this process.[27] The emphasis on community participation in the ceremonies suggests that the participation of the Catholic Church was in its role as one – but only one – of the elements of the rural community.

The pattern continued in death as in life. The approach of death was the occasion for Church intervention throughout France. To the sound of ringing church bells, the curé carried the viaticum to administer the sacrament of extreme unction to those near death, and funerals were marked by a requiem mass in the parish church. But death itself was more than a religious event, and these religious trappings were enclosed within a collection of activities and beliefs that suggest how much difficulty the Church had in controlling this event. Superstitions warned of its approach, as in the Roannais, where failure to observe the ban on marriages during May was believed to presage the death within the year of the wife. The "cult of the dead" marked both the time immediately after the funeral as well as future family events such as weddings: forty days after the funeral, a family dinner was held in memory of the deceased, and a visit to family graves marked the Sunday after a wedding. But the permeable boundary between acceptable forms of piety and popular beliefs is also apparent in the custom in a southern part of the Loire, the Jarez, of making a pilgrimage to Notre-Dame-de-Valfleury three times in the year after a death to pray for the deceased.[28]

These "folkloric" surroundings to sacramental events are but one indication of the possible disjunctions between popular piety and the boundaries set by French culture and the Catholic Church. In most instances religious authorities approved of popular practices, but were concerned about the potential for conflict with Church doctrine as they allowed an active role for country dwellers in defining their religious practices. These disjunctions can also be seen in the missions held during the Restoration. Religious missions – days of sermons, mass meetings, and the administration of the sacraments that ended with the erection of a mission cross – were a feature of Restoration religious life in France, and the archdiocese of Lyon, led by Cardinal Joseph Fesch, was a leader in this movement.

27 Van Gennep, *Le Folklore*, 39; Canard, *Folklore chrétien*, 21–22, 66; Victor Smith, "Un mariage dans le Haut-Forez en 1873," *Romania* 9 (1888), 547–560; also see Ch. 3 in this volume.

28 Philippe Ariès, *The Hour of Our Death*, trans. by Helen Weaver (New York: Random House, 1981), chs. 10, 11; Kselman, *Death and the Afterlife*, 37–124; Françoise Zonabend, *La Mémoire longue: temps et histoires au village* (Paris: Presses Universitaires de France, 1980), 217–221; Devlin, *Superstitious Mind*, 90–92; Gachon, *L'Auvergne et le Velay*, 185–189; Van Gennep, *Le Folklore*, 65–76; Taverne, *Coutumes et superstitions*, 52, 77; Canard, *Folklore chrétien*, 22–25, 78–84.

Fesch established the Society of the Fathers of the Cross in 1816 to make missions, and one held in Saint-Etienne suggests the appeal that this kind of forum could have: an estimated 17,500 people, including many from the surrounding countryside, received Communion; 9,000 received the sacrament of Confirmation.[29] Missions were held with the approval of both religious and state authorities, and their message was supportive of the regime. But the kind of response they generated, taking place outside of the normal parish setting of religious practice, suggests that there was more going on than just the revival of devotion to the doctrines and practices of the Church. Missions provided a forum for popular piety that the parish, the institution in which the Catholic Church sought to organize and contain that piety, did not.

This inability of the Church – and the French discourse about country dwellers of which it was a part – to contain popular piety is even more apparent in the controversy over popular Jansenism. A theological dispute about grace that turned into an issue of Church discipline, Jansenism had been an important part of the religious heritage of France since the conflicts over the Bull Unigenitus in the seventeenth century and royal attempts to repress Jansenism in the middle of the eighteenth century.[30] These conflicts impressed Jansenist ideas on at least some of the Catholics in the Loire, and these became rooted in the period before the Revolution due to the sympathetic attitude of the archbishop of Lyon, M. Malvin de Montazet. While not a Jansenist himself, Malvin was sympathetic to some of the tenets of Port-Royal, and he certainly refused to allow the controversy to disrupt his diocese. On the eve of the Revolution, there were some sixty curés in the archdiocese who had not adhered to the required formulary and who could be considered Jansenists, but whom Malvin allowed to remain at their posts.[31] He also brought Oratorians into the archdiocesan colleges after the expulsion of the Jesuits in 1764 and allowed priests of Jansenist tendencies to write the official *Théologie* of the archdiocese.[32] The successor to Montazet, Yves-Alexandre de Marbeuf, was in contrast an adamant anti-Jansenist, and when he took control of the archdiocese just before the Revolution he changed the *Théologie*, replaced professors in the diocesan seminary who were sympathetic to

29 Ernest Sevrin, *Les Missions religieuses en France sous la Restauration (1815–1830)* Vol. 1, *Le Missionnaire et la mission* (Saint-Mandé: Procure des prêtres de la misericorde, 1948), 300–301; Vol. 2, *Les Missions (1815–1820)* (Paris: Librairie philosophique J. Vrin, 1959), 157.

30 See Delumeau, *Catholicism between Luther and Voltaire*, 102–125; Alexander Sedgewick, *Jansenism in Seventeenth-Century France* (Charlottesville: University Press of Virginia, 1977).

31 Ledré, *Le Culte caché*, 197.

32 Ibid., 195; Gadille, *Histoire des diocèses de France*, 182–184.

Jansenist ideas, and removed those vicars general who seemed to favor the views of Jansenius.[33]

M. de Marbeuf was unable to purge his diocese completely before the Revolution, however, and the disruption of the Church during the 1790s allowed popular Jansenism to continue. After the Concordat of 1801 resolved the disputes between the Papacy and the French government, the archdiocese reasserted its control over local parishes, continuing de Marbeuf's campaign under Cardinal Joseph Fesch. But Jansenism remained a part of popular religion in some places in spite of official attempts to suppress it. The most extreme Jansenism was that of the anti-*concordataire* "Petite Eglise." This was strong in two parts of the department: several parishes north of Saint-Etienne, especially Saint-Médard (canton of Saint-Galmier), where the curé, Abbé Jacquemont, assumed the leadership of the movement; and a handful of parishes around Charlieu in the Roannais. The followers of the Petite Eglise rejected the Napoleonic Concordat and practiced an austere religion, spending Sundays reading the holy offices, observing strict rules of fasting and abstinence, saying matins and vespers each day, and avoiding public celebrations and dancing. Less extreme, but much more widespread, marking the Plaine du Forez and the cantons to the north and west of the Stephanois Valley, were those who remained in the Church in spite of the concordat but followed many of the austere practices of the Petite Eglise.[34] In Saint-Genest-Lerpt (canton of Le Chambon) the visiting archbishop found that in 1827 "there are three or four Jansenist and anti-*concordataire* families"; in Marols (canton of Saint-Jean-Soleymieux) morals were good "less a ninth part who are Jansenist, either by principle or by politics." At Saint-Médard, he found that "a third of the parish is infected with Jansenism."[35]

This continuing current of popular Jansenism under the Empire and Restoration, and the suspicions of the restored clergy after the concordat, led to a number of incidents caused by the refusal of curés to give the sacraments to suspected Jansenists in their parishes. The most notable of these in the Loire was the *affaire de Saint-Galmier,* which began on April 20, 1819, when the curé of Chazelles-sur-Lyon (canton of Saint-Galmier) refused communion to two women of the parish, declaring "I do not give communion to Jansenists! Holy things are for the holy and not for heretics!"[36] These women were not completely alone in their religious beliefs,

---

33 Ledré, *Le Culte caché,* 198.
34 Jacques Gadille, "Le Jansenisme populaire: les prolongements au XIXe siècle: le cas du Forez," *Etudes Foréziennes,* 7 (1975), 160; Benoit Laurent, *L'Eglise Janseniste du Forez* (Saint-Etienne: Imprimerie de la Loire républicaine, 1942), 135; see Langlois, *Un Diocèse bréton,* 433, for similar movements in the west of France.
35 A.A.L., *Visites pastorales* 1827.
36 A.N. F[19] 341, *Affaire de Saint-Galmier,* Acte Notarial, 21 avril 1819.

for in the following months the prefect of the Loire received a series of petitions from parishes in the Saint-Galmier region complaining that curés were refusing the sacraments, burial, and office of godparent to suspected Jansenists, expelling them from church, and demanding *billets de confession*, a certification of conformity to Church rules. The affair died down at the urging of the civil authorities, but it indicates that while most residents of the Loire were practicing Christians, there was considerable potential for conflict over religious issues even among believers. Heresy, as the curé of Chazelles described the beliefs of his would-be communicants, was a serious charge that signaled the difficulty the Church faced in controlling the piety of its members.

The challenge of Jansenism, as the curé of Chazelles well understood, lay in the unwillingness of Catholics to accept passively the instructions of the Church. But the Jansenist controversy was a luxury the Church could afford at a time when virtually all Foreziens were practicing Catholics. It was hardly a symptom of de-Christianization, and may reflect a popular revival of religious devotion after the events of the Revolution and Empire. This popular devotion remained widespread at midcentury, and similar expressions of popular piety, on the borders of the acceptable, also occurred later in the century. This is one way of reading the rash of visions, especially of the Blessed Virgin, that occurred in France in the middle third of the century, and the flourishing pilgrimage movement that marked its last part.[37] These were related: while in no instance did the apparition request that a shrine be erected and that pilgrimages be made to the spot, in most cases this occurred. With the development of a national railroad network during the Second Empire and early Third Republic, organized pilgrimages became a major source of devotion and recreation for devout Catholics. By the turn of the century, pilgrimages to Rome and even to the Holy Land had become a part of French Catholicism.[38] Visions at times provided the basis for efforts by the Catholic Church to instill piety among the faithful, but their troubling nature is apparent in the attempts by the Church hierarchy to limit the influence of apparitions as well as in the growing orthodoxy of the messages of apparitions in France.[39] As assertions that popular piety was able to define the

---

37 Thomas Kselman, *Miracles and Prophecies in Nineteenth-Century France* (New Brunswick, N.J.: Rutgers University Press, 1983), 168; Cholvy, *Religion et société*, Vol. 2: 1421–1423, connects processions and pilgrimages with the ultramontane influence after 1870, a kind of piety that emphasized sentiments rather than discipline. See also the devotions that grew up around the curé of Ars: Philippe Boutry, *Prêtres et paroisses au pays du curé d'Ars* (Paris: Cerf, 1983); and idem, "Un Sanctuaire et son saint au XIXe siècle: Jean-Marie-Baptiste Vianney, curé d'Ars," *Annales E.S.C.* 35 (1980), 353–379.
38 See A.N. F[19] 5562, *Pèlerinages, 1857–1905*.
39 Victor Turner and Edith Turner, *Image and Pilgrimage in Christian Culture: Anthro-*

bounds of belief they pushed the limits of what was acceptable to the Catholic Church itself and opposed the docility that French culture expected of "its peasants."

The sites of major apparitions – La Salette, Montligeon, and of course Lourdes – were the most obvious focus of pilgrimages and were well organized by the Church. But most localities had their own shrines to the Virgin, and these were under more popular control. The *Histoire illustrée des pèlerinages français de la très Sainte-Vièrge*[40] of 1890 lists twenty-one sites for pilgrimages to the Blessed Virgin in the archdiocese of Lyon alone. Notre-Dame-de-Fourvières in Lyon headed the list; this was not only a local shrine, but a convenient stopping point for pilgrims from northern France heading for Rome or La Salette. But most of the shrines were known only locally. It will come as no surprise that many in the Loire were located near the Monts du Forez: near Saint-Christo-en-Jarret north of Saint-Etienne, and at Saint-Genest-Lerpt, Montbrison, and La Pacaudière. But other parts of the department also had their shrines, for example in the Roannais near Saint-Symphorien in the Monts du Lyonnais, and in the Monts du Beaujolais. There is no indication of the number of pilgrimages made to these shrines, or even the origins of the pilgrims. It would be surprising, however, if they were not local Foréziens making pilgrimages for long-standing reasons, such as those made by young women for help finding a husband, by families wanting to heal sick or crippled children, or by adults seeking to cure their own illnesses.[41] The larger shrines, however, do provide some further information about the tendency of Foreziens to go on pilgrimages. Records of those healed at Lourdes, for example, suggest that pilgrims from the Loire were either frequent pilgrims or susceptible to the power of the shrine: only six departments had a greater frequency, in proportion to population, of healing at Lourdes between 1858 and 1908. The department with the highest rate was the Rhône, the other part of the Archdiocese of Lyon.[42]

Rituals, austere belief and practice, missions and pilgrimages were ways of escaping the "French" version of "peasant" piety. But in some areas of the department, in the last half of the century especially, this escape came in

pological Perspectives (Oxford: Blackwell Publisher, 1978), 3, 212, 227. Turner and Turner point out that the message at La Salette (1846) was relatively heterodox and apocalyptic, while that at Lourdes (1857) simply reinforced traditional doctrines.

40 Jean Emmanuel Drochon, *Histoire illustrée des pèlerinages français de la très-sainte Vièrge* (Paris: Plon, 1890), 1014–1020.

41 Van Gennep, *Le Folklore*, 39; Taverne, *Coutumes et superstitions*, "Les Etapes de la vie," 20–23; "Médecine populaire, sorcellerie; diable et lutins," 14; Jacques Léonard, "Les Guérisseurs en France au XIXe siècle," *Revue d'Histoire Moderne et Contemporaine* 27 (1980), 501–516.

42 Kselman, *Miracles and Prophecies*, 201–203.

what must be seen as extreme forms: secularization or de-Christianization. These are often attributed to the influence of the eighteenth-century Enlightenment and, especially in France, to the Revolution. But we must distinguish between the urban middle classes and other social groups.[43] These had different cultural patterns in the nineteenth century, and were susceptible to different influences. It may be true that Enlightenment rationalism began a move toward individualism and secularization: certainly the kind of secularism and anticlericalism that Roger Martin du Gard described in *Jean Barois* finds its origins in this intellectual tradition.[44] And, in the disputes that marked French culture in the late nineteenth century, this rationalism played a major part.

But attributing rural secularization to the spread of "French" culture is another instance of constructing rural change as a process by which "peasants" became French, in this case Voltairean bourgeois. Country dwellers' religion was enmeshed in the community in which they lived, and de-Christianization in this context seems more complex. During the Revolution, for example, the Christian model was taken over by the Republic even as Christianity and laicity formed a rough amalgamation,[45] and in the Loire there was little de-Christianization in the aftermath of the Revolution and Empire. Even given the Restoration tendency to equate proper political views with religious devotion, there was little reason for concern about a lack of religiosity from the point of view of the visiting archbishop. Rather, the problem was the presence of a small minority of Jansenists who, far from being de-Christianized, were unwilling to accept the forms of worship that the institutional Church mandated. In that it had some theological basis, Jansenism may be seen as

43 Michel Vovelle, *The Revolution against the Church*, trans. by Alan José (Columbus: Ohio State University Press, 1991); Robert R. Palmer, *Catholics and Unbelievers in Eighteenth Century France* (Princeton, N.J.: Princeton University Press, 1939); Paul Hazard, *European Thought in the Eighteenth Century*, trans. by J. Lewis May (New York: World, 1963); Peter Gay, *The Enlightenment: An Interpretation* (New York: Knopf, 1966); John McManners, *Death and the Enlightenment* (New York: Oxford University Press, 1985), ch. 6; and Ron Lesthaeghe, "A Century of Demographic and Cultural Change in Western Europe," *Population and Development Review* 9 (1983), 412–13, 429. Alain Corbin, *The Village of Cannibals: Rage and Murder in France, 1870*, trans. by Arthur Goldhammer (Cambridge, Mass.: Harvard University Press, 1992), 18, suggests the irrelevance of urban anticlericalism, stemming from philosophical atheism and free thought, for the countryside. But he describes rural attitudes as a "visceral hatred," a phrase that might be drawn from Taine.

44 Roger Martin du Gard, *Jean Barois* (Paris: Gallimard, 1921).

45 Bernard Plongeron, "A propos des mutations du 'populaire' pendant la révolution et l'Empire" in *La Religion populaire: approches historiques* (Paris: Editions Beauchesne, 1976), 129–147; Suzanne Desan, *Reclaiming the Sacred: Lay Religion and Popular Politics in Revolutionary France* (Ithaca, N.Y.: Cornell University Press, 1990); P. M. Jones, *The Peasantry in the French Revolution* (Cambridge University Press, 1988), 238–240.

characteristic of the kinds of internal quarrels that occurred until the middle of the nineteenth century. But, as Gérard Cholvy has shown for the diocese of Montpellier, and as seems to hold true for the Catholic Church throughout France, such internal divisions became infrequent later in the century, especially after the Vatican Council in 1870 had "imposed" ultramontanism on the neogallicans in the French Church, and the republican regime had begun its concerted attacks on the position of Catholicism in France.[46]

Secularization appeared slowly in the Loire in the course of the nineteenth century. At midcentury, only the industrializing urban areas broke from the mold set during the Restoration. Distinctions began to appear, however: while religion was still significant, at least in the rural areas of the department, and irreligion had not spread to the extent that the religious or civil authorities were concerned, there is an absence in much of the department of the religious fervor that marked the west and southwest of the department. There also appears to be a tendency for formal religion to lose its domination of the individual's life. This may be related to the change in the Church's approach to popular manifestations of religion: in the 1840s the Church began to accept popular devotions as long as they were under Church control. This change in approach eased the conflicts between curé and community that marked the Counter-Reformation and after; but it also allowed greater freedom for the individual, a freedom that could be used not only to organize processions and pilgrimages but also to reduce the significance for the individual of religion itself.[47] In many rural parts of the department, as well, the position of the Church had been reduced by the 1880s, and this might be described as secularization. Most still remained Christians. But we have already seen various ways in which this became less fervent. There is a significant drop in adherence to the restrictions on Lenten and Advent marriages. Religion became increasingly feminized as men ceased to practice as before. And the widespread adoption of some form of family limitation within marriage in the second half of the nineteenth century, a practice that ran directly against the teaching and advice of the Church, is a further indicator of this trend.[48] A major theme of the religious history of the Loire in the nineteenth century, therefore, appears to be the declining role of religion in the individual's life and the greater independence of many from religious control. This outcome of the process of negotiation between French and rural cultures meant a new positioning of religion in many

46 Cholvy, *Religion et société*, vol. 2: 1124.
47 Gérard Cholvy, "Le Catholicisme populaire en France au XIXe siècle," in Plongeron and Pannet, eds., *Le Christianisme populaire*, 210–211; Kselman, *Miracles and Prophecies*, 35–36, 200.
48 See Ch. 4 in this volume.

rural lives. In that it challenged earlier French versions of docile, ahistorical country dwellers, it also forced a repositioning in French culture of the "peasant." For those who saw religion as a fundamental guarantor of popular order, this was a terrifying prospect. For others, however, it opened the way, along with education, for incorporating "peasants" into a new version of the French nation.

IV

To some extent the religious history of the Loire replicated long-standing conflicts in the European countryside between the version of Catholicism that the Church sought to impose and the forms of piety that country dwellers found most attractive. In spite of the more tolerant attitude of the Church after the 1840s, significant areas remained in which the parish church was a site for contact and conflict between French and rural cultures. This difference did not necessarily mean the difference between practicing and not practicing. In the west and southwest of the department, the "backward" areas, the "peasants" were not only practicing and devout, but quiescent as well. In other areas, there were numerous ways in which country dwellers burst the bounds of the religiosity prescribed for them by the Catholic Church. But a complete rejection of religion and the supernatural was rare. For virtually all country dwellers, some kind of mystical, even if not entirely Christian, approach to the world was necessary.

Jean-Marie Mayeur has pointed out that the areas of resistance to the inventories of parish churches in 1906 have a pattern of resistance – refractory priests during the Revolution, legitimism in the course of the nineteenth century, *écoles libres* in the twentieth – that suggests a desire to maintain a "Christian civilization."[49] This way of conceiving Catholicism and the relations between politics and religion was a significant part of the French discourse about the countryside. But contention within French culture about religion led to competing versions of "peasant" and provided the opportunity for rural negotiations about the place of religion. In the course of the nineteenth century, *instituteurs* such as M. Perrin sought to assert their own preeminence in the village, and conflict with the curé was inevitable in such circumstances. For most men and women this competition came most clearly in the classroom, as Catholic and public schools fought for students' minds and hearts. There was a change in symbolism that may have been felt deeply by students in these schools: the replacement of religious education by civic, "moral" education, even

49 Jean-Marie Mayeur, "Géographie de la résistance aux inventaires (février–mars 1906)," *Annales E.S.C.*, 21 (1966), 1272.

the replacement of the crucifix and Virgin in the classroom by the tricolor and Marianne.[50] But by the Third Republic, national elections had created a forum within which this competition could be played out. In this arena of electoral politics the hopes of those like Perrin would be realized in many parts of France and the Loire.

50 For the symbolism of Marianne, see Maurice Agulhon, *Marianne au combat* (Paris: Flammarion, 1979); for conflicts in the classrooms over such symbols, see Roger Magraw, *France, 1815–1914: The Bourgeois Century* (New York: Oxford University Press, 1986), 334.

8

❧❧❧❧❧❧❧❧❧❧❧❧❧❧❧❧❧❧❧❧❧❧

A new site: electoral politics

I

The positions of churches and schools on the cultural landscape in the countryside may have changed in the course of the nineteenth century, but they were at least relatively familiar sites. The period after 1848 saw the creation of a new place of contact between "French" culture and its "peasants," the new institutions of electoral politics. From the first election of the Second Republic in 1848 into the Third Republic, these brought universal manhood suffrage into the countryside and became the principal location of political activity.

In contrast to the French discussions of "peasant" demography, economic behavior, gender, religion, and education, whose authority derived from camouflaging their imposition of a version of "peasant" on the countryside, the electoral arena was explicitly about power and its use. But electoral politics presented a particular version of politics to the countryside, one that defined its character as a site of contact between French and rural cultures by highlighting certain aspects of power and obscuring others. The electoral system of republican France was universalizing, making the substantial claim that through elections it gave power to a nation of equal citizens. The attribution of sovereignty to "the people" that lay at the heart of the Republic's promise of political participation implied the ability of those "people" to exercise that sovereignty; that is, to assume the identity of "citizens." But from the beginning of the Revolution in 1789, French culture was unable to agree on the meaning of this identity, and so the Republic was also limiting.[1] Substantial agree-

---

1 On these questions during the French Revolution, see William H. Sewell, Jr., "Le citoyen/la citoyenne: Activity, Passivity, and the Revolutionary Concept of Citizenship," in Colin Lucas, ed., *The French Revolution and the Creation of Modern Political Culture* (New York: Pergamon, 1988), vol. 2: 105–123; Patrice Gueniffey, "Les Assemblées et la représentation," in ibid., vol. 2: 233–257; Kare Tonnesson, "La Démocratie directe sous

179

ment existed on the validity of elections as expressions of political opinion, and this containment of political activity within the boundaries of the electoral system tended to define other kinds of political activity as subversive, criminal, or corrupt.[2] But it patently did not admit into participation all French adults, and it did not accept the opinions of some. Women could not vote because, having no public persona and under the influence of their husbands or priests, they did not fit the conception of "citizen." Supporters of the Republic also had memories of previous betrayals by groups perceived as not ready to be citizens. On the Left, the radical working class had seemingly demonstrated in June 1848 and in the Paris Commune of 1871 that it could not be trusted; and the patriotism – a basic component of citizenship – of the working class was questioned by many republicans. Equally troubling was the tendency of some parts of the working class to suggest alternatives to elections, such as strikes, as ways of expressing opinion.

The experience of the Second Republic and Second Empire, in which the countryside supported the opponents of the Republic and was the electoral basis of Bonapartism, made "peasants" particularly suspect.[3] In

la Révolution française – le cas des districts et sections de Paris," in ibid., vol. 2: 295–307; and Renée Waldinger, Philip Dawson, and Isser Woloch, eds., *The French Revolution and the Meaning of Citizenship* (Westport, Conn.: Greenwood, 1993).

2 See James Scott, *Weapons of the Weak* (New Haven, Conn.: Yale University Press, 1985); idem, *Domination and the Arts of Resistance* (New Haven Conn.: Yale University Press, 1990). P. M. Jones, "Common Rights and Agrarian Individualism in the Southern Massif Central, 1750–1880," in Gwynne Lewis and Colin Lucas, eds., *Beyond the Terror* (Cambridge University Press, 1983), 121–151, examines disputes over common lands. Iain Cameron, *Crime and Repression in the Auvergne and the Guyenne, 1720–1790* (Cambridge University Press, 1981), shows the kinds of disputes that marked eighteenth-century rural life. Brigandage and banditry have received a great deal of attention in recent years. Basic is Eric Hobsbawm, *Primitive Rebels* (New York: Norton, 1959). For France see Charles Tilly, *The Contentious French* (Cambridge, Mass.: Harvard University Press, 1986); Peter McPhee, "Popular Culture, Symbolism and Rural Radicalism in Nineteenth-Century France," *Journal of Peasant Studies* 5 (1978), 238–253; Richard Cobb, *Reactions to the French Revolution* (New York: Oxford University Press, 1972), 181–211; idem, *A Sense of Place* (London: Duckworth, 1975), 49–76; idem, *Paris and Its Provinces* (New York: Oxford University Press, 1975), 141–207; Gwynne Lewis, "A Cevenol Community in Crisis: The Mystery of 'L'Homme à Moustache,'" *Past and Present* 109 (1985), 144–175; John Merriman, "The Demoiselles of the Ariège" in idem, ed., *1830 in France* (New York: Watts, 1975), 87–118; and Stephen Wilson, *Feuding, Conflict and Banditry in Nineteenth-Century Corsica* (Cambridge University Press, 1988). See also Anton Blok, *The Mafia of a Sicilian Village, 1860–1960* (New York: Harper & Row, 1974).

3 John M. Merriman, *The Agony of the Republic* (New Haven, Conn.: Yale University Press, 1978); Peter McPhee, *The Politics of Rural Life* (Oxford University Press: [Clarendon Press], 1992); Theodore Zeldin, *The Political System of Napoleon III* (New York: St. Martin's, 1958); Alain Corbin, *Archaisme et modernité en Limousin au XIXe siècle* (Paris: Marcel Rivière, 1975), vol. 2: 834; William Logue, *From Philosophy to Sociology: The*

their traditional forms as scarcely human savages, different from Frenchmen, they certainly did not fit the model of a citizen of the Republic. Allowing "peasants" to be citizens therefore implied that they had to be changed. In the struggle to establish and then defend the Republic, this meant convincing them to vote for republican candidates. But there was more to it than that: they had to be transformed into members of the French nation, a project undertaken in 1848 by special representatives and schoolteachers, and in a more concerted way in the 1880s and after by the primary school.[4] The republican notion of citizenship, while admitting "peasants" into politics, therefore sought to change their identity. Participants in the Republic needed to be a part of the French nation, and the Third Republic did this by focusing the political process on elections, and by preparing country dwellers to participate in them. Even as elections became the principal form of popular political activity in France, they became a way of placing country dwellers in a particular relationship to the nation.

Among both the organizers of the system of electoral politics and later historians, a determining criterion for citizenship has been the relationship between the voter and the context of social constraints on rural voters, and in this focus the political distinctions between "peasant" and "French" have been constructed. This voting supposedly took place, in many parts of France, within the context of a hierarchical society in which local notables were able to influence the votes of their social inferiors: access to land, charity, and even salvation could depend on voting the right way. "Peasant" voters were therefore constrained in their choices; unable to select candidates on the basis of a rational consideration of policies and programs, they were influenced by local networks of kinship, clientage, and local interest. Changes in voting behavior – that is, the conversion of rural voters to the Republic – came with a loosening of these local restraints on the independence of the voter, through competition within the elite for rural votes or through education of country dwellers.[5] As political participation was extended, country dwellers were

Evolution of French Liberalism, 1870–1914 (De Kalb: Northern Illinois University Press, 1983); and Jacques Kayser, *Les Grandes batailles du radicalisme des origines aux portes du pouvoir, 1820–1901* (Paris: Marcel Rivière, 1962); and Caroline Ford, *Creating the Nation in Provincial France* (Princeton, N.J.: Princeton University Press, 1993), 97–99, 168–169.

4 See Claude Nicolet, *L'Idée républicaine en France (1789–1924)* (Paris: Gallimard, 1982), esp. 414–447; Eugen Weber, "The Second Republic, Politics, and the Peasant," *French Historical Studies* 11 (1980), 525; "Comment la Politique Vint aux Paysans: A Second Look at Peasant Politicization," *American Historical Review* 87 (1982), esp. 376.

5 Andre Siegfried, *Tableau politique de la France de l'Ouest sous la IIIe République* (Paris: Colin, 1913); Georges Dupeux, *Aspects de l'histoire sociale et politique du Loir-et-Cher, 1848–1914* (Paris: Mouton, 1962), 174, 362; Michel Denis, *Les Royalistes de la Mayenne*

expected to acquire a concern for national rather than local issues. If they did not, as several twentieth-century ethnographic studies have argued, the implication is that they remained "peasant" rather than becoming French.[6] There are disputes about the timing of this occurrence, and the Revolution, the Second Republic, and the early Third Republic all have their partisans. While I will soon argue that in much of the Loire it is this last period that seems most important, timing is less significant than that there is general agreement on the overall process, one that contrasts "archaism" with an alternative "modernity."[7]

For "archaism" we may read "peasant," and for "modernity," "French." These versions of rural political development give particular qualities to the "peasant" as a political actor, and the process of political development is conceived as one in which the "peasant" loses these qualities: development eliminated social restrictions on country dwellers' freedom of action, national concerns replaced narrow local interest, and, in Eugen Weber's phrase, "politics came to the peasant." The argument, based on an implicit contradiction between the categories "peasant" and "citizen," insists that only by giving up the identity of a "peasant" can country dwellers participate in electoral politics, and through that, in the life of the nation.

et le monde moderne (Paris: Klincksieck, 1977), 349, 417, 460–461; Pierre Barral, *Le Département de l'Isère sous la Troisième République, 1870–1940: histoire sociale et politique* (Paris: Presses de la Fondation nationale des sciences politiques, 1962), 359; Corbin, *Archaisme et modernité*, vol 2: 905, 924. See also Paul Bois, *Paysans de l'Quest* (Paris: Mouton, 1960); Maurice Agulhon, *La République au village* (Paris: Plon, 1970); and Raymond Huard, *Le Mouvement républicain en Bas-Languedoc, 1848–1881* (Paris: Presses de la Fondation nationale des sciences politiques, 1982).

6 Claude Mesliand, "Gauche et droite dans les campagnes provençales sous la IIIe république," *Etudes Rurales* 63–64 (1976), 207–234; Jean-Claude Bontron, "Transformations et permanences des pouvoirs dans une société rurale: A propos du sud du Morvan," ibid., 141–151; and Susan Carol Rogers, *Shaping Modern Times in Rural France* (Princeton, N.J.: Princeton University Press, 1991), 169–176. Ford, *Creating the Nation*, and Peter Sahlins, *Boundaries: The Making of France and Spain in the Pyrenees* (Berkeley and Los Angeles: University of California Press, 1989) are significant dissenting views of this process. See esp. 110–113, 164–167 in Sahlins.

7 Eugen Weber, *Peasants into Frenchmen* (Stanford, Calif.: Stanford University Press, 1976); David Pinkney, *Decisive Years in France, 1840–1847* (Princeton, N.J.: Princeton University Press, 1986). Corbin, *Archaisme et modernité*, frequently points out the para- doxical appearance of the relationships of various aspects of the two categories in the Limousin and portrays the conversion of the rural vote to the Republic as a process in which long-standing democratic aspirations located in small social groups joined the parliamentarism of the Third Republic. Also see Roger Price, *A Social History of Nineteenth-Century France* (New York: Holmes & Meier, 1987), 144, 187; Agulhon, *La République au village;* Bois, *Paysans de l'Quest;* and P. M. Jones, *Politics and Rural Society: The Southern Massif Central c. 1750–1880* (Cambridge University Press, 1985), 314.

II

A rural political history that escapes from the historiographical version of the French discourse about the countryside must recognize that what occurred in the elections that are our principal sources for rural political behavior was not just the determination of a national representative but also negotiation over the meaning of citizenship. In this process, the scope of negotiations was restricted. But elections, to give them their due, did provide a way for voters to affect public policies in some way. Even as the "citizen peasants" of France limited their "political" activities to the institutions of the Third Republic, therefore, they were able to force that Republic to take notice of their needs and desires.

The channeling of political activities into the electoral arena was successful in the Loire, as elsewhere in France. In much of the department there was an acceptance of not only electoral politics but also the program of moderate republicanism, and little insistence that other forms of political activity should be recognized: resistance to the inventorying of Church goods and the dispersal of religious congregations in several southwestern cantons after the turn of the century is all that is visible.[8] While in some parts of France country dwellers adopted means other than voting to register their grievances – demonstrations against the coup d'état in 1851 and the winegrowers' revolt of 1907 stand out – these movements did not touch the rural Loire. Organized demonstrations largely meant those by artisans and workers in the Loire in the second half of the nineteenth century. There does not even appear to have been much crime in the countryside.[9]

8 See James R. Lehning, *The Peasants of Marlhes* (Chapel Hill: University of North Carolina Press, 1980), 73; A.D.L. 7 M 29, *Suppressions et révocations des maires.*
9 See Ted Margadant, *French Peasants in Revolt: The Insurrection of 1851* (Princeton, N.J.: Princeton University Press, 1979), ch. 3; Laura Levine Frader, *Peasants and Protest: Agricultural Workers, Politics, and Unions in the Aude, 1850–1914* (Berkeley and Los Angeles: University of California Press, 1991), ch. 7; Yves Lequin, *Les Ouvriers de la région lyonnaise (1848–1914)* (Lyon: Presses Universitaires de Lyon, 1977); Michael Hanagan, *The Logic of Solidarity: Artisans and Industrial Workers in Three French Towns, 1871–1914* (Urbana: University of Illinois Press, 1980); and idem, *Nascent Proletarians: Class Formation in Post-Revolutionary France* (New York: Blackwell Publisher, 1989); Elinor Accampo, *Industrialization, Family Life, and Class Relations: Saint-Chamond, 1815–1914* (Berkeley and Los Angeles: University of California Press, 1989), ch. 6; and Claude Chatelard, *Crime et criminalité dans l'arrondissement de Saint-Etienne au XIXe siècle* (Saint-Etienne: Reboul Imprimerie, 1981), 30–32. At the end of the nineteenth century there was some rural unionism, in the Union du sud-est des syndicats agricoles, founded in 1888. But its efforts initially emphasized viticulture and the phylloxera crisis, and so did not affect the Loire significantly. See Gilbert Garrier, *Paysans du Beaujolais et du Lyonnais, 1800–1970* (Presses Universitaires de Grenoble, 1973), vol. 1:

Peasant and French

Table 8.1. *Participation in elections in France
and the department of the Loire, 1848—1910*

Date	Percent Voting in Loire	Percent Voting in France[a]
10 Dec. 1848	67.7	75.1
29 Feb. 1852	49.4	63.3
21 June 1857	64.9	64.5
31 May 1863	66.1	72.9
23 May 1869	70.1	78.1
2 July 1871	52.5	—
20 Feb. 1876	68.3	74.0
14 Oct. 1877	78.1	80.6
21 Aug. 1881	60.0	68.6
4 Oct. 1885	76.4	77.6
22 Sept. 1889[b]	73.2	76.6
20 Aug. 1893	55.2	71.2
8 May 1898	70.3	76.1
27 April 1902	79.5	79.2
6 May 1906	79.8	79.9
24 April 1910	74.9	77.5

[a]Lancelot, *L'Abstentionnisme électoral*, 15.
[b]First circonscription of Montbrison is missing.
— = Not available

In the place of these extraelectoral kinds of activity, elections slowly became the favored form of political activity in the department as in France as a whole. Patterns of voter participation (see Table 8.1) trace a jagged pattern in the elections between 1848 and 1910. But while the overall level of participation slowly increased, voting was very susceptible to the circumstances of a particular election, such as that of 1871, when the country was still at war with Germany, or that of 1877, when interest was high due to a crisis in Paris over the future of the regime. By the time the Third Republic was firmly established in the 1880s, most elections brought out approximately the same proportion of the electorate. But even as a 70–80 percent turnout became the norm in France and the Loire, this still meant that a significant part of the electorate was not

518–522; and idem, "L'union du sud-est des syndicats agricoles avant 1914," *Mouvement Social* 67 (1969), 17–38.

participating. This proportion could jump in elections – such as the one in 1893 – that did not arouse much excitement.[10]

Some geographic regions in France were strongholds of abstentionism: this behavior in elections in particular marked the West, the center, and the Mediterranean South. Social groups that were not well integrated into national society also tended to have high rates of abstentionism.[11] Within the Loire, there do not appear to be strong geographic or social patterns of electoral participation. This is apparent in a close analysis of the elections of 1877, 1885, and 1902. The first of these, held in October 1877,[12] followed, and helped resolve, the crisis brought about by the conflict between the president of the Republic, Marshall Phillippe MacMahon, and the republican majority elected in 1876 to the Chamber of Deputies.[13] The second, which occurred in October 1885, took place under somewhat more placid circumstances, but nevertheless was controversial because the preceding years had been marked by the passage of the Ferry Laws establishing a secular system of primary education.[14] The third, in April 1902, came in the aftermath of events such as the Wilson, Boulanger, and Panama affairs,[15] and especially the Dreyfus affair,[16] and amid growing fears by republicans that the regime was once again in danger from the

10 Alain Lancelot, *L'Abstentionnisme électoral en France* (Paris: Pressess de la Fondation nationale des sciences politiques, 1968), 98–100.

11 Ibid., 216.

12 On the election, see François Goguel, *La Politique des partis sous la Troisième république* (Paris: Le Seuil, 1946), 46–48; national results are mapped in idem, *Géographie des élections françaises de 1870 à 1951* (Paris: Colin, 1951), 19. The election is discussed from the point of view of one of the most important republican leaders, Leon Gambetta, in J. P. T. Bury, *Gambetta and the Making of the Third Republic* (London: Longman Group, 1973), 431–436. In all that follows on party affiliations, it should be kept in mind that it was only after 1910 that affiliations became relatively rigorous in the National Assembly, and that between 1871 and 1910 a deputy or senator could belong to several groups within the assembly at the same time. See Alain Bomier-Landowski, "Les Groupes parlementaires de l'Assemblée nationale et de la Chambre des députés de 1871 à 1940," in François Goguel and Georges Dupeux, eds., *Sociologie electorale: esquisse d'un bilan, guide de recherches* (Paris: Colin, 1951), 75.

13 Andre Daniel (Lebon), *L'Année politique, 1877* (Paris: Charpentier, 1878), 317. Daniel provides an extensive insider's account of the crisis on 123. See also Jean-Marie Mayeur, *La Vie politique sous la Troisième république, 1870–1940* (Paris: Seuil, 1984), 58–69; and idem, *Les Débuts de la Troisième République (1871–1898)* (Paris: Seuil, 1973), 35–54.

14 Andre Daniel (Lebon), *L'Année politique, 1885* (Paris: Charpentier, 1886), 218, 226; Goguel, *Politique des partis*, 59; Mayeur, *La Vie politique*, 115–118.

15 Frederic H. Seager, *The Boulanger Affair: Political Crossroad of France, 1886–1889* (Ithaca, N. Y.: Cornell University Press, 1969), 94–5, 102, 142; Mayeur, *La Vie politique*, 119–135. Boulanger ran a poor third in a by-election in the Loire in February 1888.

16 A summary of the conflict over the Dreyfus affair can be found in Robert L. Hoffman, *More Than a Trial: The Struggle over Captain Dreyfus* (New York: Free Press, 1980); Goguel, *Politique des partis*, 91, indicates that the affair was not an issue in the 1898 elections; see also Mayeur, *La Vie politique*, 175–186.

Right.[17] At least at the national level, then, each of these elections was seen to be of great significance, an "election of combat," and the campaigns were marked by bitterness between opponents of the Republic and those who supported it and its policies.

Most cantons of the Loire in all three elections were relatively close to the national and departmental proportions of participating voters. The department did show slight geographic variations in electoral participation, but these are not striking, nor do the cantons with low participation form a coherent bloc.[18] Several of the cantons in the western mountains, such as Saint-Bonnet-le-Chateau and Saint-Haon-le-Châtel, were among the lowest in the department in 1877 and 1885. In 1902 the cantons to the northeast – Belmont, Charlieu, Perreux, Saint-Symphorien, and Néronde – showed very high levels of participation. But what is most striking over time is the apparent incorporation into the electoral system of cantons with low levels of participation early in the Third Republic: by 1902, both Saint-Bonnet and Saint-Haon had progressively increased their levels of voting participation, actually surpassing several other cantons such as the largely industrial Le Chambon and the rural canton of Saint-Galmier north of Saint-Etienne. There is some suggestion that voting participation was dependent upon the economic characteristics of the village, but no consistent pattern across time appears (see Table 8.2). In 1877 those villages with a high proportion of proprietors – that is, the smallholding mountains – had the lowest proportion voting. By 1885, however, this factor had lost its effect and been replaced by the proportion of farmers, which in turn dropped out in 1902 to be replaced by the per capita assessment for the *impôt personnel*. There thus does not appear to be any social group in the department that was consistently refusing to participate. Rather, the factors that do appear to be significant determinants of abstentionism are those that measure, in different ways, the ability of villages to participate in a larger community. Linguistic difference was associated with low participation in 1877, although it lost influence after that date. The only factor that consistently influenced voting participation was a measure of geographic isolation – the distance from a railroad – which held up well across the three elections as a determinant of low voter turnout. This, at a minimum, represents the effect of the difficult terrain and poor avenues of transportation in more isolated parts of the department. It may also measure more nuanced aspects of integration into the nation.

17 André Daniel (Lebon), *L'Année politique, 1902* (Paris: Pierin et Cie, 1903), 120; Mayeur, *La Vie politique*, 185–186; see also Madeleine Rebérioux, *La République radicale? 1898– 1914* (Paris: Seuil, 1975), 56–61; Goguel, *La Politique des partis*, 116–117.
18 Lancelot, *L'Abstentionnisme électoral en France*, 74. For comparisons see Tony Judt, *Socialism in Provence, 1871–1914* (Cambridge University Press, 1979), 125–126; and Jones, *Politics and Rural Society*, 289.

Table 8.2. *Multiple regression analysis of determinants of proportions voting in 1877, 1885 and 1902 elections in sample villages in Loire (betas)*

	1877	1885	1902
Foncière/Capita	−0.18	−0.11	0.03
Patent/Capita	0.00	0.00	0.26
Personnel/Capita	−0.11	−0.16	−0.46***
Proprietor Percent	−0.39**	−0.12	0.23
Farmers Percent	0.07	−0.35*	−0.02
Textile Percent	0.00	−0.05	0.26
Male School Attendance 1860	−0.12	−0.10	0.20
Railroad Distance	−0.50**	−0.41*	−0.59***
South Language Area	0.36*	0.26	0.16
Multiple R	0.57	0.50	0.67
R Square	0.32	0.25	0.45

* = Significant at .05 level.
** = Significant at .01 level.
*** = Significant at .001 level.

Abstention rates are imperfect as a measure of the primacy of electoral politics but, in conjunction with the absence of other political activities in the countryside, they do suggest that the Third Republic succeeded in confining political activity to these periodic consultations, even though there were parts of the nation and places in the Loire that did not whole-heartedly accept this institution. Moreover, participation in elections could easily be forced, managed, or bought.[19] We must also inquire about the meaning of elections. A first step is to notice that not only did the country dwellers of the Loire become more regular voters, they also became predominantly republicans. In this sense the political history of the Loire can be written as a part of the gradual acceptance of the republic by "peasants." In the Loire this process was led by the cities, especially the southern industrial cities around Saint-Etienne and the major city in the north, Roanne. In these urban centers the radical and republican tradition extended back to the Revolution of 1789.[20] But much of the

19 See Weber, "Comment la Politique Vint aux Paysans," 381.
20 See especially Colin Lucas, *The Structure of the Terror* (New York: Oxford University Press, 1973). On the political history of the Loire, especially the urban working classes, later in the century, see Hanagan, *The Logic of Solidarity* and *Nascent Proletarians;* Lequin, *Les Ouvriers de la région lyonnaise;* and Accampo, *Industrialization, Family Life, and Class Relations.*

countryside opposed the Revolution, especially its more radical phases, and rural conversion to the Republic took longer, occurring only at the end of the Second Empire and in the first two decades of the Third Republic. In these years a coalition of rural voters came together in support of a moderate republicanism that excluded not only the extreme Right of monarchism and Bonapartism, but also withdrew its support from the growing working-class movement on the Left.[21]

The individuals who led this movement to the Republic were drawn from that particularly French category, "notable," and so the question must be raised of the extent to which "peasants" passively followed their social superiors or were more active influences on the views of their representatives. The entry of these men of property into French political life had been consecrated by the Constitution of 1791 and the subsequent charters of France. Until 1848, wealth was the requisite for voting as well as office holding, and this meant above all the ownership of landed property. In the Loire, those registered to vote in 1843–44 were overwhelmingly listed as proprietors, a quality that stands as significant in a society in which others (who were also no doubt the owners of land) listed themselves as "chevalier de la Légion d'honneur" or "marquis."[22] This emphasis on the importance of land as the principal form of wealth and identity in the political elite of the department was leavened by a sprinkling of professionals and businessmen among those who were elected to represent the department, especially after the extension of suffrage in 1848. Those elected under the Second Republic, particularly those who sat on the Left, were most distanced from landownership, with an industrialist, a printer, a secondary-school teacher, a civil engineer, and a journalist in the Loire's delegation.[23] Of those who sat on the Right, one had been an Orleanist administrator in the prefecture of the Loire, and the other, Fialin de Persigny, had become a professional Bonapartist after being dismissed from the army for insubordination.[24]

What these men and their successors through the rest of the century

21 See Jean Merley, "Les Elections de 1869 dans la Loire," *Cahiers d'Histoire* 6 (1961), 59–93; Sanford H. Elwitt, "Politics and Social Classes in the Loire: The Triumph of Republican Order, 1869–1873," *French Historical Studies* 6 (1969), 93–112; and idem, *The Making of the Third Republic: Class and Politics in France, 1868–1884* (Baton Rouge: Louisiana State University Press, 1975).

22 Based on A.D.L. 8 M 71, *Liste générale du Jury des electeurs pour 1843–44*, cantons of Saint-Héand, Saint-Genest-Malifaux, Bourg-Argental, Boën, Feurs, Pélussin, Saint-Georges-en-Couzan, Saint-Bonnet-le-Château, Néronde, Belmont, Charlieu, Saint-Haon-le-Châtel, La Pacaudière, Perreux, and Noirétable. I have used the microfilms of these lists in the Library of Congress, Microform #29606, reel 5. On the *notables* in general, see Andre-Jean Tudesq, *Les Grands notables en France, 1840–49* (Paris: Presses Universitaires de France, 1964).

23 Adolphe Robert, Edgar Bourloton, and Gaston Cougny, *Dictionnaire des parlementaires français 1789–1889* (Paris: Bourloton, 1891), vol. 1: 208, 206; vol. 2: 79, 440.

24 Ibid., vol. 4: 149, 599.

had in common was not so much their occupation as their roots in local society. "Parachuted" candidates from outside the department invariably lost in the rural arrondissements of the Loire, and while deputies reflected the diverse economy of the department, they usually owed their influence to their landed or industrial wealth there. Those elected under the Second Empire suggest the relative cohesiveness of that elite in spite of some tensions brought on by the development of an industrial bourgeoisie in the Stephanois region. A ribbon manufacturer like Jules Balay, deputy from 1852 to 1862, served with landed proprietors as official candidates and consistently supported the government of Napoleon III.[25] Only in the 1860s did opposition to the Empire develop, with the election in 1863 of Pierre Frédéric Dorian, a mining engineer and forge master at Saint-Etienne. The diverse backgrounds of men like Dorian seem to support the republicans' portrayal of themselves as "new men" different from the old ruling oligarchy, but in the Loire this is less credible than in other parts of the country: the political elite of the department under the Empire combined landowners and "new men" from an older generation.

Under the Third Republic, the Loire deputation continued to combine landed and industrial wealth even as it became firmly republican. The most heavily industrialized part of the department, the arrondissement of Saint-Etienne, was most likely to favor Gambetta's *couches nouvelles,* although the rural areas in the other arrondissements occasionally joined in selecting this kind of representative. In the 1870s, deputies from the Loire included journalists such as César Berthelon, nearing the end of a colorful political career that included election as a "representative of the people" in 1848 and participation in the 1871 commune in Saint-Etienne. Emile Crozet-Fourneyron, an ironmaster, and Petrus Richarme, owner of a glassworks in Rive-de-Gier, also went to Paris from the Loire. The delegation also included a civil engineer, Francisque Reymond, and a lawyer, Charles Cherpin. In later years engineers, an ironmaster, a graduate of the Ecole polytechnique, and lawyers and doctors joined the list.[26]

But if in the cities the Republic depended on an industrial bourgeoisie following in Dorian's footsteps, the adherence of rural notables to the cause of the Republic in the decades after 1870 was important in the countryside.[27] Many of these figures were ephemeral, coming and going from election to election, like Jean-Baptiste Chavassieu and Etienne

25 Elwitt, "Politics and Social Classes," 97–98; Robert, *Dictionnaire,* vol. 2: 400; vol. 1: 143; vol. 2: 473, 59.
26 A.D.L. 3 M 16, *Elections de 1877;* 3 M 21–22, *Elections de 1885;* 3 M 36–37, *Elections de 1902.*
27 Elwitt, "Politics and Social Classes," 103; David Gordon, *Merchants and Capitalists: Industrialization and Provincial Politics in Mid-Nineteenth-Century France* (University: University of Alabama Press, 1985). For the national elite under the Third Republic, see Christophe Charle, *Les Elites de la République, 1880–1900* (Paris: Fayard, 1987).

Brossard, who briefly held office in the 1870s and 1880s.[28] But in the arrondissements of Montbrison and Roanne, politics in the Third Republic was dominated by "republican notables" like Charles Dorian and Honoré Audiffred. The second Montbrison *circonscription* was the political home toward the end of the century of Charles Dorian, the son of Pierre Frédéric Dorian. He was briefly a deputy from 1887 to 1889; he was a member of the Conseil Général of the Loire, and was elected to the Chamber again in 1893 after being nominated by the Congrès républicaine of the *circonscription* in part because "he bore an illustrious democratic name."[29] He held the seat until his death in 1902, at which time it was taken over by his brother, Daniel. Honoré Audiffred, a lawyer from Saint-Pierre-la-Noaille, was the major republican political figure in the arrondissement of Roanne in the early Third Republic. Born in 1840, he was elected to the Conseil Général in 1871 and was first elected to the Chamber of Deputies in a partial election in April 1879. By the 1890s he was the president of the Conseil Général, so certain of rural support that, as was reported to the prefect in 1898, Audiffred's rural vote would drown (*noyer*) the vote in Roanne for his socialist opponent.[30] He remained a deputy until his career was crowned by election to the Senate in October 1904.

Dorian and Audiffred are typical of the deputies from the rural Loire not only in their positions as local notables but also in their relationship to national politics. Deputies from the Loire did not have particularly distinguished careers in the Palais Bourbon, and these two were not exceptions. In the Chamber, Dorian devoted himself primarily to colonial affairs, becoming known as the "deputy for the Sahara." By the turn of the century, he was a tepid supporter of the anticlerical policies of the Waldeck–Rousseau government, and declared himself a follower of Gambetta and Ferry in educational matters, calling for liberty of conscience.[31] Audiffred, while initially on the republican left, gradually adopted similarly moderated policies. In 1879 he was a member of the Gauche républicaine; in 1881 he called for revision of the Senate, although he was vague about what revisions he would support; and in 1885 he was a member of the broad republican list in the department. A supporter of colonial expansion in the Chamber in the 1890s, by 1898 he was a *progressiste* opponent of the government's religious policies. In 1898 he ran against the increasingly radical policies of the government.[32]

28 Robert, *Dictionnaire*, vol. 2: 79; Jean Jolly, ed., *Dictionnaire des parlementaires français, 1889–1940* (Paris: Presses Universitaires française, 1960), vol. 2: 780.

29 A.D.L. 3 M 30, Commissaire spécial to Prefect of the Loire, 7 août 1893.

30 A.D.L. 3 M 34, Commissaire spécial à Saint-Etienne to Prefect of the Loire, 16 mars 1898; Jolly, *Dictionnaire*, vol. 1: 410–411.

31 A.D.L. 3 M 37; Jolly, *Dictionnaire*, vol. 4: 1463.

32 André Daniel (Lebon), *L'Année politique, 1879* (Paris: Charpentier, 1880), 119; A.D.L.

Dorian, Audiffred and their colleagues not only suggest the relative mediocrity of the deputies from the Loire, they also indicate the moderate republicanism necessary for a successful political career representing the country dwellers of the department as voters became republicans. They therefore reflect the extent to which elections were negotiations between candidates and voters.[33] But just as France developed a specific electoral geography in the nineteenth century, so also different parts of the Loire adopted different political views.[34] The elections of 1877, 1885, and 1902 not only indicate the passage of the Loire into the republican camp and the formation of a firm voting bloc behind moderate republicans, but also the development of a particular electoral geography and sociology. In the center and eastern parts of the department, voters moved away from the conservatism of monarchism and Bonapartism and toward support for moderate republicans. In a good example of the republican version of rural political development, César Berthelon in 1872 described his aim as a moderate Republic in which "nobles, priests, or big capitalists" would no longer "treat us as children whom they lead by the nose."[35] But in contrast to this majority in the department, the southwestern and western mountain cantons established themselves as a home of conservative opposition to the leftward movement of the French political spectrum. In 1877, these cantons supported MacMahon against the republicans; in 1885, they voted for candidates who opposed the anticlerical policies of the government; and in 1902 the candidates who gained the most support there were opponents of the anticlerical, Dreyfusard ministry led by René Waldeck-Rousseau.

The Loire swung firmly into the republican camp in the election of 1876, when a conservative majority of deputies from the 1871 National Assembly was swept aside and replaced by republicans. All of its deputies, therefore, were among the 363 signers of the declaration of May 18, 1877, against MacMahon, and these deputies ran for reelection in 1877. They were opposed by a mixed group of conservatives, most of them royalists. All were reelected in a one-sided victory for the republicans.

Three lists of candidates presented themselves in the Loire in 1885. The

---

3 M 19, *Profession de foi de H. Audiffred, 1881;* C. M. Andrew and A. S. Kanya-Forstner, "Communication: The *Groupe Colonial* in the French Chamber of Deputies, 1892–1932," *Historical Journal* 17 (1974), 848, 851, 855, 859, list a Jean Audiffred from the Loire as a member of the *groupe;* A.D.L. 3 M 21 #141; Daniel, *L'Année politique, 1904* (Paris: Perrin et Cie, 1905), 397. A.D.L. 3 M 37 #181.

33 At the national level, the moderation of Gambetta in the first few years of the Third Republic is a prime example of this kind of behavior; see also Corbin, *Archaisme et modernité*, vol. 2: 961, for a regional example.

34 The classic study of electoral geography in France is Siegfried, *Tableau politique de la France de l'Ouest*, and this has set the basic research agenda. Among other studies, see most notably Bois, *Paysans de l'Ouest.*

35 Elwitt, "Politics and Social Classes," 103.

most conservative, the Liste Euverte, was sponsored by the Comité conservateur and consisted of a combination of the various "conservative" political views held in the early days of the Third Republic, including both royalism and Bonapartism. To their left was the Comité de l'alliance républicaine, all of whom supported the Union républicaine. Headed by Francisque Reymond, president of the department's Conseil Général, incumbent deputy and an engineer by profession, this list represented the mainstream of political life in the department and suggests how, like Dorian and Audiffred, deputies could embed themselves in that life. Six of the members of this list also sat on the Conseil général; another was a former conseiller général, and the last, Francis Laur, was adjoint to the mayor of Saint-Etienne. The last list, to the left of the Comité de l'alliance républicaine, was the Union des républicains socialistes, headed by Girodet, an incumbent deputy. The other members of the list, all on the extreme left, included several characterized by the prefect as "revolutionary anarchists" and several socialists.[36]

The elections were won by the Liste Reymonde. This victory confirmed the growing strength of the Opportunist Republicans in the Loire: building on their victories in the 1876 and 1877 elections, they continued firm political control of the department. It also, however, indicated the beginning of a disintegration of the republican bloc of the early years of the Third Republic: for the next generation, republican solidarity was broken by issues such as the assault by the Ferry Laws on the position of the Catholic Church.

This disarray is evident in the 1902 election. While in Paris the camps appeared to be clearly divided, the religious congregations that were the target of the government's policies were widespread in the Loire, and this muddied the waters for all republican candidates there. As the prefect noted in a report to the minister of the interior, no deputies put suppression of the congregations in their *professions de foi*.[37] There were also numerous candidacies. Nowhere was this more the case than in the four *circonscriptions* in the arrondissement of Saint-Etienne, where ministerial candidates had to face not only the opposition of liberal, or *progressiste*, republicans, but also an array of socialist candidates. Led by Aristide Briand, a "parachuted" candidate from Seine-et-Oise just beginning a new phase of his political career, leftist candidates won three of the four seats. In the arrondissement of Montbrison, divided into two *circonscriptions*, both incumbents were supporters of the Waldeck–Rousseau ministry, and both won. Both incumbents also won in the Roannais, but only

36 The election returns and the description of the different lists is based on documents in A.D.L. 3 M 21–22.
37 A.D.L. 3 M 37 #81.

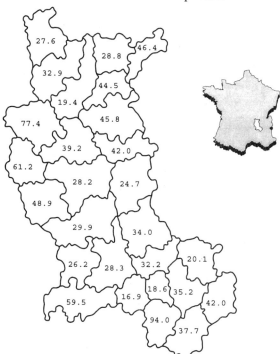

Figure 8.1   Percentage voting for conservative candidates in 1877 election for Chamber of Deputies.

one of these, the Radical Socialist Jean-Baptiste Morel, supported the ministry.[38]

The overall voting pattern of the department in each of these elections was firmly in the camp of moderate republicanism (see Figures 8.1 to 8.3 and Table 8.3). But there were some centers of conservative strength in the department. While broken by the cantons of Montbrison and Saint-Jean-Soleymieux, a broad band of conservative support extended in 1877 up the western mountainous edge of the department. The canton of Saint-Genest-Malifaux, in the southern Pilat Mountains, was also strongly conservative, along with the other Pilat cantons, Bourg-Argental and Pel-ussin. Another area of conservative support, although never reaching a majority, was in the Monts du Beaujolais, the cantons of Belmont, Per-reux, Saint-Symphorien-en-Laye, and Néronde. In contrast, the indus-trial areas of Roanne and the Stephanois region, as well as the central Plaine du Forez, were strongly republican by 1877, with only the canton

38 A.D.L. 3 M 37 #86.

Figure 8.2   Percentage voting for *Liste Euverte* in 1885 election for Chamber of
Deputies.

of Saint-Germain-Laval, in the Plaine, casting a significant percentage of
conservative votes. The cantons in the Monts du Lyonnais that were most
exposed to the influences of Lyon and the Stephanois region were also
firmly republican.

In 1885 the urban industrial areas were the strongholds of the republican Liste Reymonde: it did very well in the Stephanois Valley, polling
more than 60 percent of the vote in the two most heavily industrialized
cantons, Saint-Etienne and Le Chambon. The only industrial canton it
lost was Saint-Chamond, and here the problem was in the countryside:
the *Liste* was victorious in the city of Saint-Chamond itself. The other
area of strength for the Liste Reymonde was the center and center-east –
the cantons of Montbrison, Boen, Feurs, and Néronde – in all but the last
polling more than 60 percent of the vote.

The Liste conservateur also had its bastions of strength. The same band
of cantons in the west remained conservative in 1885 as in 1877. This began
in the low mountains south of Saint-Etienne, especially the strongly Catholic canton of Saint-Genest-Malifaux – where a remarkable 93 percent of

Figure 8.3 Percentage voting for conservative anti-ministerial candidates in 1902 election for Chamber of Deputies.

Table 8.3. *Multiple regression analysis of determinants of conservative vote in 1877, 1885 and 1902 elections in sample villages in Loire (betas)*

	1877	1885	1902
Foncière/Capita	0.20	0.17	0.07
Patent/Capita	−0.20	−0.32*	0.02
Personnel/Capita	−0.01	0.15	0.08
Proprietor Percent	0.54***	0.52***	0.50***
Farmers Percent	−0.30*	−0.02	−0.09
Textile Percent	0.13	−0.09	−0.19
Railroad Distance	0.06	0.06	−0.11
South Language Area	−0.05	−0.09	0.12
Multiple R	0.64	0.65	0.54
R Square	0.41	0.43	0.29

* = Significant at .05 level.
*** = Significant at .001 level.

the voters gave the Liste Euverte their vote – then skipped over the industrial valley to the canton of Saint-Bonnet-le-Chateau. The canton of Montbrison, extending out into the Plaine du Forez, broke the chain, but a majority vote for the conservatives resumed in the western Monts du Forez, in the cantons of Saint-Just, Noirétable, and Saint-Georges-en-Couzan. The northeastern cantons continued to give a slim majority to the republicans, and in several cantons to the northeast of Saint-Etienne, such as Saint-Galmier and Saint-Héand, the conservatives won a majority.

The elections of the 1870s and early 1880s indicate the reconstruction of a diverse alliance in France including a part of the grand bourgeoisie, the "new men" of industrializing France and workers and country dwellers, an alliance Jean-Marie Mayeur has described as a new "Third Estate." In the countryside, the construction of this alliance created new areas willing to support moderate republicans rather than conservatives.[39] The 1877 and 1885 elections in the Loire show this process, by which a consistent geographic pattern of voting was created. A significant part of the countryside was relatively moderate and was converted to the republican cause. The strength of this rural republican vote was down the center of the department, from the cantons of La Pacaudière and Saint-Haon in the north through the Plaine du Forez and toward the Stephanois Valley in the south. The schoolteacher Perrin's old commune, Marcoux, was typical of this area: it voted overwhelmingly in support of the republican candidate, Francisque Reymond, in 1877, and for the list headed by Reymond in 1885. But on the margins of this region, support for the new regime was more grudging. The commune of Verrières and its neighbors in the Monts du Forez in the canton of Montbrison, for example, moved fitfully toward the Republic: in 1877, Verrières gave a majority to Chavassieu, the republican incumbent, but Bouchetal, an opponent of the regime, did relatively well, and the conservative Liste Euverte won a majority in 1885. Similarly, the commune of Saint-Hilaire in the northeast swung only slowly toward the Republic: in 1877 it voted by a two-to-one margin for the royalist Bouillier; in 1885, it still gave a majority to the conservative Liste Euverte. Another feature of the electoral geography of the Loire in the early Third Republic was the clear demarcation of an area of strong conservative opposition to the governing mainstream of Opportunist Republicans. This extended from the southern Pilat Mountains up through the Monts du Forez, and formed a core of opposition in every election. The communes of the canton of Saint-Genest-Malifaux, in the Pilats, are the extreme cases of this bloc, with conservatives gaining virtually every vote. But if less extreme, many of the communes in the canton of Saint-Bonnet-le-Chateau are more representative of this strain,

39 Mayeur, *Les débuts de la Troisième république*, 51–54.

voting in 1877 against the incumbent republican and going strongly for the Liste Euverte in 1885.

With the significant exception of the band of cantons in the south and west, the rural Loire had become republican by the late 1880s. But we have already seen that this "republicanism" to some extent meant electing republican notables in place of the monarchist or Bonapartist notables who had represented the department earlier in the century. The question remains to what extent the voters were following or leading these notables, a crucial concern of the story of rural political development. The election of 1902, held during a major political crisis in Paris, indicated the limits to the leftward swing of the rural electorate in the Loire and suggests that the Loire's rural voters did have some "principles" even as they continued to elect comfortable local figures such as Dorian and Audiffred.

The strongest support in 1902 for the rightist candidates opposed to the ministry continued to be found in the southwestern Monts du Forez and the southern Pilat region, especially the canton of Saint-Genest-Malifaux. But the opposition vote increased in Montbrison and Saint-Jean-Soleymieux, as well as in most of the cantons of the northwestern Roannais and the Plaine du Forez. These were not votes against the Republic: the absence of antirepublican candidates made that impossible, and as we have seen, abstentionism was decreasing by 1902. Rather, they seem to be votes for the moderation of the political heirs of the republicans of the 1870s and 1880s. Even with the restricted offerings of 1902, communes in the canton of Saint-Bonnet-le-Chateau voted against the ministerial candidate, Levet, and for Jordan, the mayor of Sury-le-Comtal. Verrières had adopted the same moderate republicanism, voting for Jordan over Levet; and although Saint-Hilaire gave a plurality to Morel, the ministerial republican, there was also a heavy vote for a moderate republican from Lyon, Aulois.

The electoral geography of the Loire reflects to some extent the religious geography we have already seen and seems to link religious attitudes with voting patterns. The extremes are most apparent. The western mountains and the canton of Saint-Bonnet were strong supporters of opposition candidates, confirming the impression gained from the 1848 *Enquête* that Catholics in this region not only fulfilled their religious duties but also transferred that Catholicism into the political arena. The moderate republicanism of the center and the Monts du Lyonnais, on the other hand, suggests an additional gloss on the relationship between religion and voting. Religious practice here showed little difference from that in the western mountains. But, as suggested in the *Visites pastorales*, Catholicism in the Plaine du Forez and the eastern mountains was Blue: voters here left their religion in the church, and in the polling place showed a republicanism willing to countenance the attacks of the Opportunists on the privileged position enjoyed by the Catholic Church in French society.[40] The earlier alliance of parish priests and conservative notables seems to have lost its hold on the "peasants" in the Plaine du Forez and the Monts du Lyonnais.

But even as the 1902 election suggests the decline of the influence of local notables on voting, its principal lesson is that these moderate republican voters were not passive followers of the political winds from Paris. The threat to the Republic perceived by Waldeck–Rousseau and the Radical Republicans in Paris did not have the same impact even in the firmly republican areas of the Loire countryside. While accepting the institutions of the Republic and electoral politics, therefore, these voters seemed to be maintaining a coherent position of their own.[41]

An analysis of the determinants of conservative voting in these elections (see Table 8.3) shows that the proportion of proprietors consistently correlates with the conservative vote. While, as we have already seen, abstention was highest among smallholders, those who did vote tended to vote conservative. A consistent smallholder opposition to the republican mainstream extended from 1877 to 1885 to 1902, opposing the republican deputies in 1877, the religious policies of Ferry, and the ruling republicans of the Waldeck–Rousseau ministry. Given the preponderance of smallholders in the mountains and the strength of farming in the Plaine du Forez, it is tempting to see in this the social complement to the geographic division in the department between conservative mountain and more liberal plain. The failure of measures of isolation to support the conservative vote suggests that the growth of the alternative, republicanism, was not the result of a diffusion of republican ideas into the countryside.[42]

This development of a republican majority in the department did not mean a shift in the social background of the candidates being elected, as the same combination of landed notables and urban professionals and businessmen were successful. But there was a reshuffling of the political elite in the department, and the men who were successful suggest the moderation of rural voters. Politicians like Charles Dorian and Honoré Audiffred typified the rural areas of the Loire that were coming into the republican camp: committed republicans and supporters of Gambetta during the period of the foundation of the Third Republic, and then

---

40 Michel Lagrée, *Mentalités, religion et histoire en Haute-Bretagne au XIXe siècle: le diocèse de Rennes, 1815–1848* (Paris: Klincksieck, 1977), 73–91, defines *christianisme bleu;* see Gérard Cholvy, *Religion et société au XIXe siècle: le diocèse de Montpellier* (Lille: Université de Lille III, 1973), vol. 2: 1561, for an example of a close identity between conservatism and Catholicism; Ford, *Creating the Nation,* 222; and Huard, *Le Mouvement républicain en Bas-Languedoc,* 435, for instances of "blue" Catholicism.

41 See Ford, *Creating the Nation,* 165–166, for a similar argument concerning the 1906 election in Lower Brittany.

42 See also Corbin, *Archaïsme et modernité,* vol. 2: 991.

supporters of the educational policies of Jules Ferry, Dorian and Au-diffred adopted moderate positions in the new controversies over religion and education in the aftermath of the Dreyfus affair at the turn of the century. But while not approving of the radicalism of the government of Waldeck–Rousseau in Paris in 1902, these men were clearly not under the control of the clergy or the Catholic Church. Their anticlericalism was the moderate variety of a Victor Cousin or a Jules Ferry, distinguishing between Catholicism as a dogma and as an institution. That they were consistently reelected suggests that their constituents had also broken free from the constraints imposed by the village community of the first half of the century, dominated by church and curé.[43]

Attributing the republican victory in the rural Loire to contests between notables, while it may have some validity, assumes a passivity on the part of the "peasants" who became republicans in that it argues that, once given the alternative, country dwellers would vote for republicans. This argu-ment, while a part of contemporary and historical accounts of "how politics came to the peasant," suggests the limited notion of citizenship implicit in the Republic: although republicans like César Berthelon and later historians conceive of the process as one of empowerment, and tell the story as one in which all citizens would assume equality, they overlook the way elections placed voters in a specific place in the nation. Both urban workers and country dwellers were to vote, but that was all. It is the late-nineteenth-century version of the refusal by Godefroy Cavaignac to shake hands with his rural supporters during the July Monarchy.[44]

Viewing elections as a place of negotiation suggests that we must pay more attention to the country dwellers' side of the process, and this leads us to the benefits that made moderate republicanism attractive to rural voters. Republicanism had addressed this issue from its very beginnings: participation as citizens in the democratic and social Republic was also to provide prosperity. Given the difficult economic conjuncture in the coun-tryside during the first decades of the Third Republic, this could make it attractive. Prices for agricultural products fell in the last three decades of the nineteenth century, and the cottage industry that had supplemented the incomes of many in the countryside moved into the cities.[45] In the Loire, as elsewhere, there certainly were monarchists and Bonapartists

---

43 See Philip A. Bertocci, *Jules Simon: Republican Anti-Clericalism and Cultural Politics in France, 1848–1886* (Columbia: University of Missouri Press, 1978), 19–20, 45. See also Ford, *Creating the Nation*, 100, 134, for a case in Lower Brittany in which conflict between notables and priests opened the way for republican politics.

44 Cited by Weber, "Comment la politique vint aux paysans," 373. See also McPhee, *Politics of Rural Life*, 141.

45 Elwitt, "Politics and Social Classes," 102–103. See Ch. 4 in this volume for economic developments in the Loire after 1870, and Corbin, *Archaisme et modernité*, vol 2: 753, 824–831, for an argument concerning the importance of economic conditions in leading country dwellers to vote for republicans.

who tried to develop the means by which country dwellers could profit from the opportunities brought by urbanization and commercialization in the second half of the nineteenth century. These men had organized some improvements in the communications network of the department, and played an important role in the improvement of agriculture in the Plaine du Forez. Such constructions as the early railroad network and a bridge at Montrond over the Loire began to link this part of the department to markets in Lyon and Saint-Etienne.[46] The political ties of the Loire's deputies were important in acquiring the funds for this kind of project, and men such as the Vicomte de Meaux, a Bonapartist who represented the Montbrisonnais in the early 1870s and became a senator in 1876, were necessary links to the government in Paris. Others were also influential, such as Baron de Saint-Genest in the southern Pilat region, who organized a nightly milk caravan through the mountains down into the Stephanois Valley and obtained prizes from the Empire to be given out at agricultural fairs.[47] But Saint-Genest was active in the 1850s and 1860s, and de Meaux's career was eclipsed by his service as minister in the brief Broglie government formed during the crisis of the sixteenth of May in 1877.[48]

Men like Saint-Genest and de Meaux had access to the resources of the state for these activities during the Empire and the first few years of the Third Republic. But by the late 1870s these resources were in the hands of republicans; for these men, republicanism was not only an ideology but also a way of challenging local opponents, and republicans used the resources of the state to gain rural support. The Plan Freycinet of 1878, providing state funding for completing the railway network, was an important source of this kind of patronage. But even in lesser projects, the challengers to the conservatives were influential. A long-standing project, the irrigation canal in the Plaine du Forez, had first been planned in the 1850s. Construction began in the 1860s, but it languished in the 1870s for lack of funding. By a law of 7 August 1882, however, Francisque Reymond, the moderate republican deputy who succeeded the Vicomte de Meaux in the Chamber of Deputies, obtained state funding for the project, and this important improvement for the agriculture of the right bank of the Loire once again began moving toward completion.[49]

46 Vicomte de Meaux, *Le Progrès agricole dans la Plaine du Forez depuis cinquante ans* (Montbrison: Imprimerie d'Eleuthese Brassart, 1895), 9–10.
47 On the Baron de Saint-Genest, see Lehning, *Peasants of Marlhes*, 25, 43–44; and Pierre du Maroussem, *Fermiers montagnards du Haut-Forez* (Paris: Ouvriers des Deux Mondes, 1894), 469–470.
48 Robert, *Dictionnaire*, vol. 4: 330; Lehning, *Peasants of Marlhes*, 14–15.
49 Jones, *Politics and Rural Society*, 273, 281, 295–6; Elwitt, *Making of the Third Republic*, 305; Vicomte de Meaux, *Le Progrès agricole*, 31–36.

Such patronage can hardly be viewed as disinterested, either on the part of Bonapartists during the Second Empire, the Opportunists during the Third Republic, or, we must stress, the recipients of state assistance. The coincidence of the stagnant agricultural economy, the decline of rural by-industries, and the move toward republican opinion in the areas of the department most exposed to outside markets suggests that in the Loire, as in the Loir-et-Cher that Georges Dupeux studied, the Republic was able to profit from the uncertainties created by these factors. It thus acquired a meaning in the countryside, less an ideology than the promise of material benefits. The Republic was accepted because of its active intervention in the countryside, not just in various coercive ways, but also with "the ample pecuniary resources of the state."[50] Republican ideology may have been important in Paris, although it would be naive to suggest that there it was not assisted by material interest. In the rural Loire, support for national regimes was negotiated in the electoral arena around the economic concerns of the voters.

III

There is no doubt that the French countryside experienced significant political change in the period after the Revolution, and in many parts of the country, including the Loire, this came in the second half of the nineteenth century. For many contemporaries, as for most historians of rural politics, this process was shaped by the French discourse about the countryside, which constructed a place without politics. This has taken different forms: the passive, docile peasant of conservative utopias, the peasant dependent on priest and château of republican fears, the "demobilized" peasant of modern social science. These different forms implied different kinds of rural political change. In the 1840s, in the Mayenne, a memoir presented to the government noted that "the railroad, in reducing [the effects of] distances, will carry civilization into the countryside," but Abbé Gérault feared that railroads would bring "doctrines of disorder" to the people and precipitate "the ruin of society." In the first half of the twentieth century, the republican student of politics Andre Siegfried described the Ardèche as a place in which religion and the Catholic clergy overrode all other considerations, economic or social, in the mountains, whereas religious practice was weak and the priest ignored in the foothill areas where Catholics took "advanced" political positions. And in the 1970s Eugen Weber spoke of "politics coming to the peasants."[51] Differ-

---

50 Dupeux, *Aspects de l'histoire*, 29; Jones, *Politics and Rural Society,* 295.
51 Denis, *Les Royalistes de la Mayenne*, 243, 351; Andre Siegfried, *Géographie electorale de l'Ardèche sous la Troisième république* (Paris: Colin, 1949), 61, 62, 65, 113; Weber, "Comment la politique vint aux paysans."

ent in form, these versions of rural political history are similar in their assumption of forces acting upon country dwellers to transform them. Electoral politics in these constructions easily becomes grafted onto differences in other forms of behavior. This is a common feature of French representations of Brittany, and it appears even within departments.[52] In the Loire it is reflected in the contrast between the western Monts du Forez, on the one hand, and the Plaine du Forez and the eastern Monts du Lyonnais on the other. In politics as in demographic behavior, economic development, and religion, the Monts du Forez were typed as not only conservative but also backward and undeveloped. In contrast, the Plaine and the Monts du Lyonnais, the home of both material progress and republican sentiment, acquired several layers of progressive coding. In the discourse of politics in the early Third Republic, these codings acquired a vital coloration that placed the "peasants" to whom they referred in a specific relationship to the French nation.

This placement in the nation best describes the political changes that occurred in the countryside in this period. The early Third Republic constructed the arena in which this came about – electoral politics – and we must acknowledge the French side of this construction as a triumph of discursive power. Those who did not vote, or who voted for the wrong candidates, were still under the domination of notables and priests, and were not "citizens." The destruction of these forms of domination meant the integration of country dwellers into the Republic and the nation. But we must recognize that even after this transformation these "peasant citizens" had only the limited power of voting for republican candidates.

Hovering over this process of political change is the shadow of the *instituteur* of Marcoux, Perrin, who wished country dwellers to receive an education so that they could profit from the economic changes occurring around them, and who railed at the local curés, who feared instruction because it would undercut their influence.[53] His limited vision for the "peasants" of Marcoux aptly describes the moderate Republic a generation later: it was certainly about loosening traditional controls on country dwellers, but it was also about material progress, and we might imagine an elderly Perrin proudly watching the votes counted in 1902 as his former students resoundingly voted to reelect Charles Dorian.

Because of the assumed passivity of "peasants" who had no politics, this construction of rural political development was not likely to notice the country dwellers' part in the process. From the point of view of the "peasants," conflicts between notables opened up new alternatives even as

52 Ford, *Creating the Nation*, 97–99; see also the distinction made by Auguste Rivet for the Haute-Loire in *La Vie politique dans le département de la Haute-Loire de 1815 à 1974* (Le Puy: Cahiers de la Haute-Loire, 1979), 364.

53 A.N. F¹⁷ 10780, *Mémoire* of Perrin, instituteur at Marcoux, 1 février 1861.

elections monopolized politics. An *instituteur* who refused to take instructions from the curé and who actively challenged his preeminence was a pole around which opposition to the curé could form. A republican politician who challenged the conservative notable and was able to deliver resources from the national government could perform the same function. But seeing these aspects of rural politics not only as a gift offered to "its peasants" by the French Republic, but also as a price exacted by country dwellers for their participation in the nation, collapses the distinctions typically made between "peasant" and "French" political behavior. Electoral politics was a space in which local interests – which were not necessarily "archaic" – could be mixed with national issues – which were not necessarily "modern" – by those who lived in the countryside. The Third Republic succeeded in limiting discussions of power to the electoral arena, but in so doing it became dependent on popular support. The "milch-cow Republic" rarely lived up to the idealism of 1793 or 1848, and the Third Republic's reputation has suffered from this apparent fall from grace.[54] But, in the Loire and elsewhere, its reconstruction of country dwellers made it a peasants' republic. In this way, at least, country dwellers at last became a part of the French nation.

54 Jones, *Politics and Rural Society,* 314. The term is used by Jones, 295–304. See also Stanley Hoffman, *In Search of France* (New York: Harper & Row, 1965), 3–21; Ford, *Creating the Nation,* 226–227; Suzanne Berger, *Peasants against Politics: Rural Organization in Brittany, 1911–1967* (Cambridge, Mass.: Harvard University Press, 1972); and Gordon Wright, *Rural Revolution in France* (Stanford, Calif.: Stanford University Press, 1964).

9

Conclusion: toward
a new rural history

The notes to this book indicate the extent to which the nineteenth-century countryside has become a focus of study in the past several decades. This monographic literature has helped create a pervasive version of that history. Peasant society in this telling was isolated until the nineteenth century. It then experienced increased contact with the outside world thanks to better transportation, elective politics, migration, conscription, and education. As a result of this contact, peasant society became integrated into the French nation.

While many political historians have placed this transformation around the middle of the century, the most powerful and influential recent articulation of this orthodoxy is Eugen Weber's *Peasants into Frenchmen*, and he places the inflection in the early years of the Third Republic. For Weber, the last decades of the nineteenth century saw "the wholesale destruction of traditional ways," and tradition itself died.[1] This story appears as well in a number of other works aimed at more general readers. The multiauthor *Histoire de la France rurale* rejects a static "peasant civilization" but spells out a process similar to the one Weber describes. The Second Empire and the first decade of the Third Republic witnessed the effloresence – the "apogee" – of rural society, helped by the prosperity of the Empire. But external impulses from the city and the national market in general made the following decades a period in which the peasant society of the third quarter of the century began to break up.[2] In the same vein, Roger Price has emphasized the way "a series of changes, in particular roads and railways and the development of a more commer-

---

1 Eugen Weber, *Peasants into Frenchmen* (Stanford, Calif.: Stanford University Press, 1976), 471.
2 Maurice Agulhon, Gabriel Desert, and Robert Specklin, *Histoire de la France rurale* (Paris: Seuil, 1976), vol. 3, especially Parts 2 ("Les Campagnes à leur apogée, 1852–1880") and 3 (L'Ebranlement, 1880–1914").

cial economy, transformed rural life."[3] The prosperity of the 1860s made that decade the "apogee" of traditional rural civilization, but thereafter increased competition caused a crisis of adaptation, heightened by falling agricultural prices, the decline of the village artisanate and rural industry, and an increased sense that rural living standards were lower than in towns and cities. Rural society – "peasant" society – was dissolved by its increased integration into the national economy, shifting the balance within rural communities "from continuity to change."[4] A similar view of the third quarter of the century as the peak of rural civilization, and the tragic consequences of changes that were beginning to become apparent in that period, is found in Peter McPhee's *A Social History of France 1780–1880*. McPhee writes, "A rather more prosperous rural population continued to live within a rich variety of local cultures and ecologies," but adds that "the seeds were sown for the destruction of a civilization which was to prove incompatible with the interrelated forces of state centralization and capitalism." "Happily," he says, this was to be a slow and incomplete process.[5]

The many "little narratives" that make up this book can be easily fitted into this story, at least as far as it goes. In the Loire, economic development, demographic change, education, secularization, and increased political participation brought many of the country dwellers of the department into more frequent contact with the world outside of their particular village or surrounding ones. Their agriculture became less aimed at autoconsumption and more market oriented. Their patterns of family formation, featuring earlier marriage and fewer children within marriage, seemed to be more like those of urban France. They sent their children to schools, and schooling became a part of growing up for everyone. They may have continued to go to church on Sunday, but many adopted a more secularized approach to life. And they learned to vote in ways that forced the national government to help them better their lives.

As a story, this version of rural history is organized in particular ways with specific characters. Priests, politicians, schoolteachers, notables, administrators, and "peasants" inhabit the countryside as it is opened up to "French" culture. After several decades the story ends with peasants ceasing to exist. Eugen Weber writes bluntly about the result. If there are no peasants, there are only French: "We are talking about the process of

---

3 Roger Price, *The Social History of Nineteenth-Century France* (New York: Holmes & Meier, 1987), 143–144. See also *The Modernization of Rural France: Communications Networks and Agricultural Market Structures in Nineteenth-Century France* (New York: St. Martin's, 1983).

4 Price, *Social History,* 146, 174.

5 Peter McPhee, *A Social History of France, 1780–1880* (New York: Routledge, 1992), ch. 11, esp. the summing up on 243.

acculturation: the civilization of the French by urban France, the disintegration of local cultures by modernity and their absorption into the dominant civilization of Paris and the schools."[6]

This plot can be written in several different forms. One is as Comedy: the story can be one in which the centralizing political, economic, and social structures that developed in the past brought peasants from a savage, inhospitable environment into the civilizing culture of bourgeois, urban France. Rural families adopted the wise, rational structures and reproductive behavior of bourgeois French families. Country dwellers became more attuned to the market and adapted their agricultural techniques and production to market forces. Rural men began to vote, and many became converted to the Republic; many of them also left the sway of the Catholic Church. Schoolteachers brought French civilization into the countryside.

The same characters and plot elements, however, can be written as Tragedy: the moral virtue of the rural family was destroyed by urban values, and *pères de familles* lost the respect and support of their egoistic children. Secularization deprived country dwellers of God's wisdom and grace, and undercut the position of the natural leader of the rural community, the curé; secularized schooling encouraged peasant children to leave the countryside for the vices of the city; the Republic destroyed the paternalistic relationships that had existed in the countryside for generations. In short, a vice-ridden urban society destroyed the seat of virtue in French civilization, the "peasants" who embodied everything that was good about the society.

That the same story can have at least two different morals should alert us to the problematic nature of such accounts, and to the fact that both versions are a part of a larger story, a metanarrative, that overdetermines stories of contact between a "developed" society and an "underdeveloped" one. Whether called "progress," as did the leaders of the Empire and Republic; "development," as did international agencies after the Second World War; or "modernization," as did social science in the last generation, it is the same story, and recent histories of rural France have told it just as consistently as did bourgeois Frenchmen, United Nations officials, and social scientists.

It is, however, a metanarrative that deserves to be questioned and, if possible, refashioned. As James Clifford has noted, "Stories of cultural contact and change have been structured by a pervasive dichotomy: absorption by the other or resistance to the other. . . . Yet what if identity is conceived not as a boundary to be maintained but as a nexus of relations

6 Weber, *Peasants into Frenchmen*, 486.

and transactions actively engaging a subject? . . . How do stories of contact, resistance, and assimilation appear from the standpoint of groups in which exchange rather than identity is the fundamental value to be sustained?"[7] The questions are as valid for a story of contact between urban and rural Frenchmen in the late nineteenth century as they are for Western ethnographers studying African or Pacific peoples. Susan Carol Rogers has suggested a way in which the questions might be answered. Rogers argues that "peasant" is not so much a reality as a symbol, one that can be (and is) manipulated for various purposes in French culture. In particular, this symbol serves as a way of expressing and managing a central tension in French society, between the unified identity of a centralized French nation and an identity rooted in the diverse rural societies that coexist on the national territory. In art, history, and political discourse, "peasants" are used to express either positive or negative feelings about France in general, and modernity and change in particular.[8]

Acknowledging that "peasant" is not so much real as symbolic allows us to step outside the existing narrative of rural history and see it as a partial history that has operated to place the countryside and its inhabitants in a specific, and subordinate, relationship to French culture, marginalizing or excluding from sight those who did not fit within its limits. The "problem" of rural history then becomes one of understanding a series of particular historical moments in the exchanges between two cultures that, in the course of contact with each other, articulate themselves and use each other as a part of that process of articulation. The question can be usefully framed in terms of the processes of cultural conflict that Richard Terdiman has applied to various written forms of culture in nineteenth-century France. Terdiman shows the difficulty of moving completely outside of a dominant discourse, and most counter-discursive activity therefore takes the form of what he calls "re/citation": those in opposition to the dominant discourse seek to "surround their antagonist and neutralize or explode it." The process is one in which an involuntary duplication of the dominant discourse is linked with an intended mockery: "the process of re/citation represents a meditation on recurrence which can only achieve its effectiveness by introducing some principle of alterity into the discursive circuit, by forcibly interrupting its apparent seamlessness." In this fashion, the drawings of Daumier in *Le Charivari* were able to stand as an alternative to the uses of words in the mass-circulation newspapers that were a part of nineteenth-century bour-

7 James Clifford, *The Predicament of Culture: Twentieth-Century Ethnography, Literature, and Art* (Cambridge, Mass.: Harvard University Press, 1988), 344.
8 Susan Carol Rogers, "Good to Think: The 'Peasant' in Contemporary France," *Anthropological Quarterly* 60 (1987), 57.

geois discourse.[9] Although *Le Charivari* used the form of a newspaper, it "turned" that form against the dominant discourse.

Terdiman's formulation has the value of highlighting the ways in which dominated peoples can "turn" their rulers' versions of the world into critiques of that world, but also of recognizing that dominant discourses are powerful entities and that resisting them is a very difficult matter. "At stake in this discursive struggle," he notes, "are the paradigms of social representation themselves."[10] It suggests that one partial story of country dwellers is as individuals, families, and communities that did not passively accept their place in the dominant discourse, and who therefore have a history that is an ongoing relationship to the culture that kept insisting that they were a part of "France." The suggestion of this book has been that focusing on the processes of cultural contact allows us to reread the history of "peasants" as something other than a part of the development or modernization (or destruction) of a "traditional" society. This rereading does not dramatically change the chronology of French rural history – the Second Republic, Second Empire, and early Third Republic remain of great importance – as much as it alters the description of that history. Instead of disappearing, "peasant" changed meaning and acquired different resonances in French culture.

The landscape as a metaphor for the culture of the countryside, a space on which individuals make meaning as they live their lives, is a way of seeing that different history. It has led this story to certain sites on that landscape – the land, farmhouse, school, church, and electoral politics – that at times seem to hold a particularly significant place and whose movement on that landscape, from foreground to background or otherwise, has been the "action" of this account. Starting from this metaphor, I have argued that what was going on in the second half of the nineteenth century was a struggle at different places on the landscape over the attempt by French culture to impose a category – "peasant" – on the individuals who lived in the countryside. At every moment in this encounter, relations of power were operating, even if those relations and their character were often being denied by all participants. The narrative recounted here, then, is not one in which the country dwellers in the Loire adopted the attitudes of their more "modern" urban neighbors, under the onslaught of greater contact with national economic, political, and educational systems. It is also not about how sites on the landscape were lost for "peasants" and taken over by "France." It is rather how

---

9 Richard Terdiman, *Discourse/Counter-Discourse: The Theory and Practice of Symbolic Resistance in Nineteenth-Century France* (Ithaca, N.Y.: Cornell University Press, 1985), 68, 210, 3.
10 Ibid., 149.

certain sites were forced into the background and others pulled into the foreground, as tactical maneuvers in the contact between French and country dweller. The power of France was to be able to decide where contact would take place, what the terrain would look like, and who would be present. Placed at such a disadvantage, country dwellers had few options. They could refuse to accept that definition, and act as if fields were only to feed families, not to maximize profit; as if churches were still to find guidance in every aspect of life; and as if elections were to support the long-standing leaders of the countryside. The consequence of these positions was marginalization, as was the case with regions like the West of France and the southwestern mountains in the Loire. In these places economic, demographic, religious, and political behavior marked country dwellers – in the eyes of the government, much of the French elite, and especially the Third Republic – as backward, dangerous, and archaic: Vendées. The alternative, adopted by most of the rural Loire and the country, was to seek to make the sites selected by French culture their own: to turn economic development, demographic change, schooling, and above all electoral politics, the chosen sites of French culture, to their own ends, in the same way that Daumier and his colleagues turned the newspaper form to their own aims.

Another part of this history must emphasize the way in which the French discourse about the countryside was being reworked as a result of the contact with that countryside brought by economic development, secularization, education, and political change. My suggestion is that this was not so much a process by which "peasants became Frenchmen" but one in which France created the version of "peasants" that it would use for a particular part of its history.[11] This reading suggests that the ancien régime and the early nineteenth-century version of "peasant" – isolated, religious, ignorant, violent, and bordering on savage, the version of Michelet and Balzac – was no longer useful for French culture in the second half of the nineteenth century. The economic, social, and political conflicts of late-nineteenth-century France required a different "peasant," one who, with help from the state, could be peaceful, literate, secularized, a patriotic republican, and the repository of French values against the radical working class. The construction at the level of French culture of this "peasant" was a slow process that is apparent on several levels: the shift in republican views of the peasant between 1851 and the late 1870s, as they became not the enemy but the support of the Republic; the prominence of agrarians like Jules Méline, for whom rural civilization needed to be protected; or the depictions of country dwellers in novels,

---

11 As the creation of "the Orient" helped "the West" create its own image of itself. See Edward Said, *Orientalism* (New York: Pantheon, 1979).

denizens of a world that was more menaced than menacing.[12] This version of "peasant" became fundamental to the French perception of its identity as the nineteenth century turned into the twentieth, and its continued importance is apparent in both the frequent references to "peasants" in recent French discourse and the ongoing concern about the "end of the peasants." It worked in a particular way, as a part of the ongoing need to resolve questions in French culture about national identity.[13] As Henri Mendras asked during the early Fifth Republic, "What will a world without peasants be like?" Because difference from "peasants" helped to define national identity, the answer seems to be one in which it is difficult to be French.[14]

These partial stories derive from a focus on the contact between a dominant discourse that defined the "peasants" who lived in the nineteenth-century Loire and the counterdiscourses represented in the behavior of country dwellers in the different parts of the department. They make apparent the unresolvable contradictions of the French discourse about "peasants." Country dwellers needed to lose old customs and acquire new ones, but they still had to be "peasants." This contradiction opened up spaces for negotiation by country dwellers, not least in the electoral arena established in 1848 and brought to its peak in the Third Republic. By becoming "citizen peasants" they forced themselves on the republicans, and the Republic became committed to retaining the support of those "citizens" without destroying their identity as "peasants." Not only the Republic but the identity of France became dependent on maintaining that identity. If the happy endings of Comedy and the sad stories of Tragedy have been the usual forms of French rural history thus far, perhaps we should consider Irony.

12 Agulhon, Desert, and Specklin, *Histoire de la France rurale*, vol. 3: 529; Pierre Barral, *Les Agrariens français de Méline à Pisani* (Paris: Colin, 1968); M. Augé-Laribé, *La Politique agricole de la France de 1880 à 1940* (Paris: Presses Universitaires de France, 1950).

13 Rogers, "Good to Think;" Henri Mendras, *The Vanishing Peasant*, trans. by Jean Lerner (Cambridge, Mass.: MIT Press, 1970); Henri Mendras and Alistair Cole, *Social Change in Modern France* (Cambridge University Press, 1991), 15–22.

14 Mendras, *Vanishing Peasant*, 246. The connection between French national identity and defense of "peasants" is evident, most recently, in the dispute between France and both the European Community and the United States over supports to agriculture in the revision of the General Agreement on Tariffs and Trade in November 1992.

Sources and references

I. ARCHIVAL SOURCES

A. Archives nationales de France (Paris).
BB[18]: Versements du Ministère de justice.
    37: Inspection général de la gendarmerie nationale, Loire.
C: Assemblée nationale.
    956: Enquête sur le travail agricole et industriel du 25 mai 1848.
F[11]: Subsistances.
    2705 42 (Loire): Enquête agricole décennale, 1862.
F[17]: Instruction publique.
    116: Enquête sur l'instruction primaire, 1833.
    9176–9187: Laicisations des écoles publiques.
    9306–9369: Rapports des inspecteurs primaires.
    10356–10365: Statistique générale de l'instruction primaire.
    10368–10406: Statistique générale de l'instruction primaire.
    10413, 10493, 10589: Etats de situation des écoles primaires publiques et libres et des écoles maternelles, 1860, 1872, 1882.
    10780: Mémoires sur les besoins de l'instruction primaire.
F[19]: Cultes.
    341: Affaire de Saint-Galmier.
    5562: Pèlerinages, 1857–1905.
    6307: Etat Général des communautés religieuses de femmes, situation au 1er décembre 1831.
F[20]: Statistiques.
    731: Recensement des communautés religieuses, 1861.
Series H
    1510[1]: Montrouge, *Observations sur les diffautes de la culture employée dans la Plaine de Forez* (1764).
B. Archives départementales de la Loire (Saint-Etienne).
Series M: Personnel et administration générale.

3 M. Elections législatives et sénatoriales
7 M. Maires et adjoints.
8 M. Listes électorales.
10 M. Evénements et affaires politiques.
21 M. Rapports de police.
37 M. Epidémies.
46 M. Divisions administratives et territoriales.
48 M. Mouvement de la population.
49 M. Dénombrement de la population.
55 M. Statistique agricole.
56 M. Statistique industrielle.
57 M. Concours et comices agricoles.
58 M. Foires et marchés.
66 M. Questions agricoles, renseignements, rapports, enquêtes.
85 M. Salaires.
Series T. Enseignement.
438–508: Instruction primaire.
1537–1546: Instruction primaire: rapports.
Series 3 E. Etat civil.
Series L.
974–1029. Affaires religieuses et enseignement.
Series V. Cultes.
4: Troubles survenus à l'occasion de l'installation d'ecclésiastiques.
C. Archives de l'archdiocèse de Lyon (Lyon).
Visites pastorales, 1826–28; 1844–49; 1879–96.
D. Archives de la Diana (Montbrison).
Bréasson, Andre. "Maisons paysannes d'un coin du Froez," type-script dated January 1964.
E. Musée des arts et traditions populaires (Paris).
Enquête sur l'ancienne agriculture, 13 avril 1937.

II. PRINTED SOURCES AND REFERENCES

Accampo, Elinor. *Industrialization, Family Life, and Class Relations: Saint-Chamond, 1815–1914.* Berkeley and Los Angeles: University of California Press, 1989.
Acomb, Evelyn M. *The French Laic Laws (1979–1889).* New York: Columbia University Press, 1941.
Agulhon, Maurice. "Conscience nationale et conscience régionale en France de 1815 à nos jours." In *Histoire Vagabonde,* vol. 2: 144–174. Paris: Gallimard, 1983.
. *Marianne au combat.* Paris: Flammarion, 1979.
. *La République au village.* Paris: Plon, 1970.

Alonso, Ana Maria. "Gender, Power, and Historical Memory: Discourses of Serrano Resistance." In *Feminists Theorize the Political,* eds. Judith Butler and Joan Wallach Scott, 404–425. New York: Routledge. 1992.

Anderson, Benedict. *Imagined Communities.* 2d ed. New York: Verson, 1991.

Anderson, R. D. *Education in France, 1848–1870.* Oxford University Press (Clarendon Press), 1975.

Andrew, C. M., and A. S. Kanya-Forstner. "Communication: The *Groupe Colonial* in the French Chamber of Deputies, 1892–1932." *Historical Journal* 17 (1974): 837–866.

Annuaire du département de la Loire pour 1846. Montbrison: Département de la Loire, 1846.

Ariès, Philippe. *The Hour of Our Death.* Translated by Helen Weaver. New York: Random House, 1981.

——. "Culture orale et culture ecrite." In *Le Christianisme populaire: les dossiers de l'histoire,* 227–240. Paris: Centurion, 1976.

Armengaud, Andre. *Les Populations de l'Est Aquitaine au début de l'époque contemporaine.* Paris: Mouton, 1961.

Augé-Laribé, M. *La Politique agricole de la France de 1880 à 1940.* Paris: Presses Universitaires de France, 1950.

Aulard, Alphonse. *Histoire politique de la Révolution française.* 5th ed. Paris: Colin, 1913.

Balibar, R. *Les Français fictifs.* Paris: Hachette, 1974.

Balibar, R., and D. Laporte. *Le Français national: politique et pratique de la langue nationale sous la Révolution.* Paris: Hachette, 1974.

Balzac, Honoré de. *Les Chouans.* In *La Comédie humaine,* vol. 5: 627–741. Paris: Seuil, 1966.

——. *Les Paysans.* In *La Comédie humaine,* vol. 6: 9–120. Paris: Seuil, 1966.

Barral, Pierre. *Les Agrariens français, de Méline à Pisani.* Paris: Colin, 1968.

——. *Le Département de l'Isère sous la Troisième république, 1870–1940: histoire sociale et politique.* Paris: Presses de la Fondation nationales des sciences politiques, 1962.

——. "Note historique sur l'emploi du terme 'paysan.'" *Etudes Rurales* 21 (1966): 72–80.

Barrows, Susanna. *Distorting Mirrors: Visions of the Crowd in Late 19th-Century France.* New Haven, Conn.: Yale University Press, 1981.

Bataille, Leon, ed. *A Turning Point for Literacy.* New York: Pergamon, 1976.

Bazin, René. *La Terre qui meurt.* Paris: Calmann-Lévy, 1987.

Bell, Susan Groag, and Karen M. Offen, eds. *Women, the Family, and*

Freedom: The Debate in Documents. Stanford, Calif.: Stanford University Press, 1983.

Berenson, Edward. *Populist Religion and Left-Wing Politics in France, 1830–1852.* Princeton, N.J.: Princeton University Press, 1984.

Berger, Peter. *The Sacred Canopy.* Garden City, N.Y.: Doubleday, 1967.

Berger, Suzanne. *Peasants against Politics: Rural Organization in Brittany, 1911–1967.* Cambridge, Mass.: Harvard University Press, 1972.

Berkner, Lutz K., Jr. "Household Arithmetic: A Note." *Journal of Family History* 2 (1977): 159–163.

Bertocci, Philip A. *Jules Simon: Republican Anti-Clericalism and Cultural Politics in France, 1848–1886.* Columbia: University of Missouri Press, 1978.

Bidelman, Patrick Kay. *Pariahs Stand Up! The Founding of the Liberal Feminist Movement in France, 1858–1889.* Westport, Conn.: Greenwood, 1982.

Bloch, Marc. *Caractères originaux de l'histoire rurale française.* Oslo: H. Aschehough, 1931.

Blok, Anton. *The Mafia of a Sicilian Village, 1860–1960.* New York: Harper & Row, 1974.

Bodiguel, Maryvonne. *Le Rural en question: politiques et sociologues en quête d'objet.* Paris: Harmattan, 1986.

Bois, Paul. *Paysans de l'Ouest.* Paris: Mouton, 1960.

Bomier-Landowski, Alain. "Les Groupes parlementaires de l'Assemblée nationale et de la Chambre des députés de 1871 à 1940." In *Sociologie électorale: esquisse d'un bilan, guide de recherches,* ed. François Goguel and Georges Dupeux, 75–88. Paris: Colin, 1951.

Bontron, Jean-Claude. "Transformations et permanences de pouvoirs dans une société rurale: à propos du sud du Morvan." *Etudes Rurales* 63–64 (1976): 141–151.

Bouiller, Robert, and Madeleine Bouiller. *Les Constructions traditionelles dans le Département de la Loire.* Ambierle: Musée forézien, 1977.

Boulard, Fernand, and Jean Remy. *Pratique religieuse urbaine et régions culturelles.* Paris: Ouvrières, 1968.

Bouret, Jean. *The Barbizon School and 19th Century French Landscape Painting.* Greenwich, Conn.: New York Graphic Society, 1973.

Bourguet, Marie-Noelle. *Déchiffrer la France: la Statistique départementale à l'epoque napoléonienne.* Paris: Archives contemporaines, 1988.

——. "Race et folklore: l'image officielle de la France en 1800." *Annales: Economies. Sociétés. Civilisations.* 31 (1977): 802–823.

Boutry, Philippe. *Prêtres et paroisses au pays du curé d'Ars.* Paris: Cerf, 1983.

——. "Un Sanctuaire et son saint au XIXe siècle: Jean-Marie-Baptiste

Vianney, curé d'Ars." *Annales: Economies. Sociétés. Civilisations.* 35 (1980): 353–379.

Bowman, Mary Jean, and C. Arnold Anderson. "Concerning the Role of Education in Development." In *Old Societies and New States: The Quest for Modernity in Asia and Africa*, ed. Clifford Geertz, 247–279. New York: Free Press, 1963.

Boxer, Marilyn J. "Socialism Faces Feminism: The Failure of Synthesis in France, 1879–1914." In *Socialist Women*, ed. Marilyn J. Boxer and Jean H. Quataert, 75–111. New York: Elsevier, 1978.

Braudel, Fernand. *The Identity of France*. Translated by Sian Reynolds. New York: Harper & Row, 1988.

Bréasson, Andre. "Maisons paysannes des environs de Saint-Didier-sur Rochefort." *Bulletin de la Diana* 39 (1965): 50–68.

Brettell, Richard, and Caroline Brettell. *Painters and Peasants in the Nineteenth Century.* New York: Rizzoli, 1983.

Brooke, Michael. *Le Play: Engineer and Social Scientist.* London: Longman Group, 1970.

Brooks, Charles William. "Jean Renoir's *The Rules of the Game.*" *French Historical Studies* 7 (1971): 264–283.

Brossard, E. *Histore du département de la Loire pendant la Révolution française, 1789–1799.* Paris: H. Champion, 1904–1907.

Brubaker, Rogers. *Citizenship and Nationhood in France and Germany.* Cambridge, Mass.: Harvard University Press, 1992.

Burke, Peter, and Roy Porter, eds. *The Social History of Language.* Cambridge University Press, 1987.

Bury, J. P. T. *Gambetta and the Making of the Third Republic.* London: Longman Group, 1973.

Cameron, Iain. *Crime and Repression in the Auvergne and the Guyenne, 1720–1790.* Cambridge University Press, 1981.

Canard, J. *Folklore chrétien: coutumes d'origine religieuse, disparues ou en voie de disparition, en Forez et en Lyonnais.* Roanne: Imprimerie Sully, 1952.

Catéchisme imprimé par l'ordre de S. E. Monseigneur le Cardinal Fesch, archévêque de Lyon, primat des gaules; pour être seul enseigné dans son diocèse. Lyon: Chez Lambert-Gentot, 1823.

Cayez, Pierre. *Métiers jacquards et hauts fourneaux: aux origines de l'industrie lyonnaise.* Lyon: Presses Universitaires de Lyon, 1978.

Certeau, Michel de, Dominique Julia, and Jacques Revel. *Une Politique de la langue.* Paris: Gallimard, 1975.

Charbit, Yves, and Andre Béjin. "La Pensée démographique." In *Histoire de la population française*, ed. Jacques Dupâquier, vol. 3: 465–501. Paris: Presses Universitaires de France, 1988.

Charle, Christophe. *Les Elites de la République, 1880–1900.* Paris: Fayard, 1987.

Chassagne, Serge. "La Diffusion rurale de l'industrie cotonnière en France (1750–1850)." *Revue du Nord* 240 (1979): 97–114.

Chatelain, Abel. *Les Migrants temporaires en France de 1800 à 1914.* Villeneuve-d'Ascq: Université de Lille III, 1976.

Chatelard, Claude. *Crime et criminalité dans l'arrondissement de Saint-Etienne au XIXe siècle.* Saint-Etienne: Reboul Imprimerie, 1981.

Chaunu, Pierre. "Une histoire religieuse serielle." *Revue d'Histoire Moderne et Contemporaine* 12 (1965): 5–34.

Chayanov, A. V. *The Theory of the Peasant Economy,* ed. Daniel Thorner, B. Kerblay, and R. E. F. Smith. Homewood, Ill.: Irwin, 1966.

Cholvy, Gérard. "Le Catholicisme populaire en France au XIXe siècle." In *Le Christianisme populaire: les dossiers de l'histoire,* ed. Bernard Plongeron and Robert Pannet, 199–223. Paris: Centurion, 1976.

. "Réalités de la religion populaire dans la France contemporaine, XIXe–début XXe siècles." In *La Religion populaire: approches historiques,* ed. Bernard Plongeron, 149–193. Paris: Beauchesne, 1976.

. *Religion et société au XIXe siècle: le diocèse de Montpellier.* Université de Lille III, 1973.

Clark, Linda L. *Schooling the Daughters of Marianne: Textbooks and the Socialization of Girls in Modern French Primary Schools.* Albany, N.Y.: SUNY Press, 1984.

Clark, T. J. *Image of the People: Gustave Courbet and the Second French Republic, 1848–1851.* Greenwich, Conn.: New York Graphic Society, 1973.

. *The Absolute Bourgeois: Artists and Politics in France, 1848–1851.* London: Thames & Hudson, 1973.

Clifford, James. *The Predicament of Culture.* Cambridge, Mass.: Harvard University Press, 1988.

Coale, Ansley J., and Roy Treadway. "A Summary of the Changing Distribution of Overall Fertility, Marital Fertility, and the Proportion Married in the Provinces of Europe." In *The Decline of Fertility in Europe,* ed. Ansley J. Coale and Susan Cotts Watkins, 31–182. Princeton, N.J.: Princeton University Press, 1986.

Cobb, Richard. *Reactions to the French Revolution.* New York: Oxford University Press, 1972.

. *A Sense of Place.* London: Duckworth, 1975.

. *Paris and Its Provinces.* New York: Oxford University Press, 1975.

Cohen, Anthony P. *The Symbolic Construction of Community.* New York: Tavistock, 1985.

Cohen, William B. *The French Encounter with Africans: White Response to Blacks, 1530–1880.* Bloomington: Indiana University Press, 1980.

Cohn, Bernard. "The Census, Social Structure and Objectification in South Asia." In *An Anthropologist Among the Historians and Other Essays*, 224–254. New York: Oxford University Press, 1987.

Coleman, William. *Death Is a Social Disease: Public Health and Political Economy in Early Industrial France.* Madison: University of Wisconsin Press, 1982.

Cook, Malcolm C. "Politics in the Fiction of the French Revolution, 1789–1794." *Studies on Voltaire and the Eighteenth Century* 201 (1982): 233–340.

Corbin, Alain. *Archaisme et modernité en Limousin au XIXe siècle, 1845–1880.* Paris: Marcel Rivière et Cie, 1975.

. *Les Filles de noce.* Paris: Flammarion, 1982.

. *The Village of Cannibals: Rage and Murder in France, 1870.* Translated by Arthur Goldhammer. Cambridge, Mass.: Harvard University Press, 1992.

Cranston, Maurice. "The Sovereignty of the Nation." In *The French Revolution and the Creation of Modern Political Culture*, ed. Colin Lucas, vol. 2: 97–104. New York: Pergamon, 1988.

Crubellier, Maurice. "D'Une culture populaire à une autre: l'école de la Troisième république." In *Popular Traditions and Learned Culture in France*, eds. Jacques Beauroy, Marc Bertrand, and Edward T. Gargan, 149–162. Saratoga, Calif.: Anma Libri, 1985.

Daniel (Lebon), André. *L'Année politique, 1879.* Paris: Charpentier, 1880.

. *L'Année politique, 1877.* Paris: Charpentier, 1878.

. *L'Année politique, 1885.* Paris: Charpentier, 1886.

. *L'Année politique, 1902.* Paris: Perrin et Cie, 1903.

. *L'Année politique, 1904.* Paris: Perrin et Cie, 1905.

Darmon, Jean-Jacques. *Le Colportage de libraire en France sous le Second empire: grands colporteurs et culture populaire.* Paris: Plon, 1972.

Davis, Natalie Zemon. *Society and Culture in Early Modern France.* Stanford, Calif.: Stanford University Press, 1975.

Dechelette, Charles. *L'Industrie cotonnière à Roanne.* Roanne: Imprimerie Souchier, 1910.

Delumeau, Jean. *Catholicism between Luther and Voltaire: A New View of the Counter-Reformation.* Translated by Jeremy Moiser. Philadelphia: Westminster, 1977.

Dening, Greg. *Islands and Beaches: Discourse on a Silent Land: Marquesas, 1774–1880.* Honolulu: University of Hawaii Press, 1980.

Denis, Michel. *Les Royalistes de la Mayenne et le monde moderne.* Paris: Klincksieck, 1977.

Desan, Suzanne. *Reclaiming the Sacred: Lay Religion and Popular Politics in Revolutionary France.* Ithaca, N.Y.: Cornell University Press, 1990.

. "Redefining Revolutionary Liberty: The Rhetoric of Religious Revival during the French Revolution." *Journal of Modern History* 60 (1988): 1–27.

Devlin, Judith. *The Superstitious Mind: French Peasants and the Supernatural in the Nineteenth Century.* New Haven, Conn.: Yale University Press, 1987.

DeVries, Jan. "Peasant Demand Patterns and Economic Development: Friesland, 1550–1740." In *European Peasants and their Markets*, eds. William N. Parker and Eric Jones, 205–266. Princeton, N.J.: Princeton University Press, 1975.

Donzelot, Jacques. *The Policing of Families.* Translated by Robert Hurley. New York: Pantheon, 1979.

Douglas, Mary. "Deciphering a Meal." In *Implicit Meanings: Essays in Anthropology*, 249–275. London: Routledge & Kegan Paul, 1975.

Drochon, Jean Emmanuel. *Histoire illustrée des pèlerinages français de la très-sainte Vièrge.* Paris: Plon, 1890.

Duby, George, ed. *Histoire de la France rurale.* Paris: Seuil, 1975–76.

Duggett, Michael. "Marx on Peasants." *Journal of Peasant Studies* 2 (1975): 159–182.

Dupâquier, Jacques, and Michel Dupâquier. *Histoire de la démographie.* Paris: Perrin, 1985.

Dupâquier, Jacques, and René Le Mée. "La Connaissance des faits démographiques de 1789 à 1914." In *Histoire de la population française*, ed. Jacques Dupâquier, vol. 3: 15–61. Paris: Presses Universitaires de France, 1988.

Dupeux, Georges. *Aspects de l'histoire sociale et politique du Loir-et-Cher, 1848–1914.* Paris: Mouton, 1962.

Duplessy, Joseph. *Annuaire du département de la Loire.* Montbrison: Cheminal, 1818.

Ekloff, Ben. "Peasant Sloth Reconsidered: Strategies of Education and Learning in Rural Russia before the Revolution." *Journal of Social History* 16 (1981): 355–385.

Elwitt, Sanford H. "Politics and Social Classes in the Loire: The Triumph of Republican Order, 1869–1873." *French Historical Studies* 6 (1969): 93–112.

. *The Making of the Third Republic.* Baton Rouge: Louisiana State University Press, 1975.

Estier, Robert. "Productions agricoles et industries rurales: l'example du roannais textile au XIXe siècle." In *Des Economies traditionelles aux sociétés industrielles*, ed. P. Bairoch and A-M. Pinz, 237–256. Geneva: Droz, 1985.

Faure, Christian. "Le Film documentaire sous Vichy: une promotion du terroir." *Ethnologie Française* 18 (1988): 283–290.

. *Le Projet culturel de Vichy: folklore et révolution nationale, 1940–1944.* Lyon: Presses Universitaires de Lyon, 1989.

Fitch, Nancy. "Mass Culture, Mass Parliamentary Politics, and Modern Anti-Semitism: The Dreyfus Affair in Rural France." *American Historical Review* 97 (1992): 55–95.

Fleury, Michel, and Louis Henry. *Nouveau manuel de dépouillement et d'exploitation de l'état civil ancien.* Paris: Institut nationale d'etudes démographiques, 1976.

Ford, Caroline. *Creating the Nation in Provincial France.* Princeton, N.J.: Princeton University Press, 1993.

Fortier-Beaulieu, Paul. *Mariages et noces campagnards.* Paris: G. P. Maisonneuve, 1937.

Foucault, Michel. *The Discourse on Language.* In *The Archaeology of Knowledge.* Translated by Rupert Swyer. New York: Pantheon, 1972.

. *The History of Sexuality.* Translated by Robert Hurley. New York: Random House, 1978.

Fournial, Etienne and Jean-Pierre Gutton. *Cahiers de doléances de la province de Forez.* Saint-Etienne: Centre d'études foréziennes, 1974. 2 Vols.

Fox-Genovese, Elizabeth. *The Origins of Physiocracy.* Ithaca, N.Y.: Cornell University Press, 1976.

Frader, Laura Levine. *Peasants and Protest: Agricultural Workers, Politics, and Unions in the Aude, 1850–1914.* Berkeley and Los Angeles: University of California Press, 1991.

Fried, Michael. *Courbet's Realism.* University of Chicago Press, 1990.

Fuchs, Rachel. *Poor and Pregnant in Paris.* New Brunswick, N.J.: Rutgers University Press, 1992.

Furet, François, and Jacques Ozouf. *Lire et écrire: L'alphabétisation des français de Calvin à Jules Ferry.* Paris: Minuit, 1977.

Gachon, Louis. *L'Auvergne et le Velay.* Paris: G. P. Maisonneuve, 1975.

Gadille, Jacques. *Histoire des diocèses de France: Lyon.* Paris: Beauchesne, 1983.

. "Le Jansenisme populaire: les prolongements aux XIXe siècle: le cas du Forez." *Etudes Foréziennes,* 7 (1975): 157–167.

Galpern, A. N. *The Religions of the People in Sixteenth-Century Champagne.* Cambridge, Mass.: Harvard University Press, 1976.

Garden, Maurice. *Lyon et les lyonnais au XVIIIe siècle.* Paris: Belles lettres, 1970.

Gardette, Pierre et al. *Atlas linguistique et ethnographique du lyonnais.* Lyon: L'Institut de linguistique romane des facultés catholiques de Lyon, 1956.

. "Carte linguistique du Forez." *Bulletin de la Diana* (1943): 269–281.

Gargan, Edward T. "The Priestly Culture in Modern France." *Catholic Historical Review* 57 (1971): 1–20.

Garrier, Gilbert. "La Formation d'un complexe economico-social de type 'Rhôdanien': Champonost (1730–1822)." In *Structures économiques et problèmes sociaux du monde rural dans la France du Sud-Est*, ed. Pierre Léon 315–369. Paris: Belles lettres, 1966.

. *Paysans du Beaujolais et du Lyonnais*. Presses Universitaires de Grenoble, 1973.

. "L'union du Sud-Est des syndicats agricoles avant 1914." *Mouvement Social* 67 (1969): 17–38.

Gay, Peter. *The Bourgeois Experience*. New York: Oxford University Press, 1984.

. *The Enlightenment: An Interpretation*. New York: Knopf, 1966.

Geertz, Clifford. *Works and Lives: The Anthropologist as Author*. Stanford, Calif.: Stanford University Press, 1988.

Genovese, Eugene D. *Roll, Jordon, Roll*. New York: Random House, 1972.

Gide, Charles, and Charles Rist. *Histoire des doctrines économiques*. Paris: Société du Recueil Sirey, 1922.

Gildea, Robert. *Education in Provincial France, 1800–1914*. Oxford University Press: (Clarendon Press), 1983.

Gille, Bertrand. *Les Sources Statistiques de l'Histoire de France*. Paris: Minard, 1964.

Gillis, John. *For Better, For Worse: British Marriages, 1600 to the Present*. New York: Oxford University Press, 1985.

Goguel, François. *La Politique des partis sous la Troisième république*. Paris: Seuil, 1946.

. *Géographie des élections françaises de 1870 à 1951*. Paris: Colin, 1951.

Gontard, Maurice. *Les Ecoles primaires de la France bourgeoise (1833–1875)*. Toulouse: Service de reprographie, Académie de Toulouse, 1976.

. *L'Enseignement primaire en France de la Révolution à la loi Guizot (1789–1833)*. Paris: Belles lettres, n.d.

Goode, William. *World Revolution and Family Patterns*. New York: Free Press, 1963.

Gordon, David. *Merchants and Capitalists: Industrialization and Provincial Politics in Mid-Nineteenth-Century France*. University: University of Alabama Press, 1985.

Goubert, Pierre. *The Ancien Régime: French Society, 1600–1750*. Translated by Steve Cox. New York: Harper & Row, 1973.

. *Beauvais et les Beauvaisis de 1600 à 1730*. Paris: S.E.V.P.E.N., 1960.

Graff, Harvey. *The Legacies of Literacy: Continuities and Contradictions in Western Culture and Society*. Bloomington: Indiana University Press, 1987.

Grantham, George W. "Scale and Organization in French Farming, 1840–1880." In *European Peasants and their Markets*, eds. William

Parker and Eric Jones, 293–326. Princeton, N.J.: Princeton University Press, 1975.

Gras, Louis-Jean. *Histoire de la rubannerie.* Saint-Etienne: Théolier, 1906.

. *Histoire des premiers chemins de fer français et du premier tramway de France.* Saint-Etienne: Théolier, 1924.

. *Histoire du commerce local et des industries qui s'y rattachent dans la région stéphanoise et forézienne.* Saint-Etienne: Théolier, 1910.

. *Les Routes du Forez et du Jerez.* Saint-Etienne: Théolier, 1925.

Gras, Louis-Pierre. *Dictionnaire du patois forezien.* Lyon: A. Brun, 1863.

Gravier, J.-F. *Paris et le désert français.* 2d ed. Paris: Flammarion, 1958.

Grayzel, Susan R. "Writers of *la Grande Guerre:* Gender and the Boundaries Between the Fronts." *Proceedings of the Western Society for French History* 21 (1994), 181–189.

Greenblatt, Stephen J. "Learning to Curse: Aspects of Linguistic Colonialism in the Sixteenth Century." In *Learning to Curse: Essays in Early Modern Culture,* 16–39. New York: Routledge, 1990.

Greenfeld, Liah. *Nationalism: Five Roads to Modernity.* Cambridge, Mass.: Harvard University Press, 1992.

Grew, Raymond. "Picturing the People: Images of the Lower Orders in Nineteenth-Century French Art." *Journal of Interdisciplinary History* 17 (1986): 203–231.

Grew, Raymond, and Patrick J. Harrigan. *School, State, and Society.* Ann Arbor: University of Michigan Press, 1991.

Grillo, R. D. *Dominant Languages: Language and Hierarchy in Britain and France.* Cambridge University Press, 1989.

Gueniffey, Patrice. "Les assemblées et la représentation." In *The French Revolution and the Creation of Modern Political Culture,* ed. Colin Lucas, vol. 2: 233–257. New York: Pergamon, 1988.

Guha, Ranajit, and Gayatri Chakravorty Spivak, eds. *Selected Subaltern Studies.* New York: Oxford University Press, 1988.

Guillaumin, Emile. *The Life of a Simple Man.* Translated by Margaret Crosland. Hanover, N.H.: University Press of New England, 1983.

Guizot, François. *Mémoires pour servir à l'histoire de mon temps.* Paris: Michel Levy Frères, 1860.

Gullickson, Gay L. *Spinners and Weavers of Auffay.* Cambridge University Press, 1986.

Gutton, Jean-Pierre. *La Sociabilité villageoise dans l'ancienne France.* Paris: Hachette, 1979.

Hajnal, John. "European Marriage Patterns in Perspective." In *Population in History,* eds. D. V. Glass and D. E. C. Eversley, 101–146. London: E. Arnold, 1965.

. "Two Kinds of Pre-Industrial Household Formation System." *Population and Development Review* 8 (1982): 449–494.

Hanagan, Michael. *The Logic of Solidarity: Artisans and Industrial Workers in Three French Towns, 1871–1914.* Urbana: University of Illinois Press, 1980.

. *Nascent Proletarians: Class Formation in Post-Revolutionary France.* New York: Blackwell Publisher, 1989.

. "Proletarian Families and Social Protest: Production and Reproduction as Issues of Social Conflict in Nineteenth-Century France." In *Work in France: Representations, Meaning, Organization, and Practice,* eds. Steven Laurence Kaplan and Cynthia J. Koepp, 418–456. Ithaca, N.Y.: Cornell University Press, 1986.

Harsin, Jill. *Policing Prostitution in Nineteenth-Century Paris.* Princeton, N.J.: Princeton Unversity Press, 1985.

Hause, Steven C., and Anne R. Kenney. *Women's Suffrage and Social Politics in the French Third Republic.* Princeton, N.J.: Princeton University Press, 1984.

Hazard, Paul. *European Thought in the Eighteenth Century.* Translated by J. Lewis May. New York: World, 1963.

Hélias, Pierre Jakez. *Le Cheval d'orgueil.* Paris: Plon, 1975.

Herbert, Robert L. "City vs. Country: The Rural Image in French Painting." *Artforum* 8 (1970): 44–55.

Higonnet, Patrice. "The Politics of Linguistic Terrorism and grammatical Hegemony during the French Revolution." *Social History* 5 (1980): 41–69.

Hilaire, Yves-Marie. *Une Chrétienté au XIXe siècle? La Vie religieuse des populations du diocèse d'Arras (1840–1914).* Villeneuve d'Asq: Université de Lille III, 1977.

Hobsbawm, Eric. *Echoes of the Marseillaise: Two Centuries Look Back on the French Revolution.* New Brunswick, N.J.: Rutgers University Press, 1990.

. *Nations and Nationalism since 1780.* Cambridge University Press, 1990.

. *Primitive Rebels.* New York: Norton, 1959.

Hoffman, Philip. *Church and Community in the Diocese of Lyon.* New Haven, Conn.: Yale University Press, 1984.

Hoffman, Robert L. *More than a Trial: The Struggle over Captain Dreyfus.* New York: Free Press, 1980.

Hoffman, Stanley. *In Search of France.* New York: Harper & Row, 1965.

Hohenberg, Paul. "Change in Rural France in the Period of Industrialization." *Journal of Economic History* 32 (1972): 219–240.

Houdaille, Jacques. "Un Indicateur de pratique religieuse: la célébration saisonnière des mariages avant, pendant et après la Révolution française (1740–1829)." *Population* 33 (1978): 367–380.

Huard, Raymond. *Le Mouvement républicain en Bas-Languedoc, 1848–1881.* Paris: Presses de la Fondation nationale des sciences politiques, 1982.

Hufton, Olwen. *The Poor of Eighteenth-Century France, 1759–1789.* Oxford University Press (Clarendon Press), 1974.

. "Women without Men: Widows and Spinsters in Britain and France in the Eighteenth Century." *Journal of Family History* 9 (1984): 355–376.

Hunt, Lynn. *The Family Romance of the French Revolution.* Berkeley and Los Angeles: University of California Press, 1991.

Hutton, Patrick. "The Role of Memory in the Historiography of the French Revolution." *History and Theory* 30 (1991): 56–69.

Inkeles, Alex, and David Smith. *Becoming Modern.* Cambridge, Mass.: Harvard University Press, 1974.

Jaurès, Jean. *Histoire socialiste.* Paris: Jules Roff et Cie, 1900–02.

Jolly, Jean, ed. *Dictionnaire des parlementaires français, 1889–1940.* Paris: Presses Universitaires Française, 1960.

Jones, P. M. "Common Rights and Agrarian Individualism in the Southern Massif Central, 1750–1880." In *Beyond the Terror,* eds. Gwynne Lewis and Colin Lucas, 121–151. Cambridge University Press, 1983.

. *The Peasantry in the French Revolution.* Cambridge University Press, 1988.

. *Politics and Rural Society: The Southern Massif Central c. 1750–1880.* Cambridge University Press, 1985.

Judt, Tony. *Past Imperfect: French Intellectuals, 1944–1956.* Berkeley and Los Angeles: University of California Press, 1992.

. *Socialism in Provence, 1871–1914.* Cambridge University Press, 1979.

Kaplan, Steven L. *Bread, Politics and Political Economy in the Reign of Louis XV.* The Hague: Martinus Nijhoff, 1976.

Kayser, Jacques. *Les Grandes batailles du radicalisme des origines aux portes du pouvoir, 1820–1901.* Paris: Marcel Rivière, 1962.

Keylor, William. *Academy and Community: The Foundation of the French Historical Profession.* Cambridge, Mass.: Harvard University Press, 1975.

Kondo, Dorinne K. *Crafting Selves: Power, Gender, and Discourses of Identity in a Japanese Workplace.* University of Chicago Press, 1990.

Kselman, Thomas. *Death and the Afterlife in Modern France.* Princeton, N.J.: Princeton University Press, 1993.

. *Miracles and Prophecies in Nineteenth-Century France.* New Brunswick, N.J.: Rutgers University Press, 1983.

Kussmaul, Ann. *Servants in Husbandry in Early Modern England.* Cambridge University Press, 1981.

Lagrée, Michel. *Mentalités, religion et histoire en Haute-Bretagne au XIXe siècle: le diocèse de Rennes, 1815–1848.* Paris: Klincksieck, 1977.

Lancelot, Alain. *L'Abstentionnisme électoral en France.* Paris: Presses de la Fondation nationale des sciences politiques, 1968.

Landes, Joan B. *Women and the Public Sphere in the Age of the French Revolution.* Ithaca, N.Y.: Cornell University Press, 1988.

Langlois, Claude. *Le Catholicisme au féminin: les congrégations françaises à supérieure générale au XIXe siècle.* Paris: Cerf, 1984.

. *Un Diocèse bréton au début du XIXe siècle: le diocèse de Vannes au XIXe siècle, 1800–1830.* Paris: Klincksieck, 1974.

Laqueur, Thomas. *Making Sex: Body and Gender from the Greeks to Freud.* Cambridge, Mass.: Harvard University Press, 1990.

Laslett, Peter. *Family Life and Illicit Love in Earlier Generations.* Cambridge University Press, 1977.

Laurent, Benoit. *L'Eglise janseniste du Forez.* Saint-Etienne: Imprimerie de la Loire républicaine, 1942.

Lebovics, Herman. *True France: The Wars over Cultural Identity, 1900–1945.* Ithaca, N.Y.: Cornell University Press, 1992.

Le Bras, Gabriel. *Etudes de sociologie religieuse.* Paris: Presses Universitaires de France, 1955–56.

Le Bras, H. "La Statistique générale de la France." In *Les Lieux de mémoire,* vol. 2, *La Nation,* ed. Pierre Nora, vol. 2: 317–353. Paris: Gallimard, 1986.

Lebrun, François. *La vie conjugale sous l'ancien régime.* Paris: Hachette, 1976.

Ledré, Charles. *Le Culte caché sous la Révolution: les missions de l'abbé Linsolas.* Paris: Bonne Presse, 1949.

Lefebvre, Georges. *Les Paysans du nord pendant la révolution française.* Bari: Laterza, 1959.

. *The Coming of the French Revolution.* Translated by R. R. Palmer. Princeton, N.J.: Princeton University Press, 1947.

Lehning, James R. "Family Life and Wetnursing in a French Village." *Journal of Interdisciplinary History* 12 (1982): 645–656.

. "The Decline of Marital Fertility: Evidence from a French Department, la Loire, 1851–1891." *Annales de Démographie Historique* (1984): 201–217.

. "Literacy and Demographic Behavior." *History of Education Quarterly* (1984): 545–559.

. "Nuptiality and Rural Industry: Families and Labor in the French Countryside." *Journal of Family History* 8 (1983): 333–345.

. *The Peasants of Marlhes.* Chapel Hill: University of North Carolina Press, 1980.

. "Socioeconomic Change, Peasant Household Structure and Demographic Behavior in a French Department." *Journal of Family History* 17 (1992): 161–181.

. "The Timing and Prevalence of Women's Marriage in the French Department of the Loire, 1851–1891." *Journal of Family History* 13 (1988): 307–323.

Léonard, Jacques. "Les Guérisseurs en France au XIXe siècle." *Revue d'Histoire Moderne et Contemporaine* 27 (1980): 501–516.

Le Play, Frédéric. *L'Organisation de la famille.* Paris: Tequi, 1871.

. *L'Organisation du travail.* Tours: Mame, 1870.

Lequin, Yves. *Les Ouvriers de la région lyonnaise (1848–1914).* Lyon: Presses Universitaires de Lyon, 1977.

Lerner, Gerda. *The Creation of Patriarchy.* New York: Oxford University Press, 1986.

Le Roy, Eugène. *Jacquou le Croquant.* Paris: Calmann-Levy, 1946.

Leroy Ladurie, Emmanuel. *Les Paysans de Languedoc.* Paris: S.E.V.P.E.N., 1966.

Lesthaeghe, Ron. "A Century of Demographic and Cultural Change in Western Europe." *Population and Development Review* 9 (1983): 411–435.

Levine, David. "Education and Family Life in Early Industrial England." *Journal of Family History* 4 (1979): 368–380.

. "Illiteracy and Family Life during the First Industrial Revolution." *Journal of Social History* 14 (1979): 25–44.

Lévi-Strauss, Claude. *Tristes Tropiques.* Translated by John Russell. New York: Criterion, 1961.

Lewis, Gwynne. "A Cevenol Community in Crisis: The Mystery of 'L'Homme à Moustache.'" *Past and Present* 109 (1985): 144–175.

Logue, William. *From Philosophy to Sociology: The Evolution of French Liberalism, 1870–1914.* De Kalb: Northern Illinois University Press, 1983.

Lucas, Colin. *The Structure of the Terror.* New York: Oxford University Press, 1973.

Luckmann, Thomas. *The Invisible Religion.* New York: Macmillan, 1967.

Luria, Keith. *Territories of Grace: Cultural Change in the Seventeenth-Century Diocese of Grenoble.* Berkeley and Los Angeles: University of California Press, 1991.

Lynch, Katherine. *Family, Class, and Ideology in Early Industrial France.* Madison: University of Wisconsin Press, 1988.

Magraw, Roger. *France, 1815–1914: The Bourgeois Century.* New York: Oxford University Press, 1986.

Marcilhacy, Christianne. *Le Diocèse d'Orléans sous l'épiscopat de Mgr. Dupanloup, 1849–1879.* Paris: Plon, 1962.

Margadant, Ted. *French Peasants in Revolt: The Insurrection of 1851.* Princeton, N.J.: Princeton University Press, 1979.

Maroussem, Pierre du. *Fermiers montagnards du Haut-Forez.* Paris: Ouvriers des Deux Mondes, 1894.

Marrus, Michael R. "Folklore as an Ethnographic Source: A 'Mise au Point.'" In *The Wolf and the Lamb: Popular Culture in France,* eds. Jacques Beauroy, Marc Bertrand, and Edward T. Gargan, 109–125. Saratoga, Calif.: Anma Libri, 1977.

Martin du Gard, Roger. *Jean Barois.* Paris: Gallimard, 1921.

Marx, Karl. "The Eighteenth Brumaire of Louis Bonaparte," In *Surveys from Exile: Political Writings,* vol. 2: 143–249. New York: Vintage, 1974.

Mathiez, Albert. *La Révolution française.* Paris: Colin, 1978.

Maupassant, Guy de. "Histoire d'une fille de ferme." In *Oeuvres complètes,* vol. 1: 117–139. Paris: Art H. Piazza, 1968.

Mauss, Marcel, *The Gift.* Translated by Ian Cunnison. New York: Free Press, 1954.

Mayeur, Françoise. *L'Education des filles en France au XIXe siècle.* Paris: Hachette, 1979.

Mayeur, Jean-Marie. *Les Débuts de la Troisième république (1871–1898).* Paris: Seuil, 1973.

. "Géographie de la resistance aux inventaires (février–mars 1906)." *Annales: Economies. Sociétés. Civilisations.* 21 (1966): 1259–1272.

. *La Vie politique sous la Troisième république, 1870–1940.* Paris: Seuil, 1984.

Maynes, Mary Jo. *Schooling For the People.* New York: Holmes & Meier, 1985.

McDonald, Maryon. *We Are Not French! Language, Culture and Identity in Brittany.* New York: Routledge, 1989.

McLaren, Angus. *Sexuality and Social Order: The Debate over the Fertility of Women and Workers in France, 1770–1920.* New York: Holmes & Meier, 1983.

McManners, John. *Church and State in France, 1870–1914.* New York: Harper & Row, 1972.

. *Death and the Enlightenment.* New York: Oxford University Press, 1985.

. *The French Revolution and the Church.* New York: Harper & Row, 1969.

McPhee, Peter. *The Politics of Rural Life.* Oxford University Press (Clarendon Press), 1992.

. "Popular Culture, Symbolism and Rural Radicalism in Nineteenth-Century France." *Journal of Peasant Studies* 5 (1978): 238–253.

. *A Social History of France, 1780–1880.* New York: Routledge, 1992.

Meaudre, Jacques. "La poussée urbaine à Saint-Etienne, 1815–1872." *Diplôme d'études supérieures,* Université de Lyon, 1966.

Meaux, Vicomte de. *Le Progrès agricole dans la Plaine du Forez depuis cinquante ans.* Montbrison: Imprimerie d'Eleuthese Brassart, 1895.

Mendels, Franklin F. "La composition du ménage paysan en France au XIXe siècle: une analyse économique du mode de production domestique." *Annales: Economies. Sociétés. Civilisations.* 33 (1978): 780–802.

. *Industrialization and Population Pressure in 18th-Century Flanders.* Ann Arbor, Mich.: University Microfilms International, 1977.

. "Proto-Industrialization: The First Phase of the Industrialization Process." *Journal of Economic History* 32 (1972): 241–261.

Mendras, Henri. *The Vanishing Peasant.* Translated by Jean Lerner. Cambridge, Mass.: MIT Press, 1970.

Mendras, Henri, and Alistair Cole. *Social Change in Modern France.* Cambridge University Press, 1991.

Merley, Jean. "Les Elections de 1869 dans la Loire." *Cahiers d'Histoire* 6 (1961): 59–93.

Merriman, John M. *The Agony of the Republic.* New Haven, Conn.: Yale University Press, 1978.

. "The Demoiselles of the Ariège." In *1830 in France,* ed. John M. Merriman, 87–118. New York: Watts, 1975.

Mesliand, Claude. "Gauche et droite dans les campagnes provençales sous la IIIe république." *Etudes Rurales* 63–64 (1976): 207–234.

Messance, L. *Recherches sur la population des généralités d'Auvergne, de Lyon, de Rouen et de quelques provinces et villes du royaume.* Paris, n. p., 1766.

Michelet, Jules. *The People.* Translated by John P. McKay. Urbana: University of Illinois Press, 1973.

. *Histoire de la Révolution française.* Paris: Gallimard, 1952.

Midelfort, H. C. Erik. *Witch Hunting in Southwestern Germany, 1562–1684: The Social and Intellectual Foundations.* Stanford, Calif.: Stanford University Press, 1972.

Ministère de l'instruction publique. *Etat récapitulatif et comparatif indiquant, par département, le nombre des conjoints qui ont signé l'acte de leur mariage aux XVIIe, XVIIIe et XIXe siècles.* Paris: Ministère de l'instruction publique, n.d.

Mitrany, David. *Marx Against the Peasant.* Chapel Hill: University of North Carolina Press, 1951.

Moheau. *Recherches et considérations sur la population de la France.* Paris: Geuthner, 1912.

Monter, E. William. *Witchcraft in France and Switzerland: The Border-lands during the Reformation.* Ithaca, N.Y.: Cornell University Press, 1976.

Morin, Edgar. *Commune en France: la metamorphose de Plodémet.* Paris: Fayard, 1967.

Morineau, Michel. *Les Faux-Semblants d'un démarrage économique.* Paris: Colin, 1970.

Moses, Claire Goldberg. *French Feminism in the 19th Century.* Albany, N.Y.: SUNY Press, 1984.

Muchembled, Robert. *Popular Culture and Elite Culture in France, 1400–1750.* Translated by Lydia Cochrane. Baton Rouge: Louisiana State University Press, 1985.

Nicolet, Claude. *L'Idée républicaine en France (1789–1924).* Paris: Galli-mard, 1982.

Offen, Karen. "Depopulation, Nationalism, and Feminism in Fin-de-Siècle France." *American Historical Review* 89 (1984): 648–676.

Orr, Linda. *Headless History.* Ithaca, N.Y.: Cornell University Press, 1990.

Ozouf, Mona. *L'Ecole, l'église et la république, 1871–1914.* Paris: Colin, 1963.

Palluat de Bessat, R. "La Résistance à la constitution civile du clergé dans le district de Montbrison, 1791–1792." *Amitiés Foréziennes et Vellaves* (1926): 305–310, 398–410, 492–503.

Palmer, Bryan D. *Descent into Discourse: The Reification of Language and the Writing of Social History.* Philadelphia: Temple University Press, 1990.

Palmer, Robert R. *Catholics and Unbelievers in Eighteenth Century France.* Princeton, N.J.: Princeton University Press, 1939.

Pariset, E. *Histoire de la fabrique lyonnaise.* Lyon: A. Rey, 1901.

Parrish, William, and Moshe Schwartz. "Household Complexity in Nineteenth Century France." *American Sociological Review* 37 (1972): 154–173.

Parsons, Talcott. "The Kinship System of the Contemporary United States." *American Anthropologist* 43 (1943): 22–38.

Paxton, Robert O. *Vichy France: Old Guard and New Order, 1940–1944.* New York: Knopf, 1972.

Pinkney, David. *Decisive Years in France, 1840–1847.* Princeton, N.J.: Princeton University Press, 1986.

Plongeron, Bernard. "A propos des mutations du 'populaire' pendant la révolution et l'Empire." In *La Religion populaire: approches histori-ques,* 129–147. Paris: Editions Beauchesne, 1976.

Poitrineau, Abel. "Aspects de l'émigration temporaire et saissonière en Auvergne à la fin du XVIIIe et au début du XIXe siècle." *Revue d'Histoire Moderne et Contemporaine* 9 (1962): 5–50.

Porter, Theodore M. *The Rise of Statistical Thinking*. Princeton, N.J.: Princeton University Press, 1986.

Prakash, Gyan. *Bonded Histories: Genealogies of Labor Servitude in Colonial India*. Cambridge University Press, 1990.

Price, Richard. *Alabi's World*. Baltimore: The Johns Hopkins University Press, 1990.

. *First-Time: The Historical Vision of an Afro-American People*. Baltimore: The Johns Hopkins University Press, 1983.

Price, Roger. *The Modernization of Rural France: Communications Networks and Agricultural Market Structures in Nineteenth-Century France*. New York: St. Martin's, 1983.

. *A Social History of Nineteenth-Century France*. New York: Holmes & Meier, 1987.

Prost, Antoine. *Histoire de l'enseignement en France, 1800–1967*. Paris: Colin, 1968.

Rearick, Charles. *Beyond the Enlightenment: Historians and Folklore in Nineteenth-Century France*. Bloomington: Indiana University Press, 1974.

Rebérioux, Madeleine. *La République radicale? 1898–1914*. Paris: Seuil, 1975.

Reddy, William. *The Rise of Market Culture*. Cambridge University Press, 1984.

Reece, Jack E. *The Bretons Against France: Ethnic Minority Nationalism in 20th-Century Brittany*. Chapel Hill: University of North Carolina Press, 1977.

Renan, Ernest. "Qu'est-ce qu'une nation?" In *Oeuvres complètes*, vol. 1: 887–906. Paris: Calmann Levy, 1947.

Rétif de la Bretonne, Nicolas. *La Vie de mon père*. Paris: Garnier, 1981.

Ringer, Fritz. *Fields of Knowledge*. Cambridge University Press, 1992.

Rivet, Auguste. *La Vie politique dans le département de la Haute-Loire de 1815 à 1974*. Le Puy: Cahiers de la Haute-Loire, 1979.

Robert, Adolphe, Edgar Bourloton, and Gaston Cougny. *Dictionnaire des parlementaires français, 1789–1889*. Paris: Bourloton, 1891.

Robert, Guy. *La Terre d'Emile Zola*. Paris: Belles lettres, 1952.

Rogers, Susan Carol. "Espace masculin, espace féminin: essai sur la différence." *Etudes Rurales* 74 (1979): 87–110.

. "Good to Think: The 'Peasant' in Contemporary France." *Anthropological Quarterly* 60 (1987): 56–63.

. *Shaping Modern Times in Rural France*. Princeton, N.J.: Princeton University Press, 1991.

Rosenberg, Harriet G. *A Negotiated World: Three Centuries of Change in a French Alpine Community*. University of Toronto Press, 1988.

Rouchon, Ulysses. *La Vie paysanne dans la Haute-Loire*. Le Puy: Imprimerie de la Haute-Loire, 1933.

Sabean, David Warren. *Power in the Blood: Popular Culture and Village Discourse in Early Modern Germany*. Cambridge University Press, 1984.

Sahlins, Peter. *Boundaries: The Making of France and Spain in the Pyrenees*. Berkeley and Los Angeles: University of California Press, 1989.

Said, Edward. *Orientalism*. New York: Random House, 1978.

. "Orientalism Reconsidered." In *Literature, Politics and Theory*, eds. Francis Barker et al., 210–229. London: Methuen, 1986.

Saint-Jacob, Pierre de. *Les Paysans de la Bourgogne du Nord au dernier siècle de l'ancien régime*. Paris: Belles Letters, 1960.

Sand, George. *François le champi*. Oxford University Press (Clarendon Press), 1910.

Scott, James. *Domination and the Arts of Resistance*. New Haven, Conn.: Yale University Press, 1990.

. *Weapons of the Weak*. New Haven, Conn.: Yale University Press, 1985.

Scott, Joan Wallach. "Gender: A Useful Category of Historical Analysis." *American Historical Review* 91 (1986): 1053–1075.

. *Gender and the Politics of History*. New York: Columbia University Press, 1989.

Scott, Joan Wallach, and Louise A. Tilly. *Women, Work and Family*. New York: Holt, Rinehart, & Winston, 1978.

Seager, Frederic H. *The Boulanger Affair: Political Crossroad of France, 1886–1889*. Ithaca, N.Y.: Cornell University Press, 1969.

Sedgewick, Alexander. *Jansenism in Seventeenth-Century France*. Charlottesville: University Press of Virginia, 1977.

Segalen, Martine. *Love and Power in the Peasant Family*. Translated by Sarah Matthews. University of Chicago Press, 1983.

Seignobos, Charles. *L'Evolution de la Troisième République(1875–1914)*. Paris: Hachette, 1921.

Sevrin, Ernest. *Les Missions religieuses en France sous la Restauration (1815–1830)*. vol. 1, *Le Missionnaire et la Mission*. Saint-Mandé: Procure des prêtres de la misericorde, 1948. Vol. 2, *Les Missions (1815–1820)*. Paris: Librairie philosophique J. Vrin, 1959.

Sewell, William H. Jr. "Le Citoyen/La Citoyenne: Activity, Passivity, and the Revolutionary Concept of Citizenship." In *The French Revolution and the Creation of Modern Political Culture*, ed. Colin Lucas, vol. 2: 105–123. New York: Pergamon, 1988.

Shaffer, John. *Family and Farm: Agrarian Change and Household Organization in the Loire Valley, 1500–1900*. Albany, N.Y.: SUNY Press, 1982.

Sharp, Lynn L. "Spiritist Women Mediums: Using the Beyond to Construct the Here-and-Now." *Proceedings of the Western Society for French History* 21 (1994): 161–168.

Shorter, Edward, John Knodel, and Etienne van de Walle. "The Decline of Non-Marital Fertility in Europe, 1880–1940." *Population Studies* 25 (1971): 375–393.

. *The Making of the Modern Family.* New York: Basic, 1975.

Siegfried, Andre. *Géographie électorale de l'Ardèche sous la Troisième république.* Paris: Colin, 1949.

. *Tableau politique de la France de l'Ouest sous la IIIe République.* Paris: Colin, 1913.

Smith, Bonnie G. *Ladies of the Leisure Class: The Bourgeoises of Northern France in the Nineteenth Century.* Princeton, N.J.: Princeton University Press, 1981.

Smith, Daniel Scott. "The Meanings of Family and Household: Change and Continuity in the Mirror of the American Census." *Population and Development Review* 18 (1992): 421–456.

Smith, Victor. "Un mariage dans le Haut-Forez en 1873." *Romania* 9 (1880): 547–570.

Sowerwine, Charles. *Sisters or Citizens? Women and Socialism in France since 1876.* Cambridge University Press, 1982.

Specklin, Robert. "L'Achèvement des paysages agraires." In *Histoire de la France rurale*, ed. Georges Duby, Vol. 3, 255–305. Paris: Seuil, 1976.

Spengler, Joseph, J. *France Faces Depopulation.* New York: Greenwood, 1968.

Stendhal. *Le Rouge et le noir.* Paris: Le François 1946.

Stewart, Mary Lynn. *Women, Work, and the French State: Labour Protection and Social Patriarchy, 1879–1919.* Kingston: McGill-Queen's University Press, 1989.

Stock-Morton, Phyllis. *Moral Education for a Secular Society.* Albany, N.Y.: SUNY Press, 1988.

Strumingher, Laura. "Square Pegs into Round Holes: Rural Parents, Children and Primary Schools; France, 1830–1880." In *Popular Traditions and Learned Culture*, eds. Jacques Beauroy, Marc Bertrand, and Edward T. Gargan, 133–147. Saratoga, Calif.: Anma Libri, 1977.

. *What Were Little Girls and Boys Made Of? Primary Education in Rural France, 1830–1880.* Albany, N.Y.: SUNY Press, 1983.

Sussman, George. *Selling Mothers' Milk: The Wet-Nursing Business in France, 1715–1914.* Urbana: University of Illinois Press, 1982.

Tackett, Timothy. *Religion, Revolution, and Regional Culture in Eighteenth-Century France: The Ecclesiastical Oath of 1791.* Princeton, N.J.: Princeton University Press, 1986.

Taine, Hippolyte. *Les Origines de la France contemporaine.* Paris: Hachette, 1921–38.

Taverne, Alice. *Coutumes et superstitions foréziennes: aspects de la vie quotidienne.* Ambierle: Editions du Musée forezien, 1973.

. *Coutumes et superstitions foréziennes: les étapes de la vie.* Ambierle: Editions du Musée forezien, 1972.

. *Coutumes et superstitions foréziennes: l'habitat.* Ambierle: Editions du Musée forezien, 1973.

. *Coutumes et superstitions foréziennes: médecine populaire, sorcellerie; diable et lutins.* Ambierle: Editions du Musée forezien, 1971.

Tenand, D. "Les Origines de la classe ouvrière stéphanoise." *Diplôme d'études supérieures,* Université de Lyon II, 1972.

Terdiman, Richard. *The Dialectics of Isolation.* New Haven, Conn.: Yale University Press, 1976.

. *Discourse/Counter-Discourse: The Theory and Practice of Symbolic Resistance in Nineteenth-Century France.* Ithaca, N.Y.: Cornell University Press, 1985.

Thabault, Roger. *Education and Change in a Village Community: Mazières-en-Gatine, 1848–1914.* Translated by Peter Tregear. New York: Schocken, 1971.

Thomas, Janet. "Women and Capitalism: Oppression or Emancipation?" *Comparative Studies in Society and History* 30 (1988): 534–549.

Thompson, E. P. "The Moral Economy of the English Crowd in the Eighteenth Century." *Past and Present* 50 (1971): 71–136.

. "Rough Music: le charivari anglais." *Annales: Economies. Sociétés. Civilisations.* 27 (1972): 285–312.

. "Rough Music and Charivari: Some Further Reflections." In *Le Charivari,* eds. Jacques Le Goff and Jean-Claude Schmitt, 273–283. Paris: Mouton, 1982.

Thuillier, Guy. "Une Source à exploiter: les mémoires des instituteurs en 1861." *Revue d'Histoire Économique et Sociale* 55 (1977): 263–270.

Tilly, Charles. *The Contentious French.* Cambridge, Mass.: Harvard University Press, 1986.

. "Did the Cake of Custom Break?" In *Consciousness and Class Experience in Nineteenth–Century Europe,* ed. John M. Merriman, 17–44. New York: Holmes & Meier, 1979.

Todd, E. "Mobilité géographique et cycle de vie en Artois et en Toscane au XVIIIe siècle." *Annales: Economies. Sociétés. Civilisations.* 30 (1975): 726–744.

Todorov, Tzvetan. *The Conquest of America: The Question of the Other.* Translated by Richard Howard. New York: Harper & Row, 1984.

Tomas, François. "Géographie sociale du Forez en 1788 d'après les tableaux des 'propriétaires et habitans.'" *Bulletin de la Diana* 39 (1965): 80–117.

. "Problèmes de démographie historique: le Forez au XVIIIe siècle." *Cahiers d'Histoire* 13 (1968): 381–399.

Tonnesson, Kare. "La démocratie directe sous la Révolution française – le cas des districts et sections de Paris." In *The French Revolution and the Creation of Modern Political Culture*, ed. Colin Lucas, vol. 2: 295–307. New York: Pergamon, 1988.

Tudesq, Andre-Jean. *Les Grands notables en France, 1840–49*. Paris: Presses Universitaires de France, 1964.

Turner, Victor, and Edith Turner. *Image and Pilgrimage in Christian Culture: Anthropological Perspectives*. Oxford: Blackwell Publisher, 1978.

Van de Walle, Etienne. "Alone in Europe: The French Fertility Decline Until 1850." In *Historical Studies of Changing Fertility*, ed. Charles Tilly, 257–288. Princeton, N.J.: Princeton University Press, 1978.

. "Motivations and Technology in the Decline of French Fertility." In *Family and Sexuality in French History*, eds. Robert Wheaton and Tamara K. Hareven, 135–178. Philadelphia: University of Pennsylvania Press, 1980.

Van Gennep, Arnold. *Le Folklore de l'Auvergne et du Velay*. Paris: G. P. Maisonneuve, 1942.

Verdier, Yvonne. *Façons de dire, façons de faire: la laveuse, la couturière, la cuisinière*. Paris: Gallimard, 1979.

Vernois, Paul. *Le Roman rustique de George Sand à Ramuz*. Paris: Nizet, 1962.

Vincent, David. *Literacy and Popular Culture: England, 1750–1914*. Cambridge University Press, 1989.

Vovelle, Michel. *Piété baroque et déchristianisation en Provence au XVIIIe siècle*. Paris: Plon, 1973.

. *The Revolution against the Church*. Translated by Alan José. Columbus: Ohio State University Press, 1991.

. "Y a-t-il une révolution culturelle au XVIIIe siècle? A propos de l'education populaire en Provence." *Revue d'Histoire Moderne et Contemporaine* 32 (1975): 89–141.

Waldinger, Renée, Philip Dawson, and Isser Woloch, eds. *The French Revolution and the Meaning of Citizenship*. Westport, Conn.: Greenwood, 1993.

Warshaw, Dan. *Paul Leroy-Beaulieu and Established Liberalism in France*. De Kalb: Northern Illinois University Press, 1991.

Watkins, Susan Cotts. *From Provinces Into Nations: Demographic Integration in Western Europe, 1870–1960*. Princeton, N.J.: Princeton University Press, 1991.

Weber, Eugen. "Comment la Politique Vint aux Paysans: A Second Look at Peasant Politicization." *American Historical Review* 87 (1982): 357–389.

. *Peasants Into Frenchmen*. Stanford, Calif.: Stanford University Press, 1975.

234   *Sources and references*

. "The Second Republic, Politics, and the Peasant." *French Historical Studies* 11 (1980): 521–550.

Wilson, Stephen. *Feuding, Conflict and Banditry in Nineteenth-Century Corsica.* Cambridge University Press, 1988.

Woolf, Stuart. "French Civilization and Ethnicity in the Napoleonic Empire." *Past and Present* 124 (1989): 96–120.

. "Statistics and the Modern State." *Comparative Studies in Society and History* 31 (1989): 588–604.

Wright, Gordon. *Rural Revolution in France.* Stanford, Calif.: Stanford University Press, 1964.

Wrigley, E. A. "The Fall of Marital Fertility in 19th–Century France: Exemplar or Exception?" *European Journal of Population* 1 (1985): 31–60, 141–177.

Wylie, Laurence. *Village in the Vaucluse.* Cambridge, Mass.: Harvard University Press, 1974.

Zeldin, Theodore. *The Political System of Napoleon III.* New York: St. Martin's, 1958.

Zind, Pierre. *Les Nouvelles congrégations de frères enseignants en France de 1800 à 1830.* Saint-Génis-Laval: Chez l'auteur, 1969.

Zola, Emile. *La Terre.* In *Oeuvres complètes,* vol. 5: 761–1156. Paris: Fasquelle, 1967.

. *Germinal.* In *Oeuvres complètes,* vol. 5: 23–421. Paris: Fasquelle, 1967.

Zonabend, Françoise. *La Mémoire longue: temps et histoires au village.* Paris: Presses Universitaires de France, 1980.

Index

235